ADIRONDACK STORIES
OF
THE BLACK RIVER COUNTRY

NORTH COUNTRY BOOKS
UTICA, NEW YORK

Adirondack Stories
of
The Black River Country

William O'Hern

Based on the Diaries of
A. L. Byron-Curtiss

NORTH COUNTRY BOOKS
Utica, New York

Adirondack Stories of
The Black River Country

Copyright © 2003
by
William J. O'Hern

ISBN 0-925168-68-8

NORTH COUNTRY BOOKS
311 Turner Street
Utica, New York 13501

Dedication

*This book is dedicated to the memory of the
Reverend Arthur Leslie Byron-Curtiss,
and to all lovers of the North Woods.*

November 29, 1871 – October 30, 1959

Contents

Acknowledgments

This book about Rev. A. L. Byron-Curtiss and the Adirondacks of the Black River headwaters has been a labor of love. It has been compiled out of a profound personal interest and the wisdom to know that, once published, the effort would endure for future generations of readers whose breadth of knowledge will be broadened and who will be indebted to Rev. Byron-Curtiss for gathering the material and telling of the life of those early days.

As is usually the case, many people had a hand in the development of *Adirondack Stories of the Black River Country.* I am grateful to all those who made it possible.

The Rome Historical Society; its executive director James R. Davis; Thomas J. Kernan, researcher; and Barbara Schaffer. Without their generous support and contributions the Adirondack history contained within would never have been produced.

Acknowledgment goes to everyone who helped in every facet of my research:

I am indebted to the Adirondack Museum librarian Jerry Pepper and to Jim Meehan, Manager of Historic Photographs and Films; Sheri Amsel, Adirondack artist; Edward Blankman who provided many photographs from the collection of his father, the late Lloyd Blankman; the Adirondack League Club Archives and club historian Ted Comstock, who checked for historical inaccuracies that dealt with the Adirondack League Club; Anthony Cucchi, Editorial Assistant of *Audubon* magazine; Carolyn A. Davis, Reader Services Librarian at The George Arents Research Library, Syracuse University; Mary Cole Dickerman, Cultural Education Center, New York State Museum; and Susan Heberling; Eric Johnson, Editor of *The Northeastern Logger* magazine.

Gratitude is also extended to Walter Hastings; Thomas and Doris Kilbourn; Laura Kohl; Sara Layden; Fred R. Lindsey, Jr.; Marion McDermott; Bette O'Hern; Kerry O'Hern; Michael O'Hern; Dorothy Payton; Harold E. Schmelzle; Richard J. Raymond; Richard Smith; Charles B. and Claire Sperry; Beverly and Burton C. Sperry; and Craig Williams, Senior Curator of History at the New York State Museum.

For permission to use A. L. Byron-Curtiss' papers and records grateful acknowledgment is made to the Rome Historical Society.

For permission to use A. L. Byron-Curtiss' photos and camp diaries grateful acknowledgment is made to Tom and Doris Kilbourn.

For permission to reprint the following material by A. L. Byron-Curtiss, grateful acknowledgment is made to Anthony Cucchi, Editorial Assistant of *Audubon* magazine, for: "My Last Visit with John Burroughs," September-October 1959.

For permission to reprint the Scothon and Lindsey Collections, grateful acknowledgment is made to New York State Museum, Albany, New York.

For permission to reprint a photo from the McClusky-Yale 1899 North Lake Collection grateful acknowledgment is made to the Adirondack Museum.

I have made every effort to acknowledge the assistance of everyone who helped; any omission is an unintentional oversight.

Preface

I must confess that I look forward to reading true (and stretched) stories of lumbermen with their caulked boots and double-bitted axes; of eccentric hermits with maps of secret silver finds; of the "Dirty Dozen" trying to outwit the New York State Conservation Department and the Adirondack League Club gamekeepers; and of skillful guides with their tales of the ones that got away. You'll find them all here, along with period photographs of the Black River headwaters.

The Reverend A. L. Byron-Curtiss' arrival by buckboard in the village of Forestport, New York, in 1892 began a romance with the southwestern Adirondacks that was to last for sixty years. He felt an immediate affinity for the wild region and its people: the hardscrabble farmers, hunters, guides, and lumbermen who eked out a living in an unforgiving but majestic environment. Byron-Curtiss recorded his observations with compassion and homespun humor, painting a vibrant turn-of-the-century portrait of this little-chronicled region.

Though he gained some recognition during his lifetime with his biography of hunter and trapper Nat Foster, Byron-Curtiss' busy clerical schedule, as well as some persistent personal problems, prevented him from publishing most of his Adirondack tales. Some were generously given to author Thomas C. O'Donnell for inclusion in his 1952 book, *Birth of a River,* but most disappeared after the minister's death in 1959 until I discovered them in an unmarked and uncataloged file folder at the historical society in Rome, New York.

Compiling and editing the cleric's stories, poring over nearly illegible handwriting in camp log books, interviewing locals who had known the minister, and backpacking through the North Lake region to see Byron-Curtiss' stomping grounds with my own eyes, I have managed to preserve a part of Adirondack history that might otherwise have been lost. And in the process of bringing these writings to light, I bring their creator to life as well, showing Byron-Curtiss to have been as rich and interesting a character as the folks he wrote about.

Sharpening, clarifying, and in some cases rewriting Rev. Byron-Curtiss' stories has been an effort sprinkled with love for the Black River Headwater country, the same Adirondack territory the "Bishop of North Lake" called home for more than half a century.

I began this work in 1980. Over the next two decades I added additional research material that eventually filled two large cardboard boxes. In 1996 I tried to jettison a large measure of the accumulated matter but when it came down to using it as fire starter I could not put a match to it. Result? I dusted off the boxes and questioned how I might use the entire contents. I felt the North Lake reverend was an interesting personality.

Who was this old-time preacher? Who was A. L. Byron-Curtiss? I already had some idea from reading Byron's long out-of-print books: *Life and Adventures of Nat Foster: Trapper and Hunter of the Adirondacks* (1897) and *The Story of a Pass in the Mountains* (1917), but I wanted to learn more about the man he was.

The long and short of my interest lead to tracking whatever paper trail that was still available about "B-C." I refer to him in using those initials because my greatest lead came following two days of sifting through four boxes of author Thomas C. O'Donnell's notes: "B-C #2, B-C #14," and so forth were penciled in the margins of several notebooks.

It has been a long time since I first summited Ice Cave Mountain for a look at the so-called "ice cave" on the peak. Unbelievable as it might sound, that bushwhack eventually led to my uncovering, in an uncataloged file of a historical society's vault, a long-lost manuscript-in-progress—Byron's last effort to tell about his Adirondack world.

Soon I tracked down the current owner of Byron's Nat Foster Lodge. I rented the camp, lived lakeside, used my eyes, ears, and nose to sense what Byron liked about the territory and re-created experiences Byron wrote about in the headwaters. During my residence the final bulk of primary documents came my way. The owner and his wife graciously shared Byron's camp journals, personal photographs, and scrapbooks he chose to leave in camp at the time of the sale. Reading what he did from day to day, year to year, and how he felt provided a new perspective. It also gave me a much better idea of what I should be doing to shape this nonfiction book, a historical narrative of the memoir sort.

In writing *Adirondack Stories of the Black River Country*, from time to time I invoke an imaginary dialogue. I use Bryon's words when possible but it has been necessary to envision the old-timer (add to the image, if you like, a rocker, a warming wood stove, and Nat Foster Lodge) getting up in the dim of a November morning to rekindle the camp stove when the temperature was below freezing; sitting in a guide boat fishing with friends on North Lake in the light fog of a soon-to-be-warm summer morning; and teaming up with locals to hike to North Star camp on Horn Lake or heading off to one of Gould's lumber camps in the backwoods.

Shut your eyes, put yourself in Rev. Byron-Curtiss' shoes. There was no room in his life for boredom. Hear the songbirds in the forest, the loons calling near Cranberry Island, the shouts of glee at landing a large brook trout, the scampering of woodland creatures, and the night noise coming from Ice Cave Creek valley. I think the best memories of Rev. Byron-Curtiss have to do with camping in the Adirondacks and the people he knew.

For inspiration I have bushwhacked to every nook and cranny in the headwaters of the Black River mentioned. I saw—in my mind—Byron on a weekday afternoon clasp his hands behind his back and walk the dirt track from his camp to the State House to get his mail. I climbed Reed's Hill and saw him talking to crippled Addie Reed as they sat on the top stones of Reed's crumbling cellar foundation. I've hiked along every tributary that is part of the Black River watershed. And I have slept under the open verandah of Nat Foster Lodge and envisioned the aged gentleman. How he would sit there, rocking, for a long time, looking out across the water with which he had grown in alliance with Nature and God. The Adirondack Mountains helped him to find that which we all are seeking—contentment.

Author Jay O'Hern at Nat Foster Lodge, North Lake

Introduction

Reverend Arthur Leslie Byron-Curtiss was a youthful man of the cloth when, in 1901, he earmarked North Lake his sanctuary, his holiest of holies. A place that waited patiently just for him to come and still his mind and heal from the cares that were often too much for him. It was the second year in a new century, a year that seemed to have added significance because, aside from only twelve months lying behind it as a unit of time, there lay ninety-nine years of the twentieth century stretched ahead, fresh and ready for brand-new experiences.

From 1901 until 1950, few years passed during which he had not spent several uninterrupted months at the Nat Foster lodge. He heard many old tales about the people and the fishing to be found there, and he had come to feel as much at home in long woolen underclothes, a cotton shirt and overalls (except when he conducted Sunday Christian services or on a holiday) than in a Roman collar.

I suppose he had as many friends among backwoods Adirondack natives as he had among city folks and nationally known figures. I know that he found talk of trout, fox, black bear, and deer far more interesting than talk of the political doings of the American government. And perhaps he had learned as much about people and about human life in general from these mountain folks with whom he dwelled for more than forty years as he ever had from his own persuasion.

At camp, Byron-Curtiss was always in high spirits and entertained hundreds of guests yearly with his stories until they ultimately fell into a heavy slumber from a full belly of trout, bacon, booze, physical exercise, a lack of sleep, or from a combination of all.

Perhaps storytelling lead him to put pen to paper. He was always full of ideas. Recording cherished tales gave the reverend an outlet for his energy and a dash of adventure. His stories and observations are of real happenings. He knew that the world was wonderful and that he felt on top of it. Byron-Curtiss was an able writer, but writing was to him a hobby and not a vocation. There was no sacred flame of journalism burning bright in him. The Reverend Byron-Curtiss was a contented man, writing about the Adirondack Mountains that he loved so well.

Simply, I say Rev. A. L. Byron-Curtiss was a good teller of tales.

He wrote from the perspective of one who lived the life. He wore many hats: Adirondack preacher, social philosopher, political activist, a believer in living as nonmaterialistically as possible. He was also a thief, a fish hog, a tippler, a scofflaw, and a nature lover. These are the elements that make good reading and a fascinating main character to me.

The spirit of North Lake's "bishop" lives on through these chronicles. So, too, does the hardened band of guides, woodsmen, and mountain people he kept pace with. Their knowledge of backwoods living steers the reader into a time that has almost vanished, but will never be forgotten because of how vividly Byron-Curtiss recalls mountain life in America as it was from the turn of the century through the Great Depression. With excitement and wit, the reverend writes about his confidants, the doctors, the teamsters, the lumbermen, and his own trials as a country preacher.

North Lake is a very special place in the Adirondack Mountains for me, too. The grandness Byron saw still exists. The peace and quiet continues, as does the contentment that comes from one being in tune with the natural world: a hawk circling high, serenading birds, a loon's haunting call, a beaver slapping its tail on a quiet isolated pond. The best things in life really are free—the love of God and the beauty and splendor of His creation.

Not unlike people today, Byron-Curtiss found solace in the woods and on the water beneficial to growing spiritually as a human being. All who treasure the Adirondack Park need to recognize the task of protecting it is complex and arduous—a lifelong effort.

The real purpose of this collection of Adirondack stories is to showcase what an extraordinary collector of human history and lore Byron-Curtiss was. It is also the answer to a dream he hoped would someday come true. For those of all ages who have a curiosity about it, here is a delightful glimpse into the early Adirondack life of A. L. Byron-Curtiss.

Enjoy the ride.

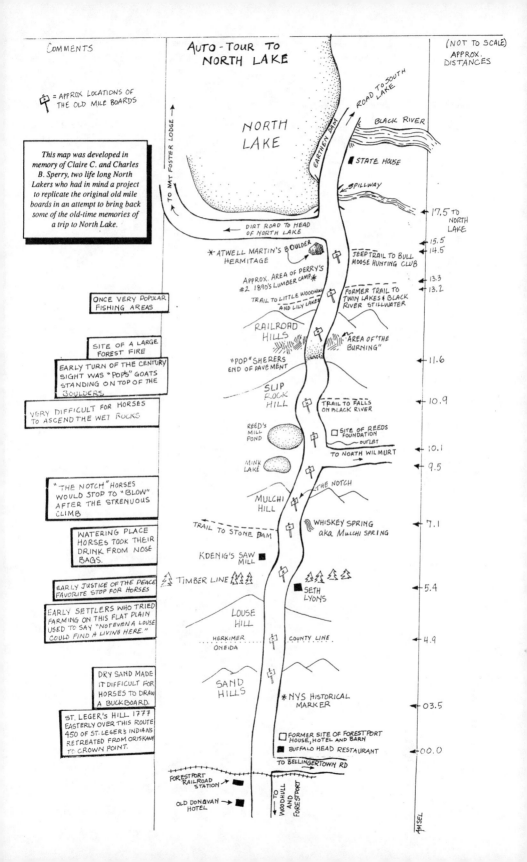

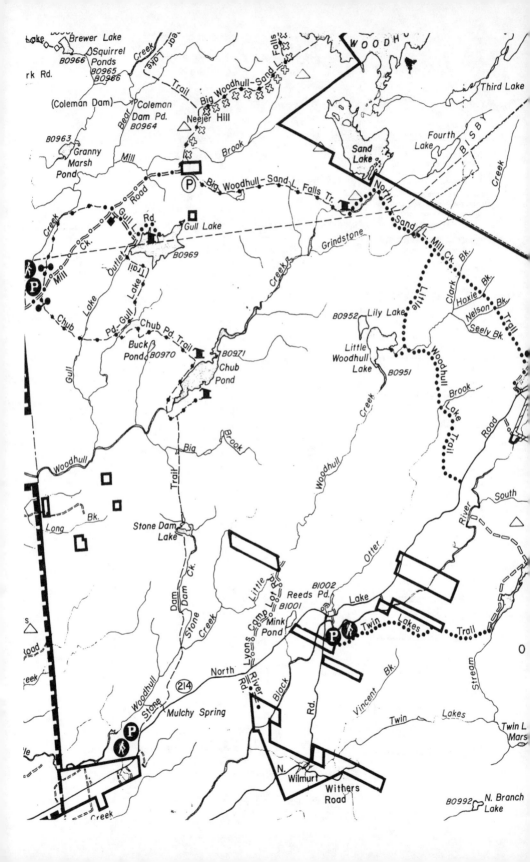

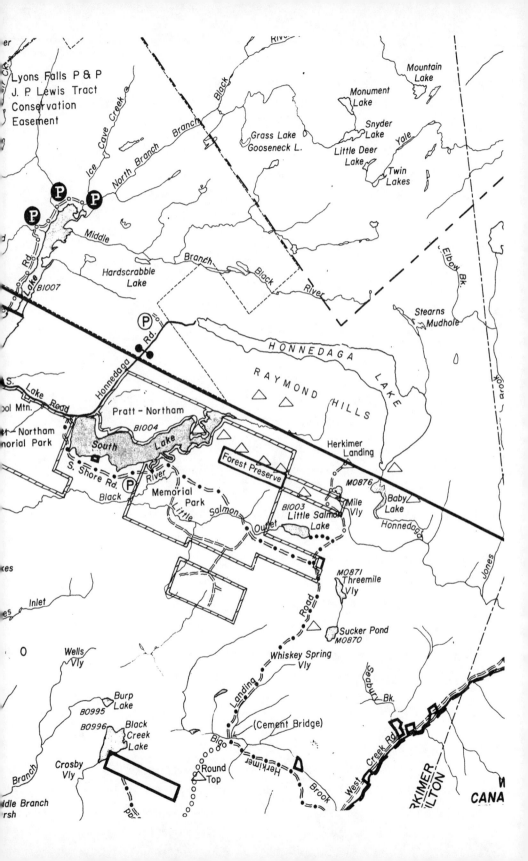

Clerical Adventures

Forestport was still a rip-roaring Adirondack community complete with water-powered sawmills, a steam-powered stavemill, and a steam-powered sawmill when the Reverend Byron-Curtiss came to town in 1892. Nearby on Bear Creek, Big Woodhull and Little Woodhull Creek were more mills. Tens of millions of board feet of lumber were harvested every year. In 1894 alone, Gid Perry contracted with Denton & Waterbury and the Forestport Lumber Company to cut twelve million feet of hardwood just from the forests in the North Lake Country. Rev. Byron-Curtiss was on hand to observe the lumbermen's activities. He visited the lumber camp, listened to the tales, and took in the colorful picture of late nineteenth century life in the area.

Days of the log drives; buckboard rides on rough, rocky tote roads; picturesque hermits who made their homes in the woods in bark and pole lean-tos; tales of old isolated communities, now no longer on the map, that still retained the flavor of the pioneers—places such as Farrtown, Wheelertown, Pony Bob's, Reed's Mill and Enos; a local group known as the "Dirty Dozen" who found sport in harassing the game wardens assigned to patrol the newly posted lands of the Adirondack League Club; these were all part of the reverend's North Woods experience.

Byron-Curtiss tapped the local lore of turn-of-the-century upstate mountain life. He made no bones about admitting where his sympathies lay. The man-of-the-cloth had a most intriguing side to his personality. He supported the early judges in and around Forestport who gave the game protectors a bad time. He was not above floating (driving deer into the water then shooting them), a practice now outlawed, or salting stumps. He knew of the many ingenious ways poachers beat the law. He himself was a self-admitted irregular poacher on the Adirondack League Club land. He fit in well. He had a serious side but he could and did laugh at himself. That point is illustrated when he tells when guide Del Bellinger played a practical joke on him. The preacher had very nearly "buried" a couple instead of "marrying" them.

1

I constructed "Clerical Adventures" the way a patchwork quilt is pieced together. Select, expressive swaths of previously published auto-biographical sketches that A. L. Byron-Curtiss wrote in now-out-of-print magazines, newspaper interviews, correspondence between the reverend and Thomas Kilbourn, and notations Byron-Curtiss made in his camp logs have been threaded as one. I used my editorial liberty to compose the piece to sound like a narrative. Events and facts are real. Quoted conversation is the reverend's. Every effort was made to endeavor to retain the sound of Byron-Curtiss' voice.

On December 20, 1892, I went to Forestport as a young deacon with the oil of consecration fresh on my forehead to take charge of Christ Episcopal. I had been ordained two days before in St. Paul's Church of Syracuse—less than a month after my twenty-first birthday. I spent the next two days with kinfolk in Utica and then I started for Forestport by way of Alder Creek. There was about a foot of snow on the ground and it was bitter cold, but the day itself was fine. I remember that during the two-and-one-half mile drive to the village in an open cutter with a good span of horses my ears began to feel stiff and frozen, but I was young. I tolerated the biting cold and paid little heed to the discomfort.

As I reached the dip of the hill on the Alder Creek Road that crosses the feeder of the Black River Canal, I saw two huge sawmills loom on my right as the zip and the screech of the saws greeted my numb ears. Making its way into my cold nostrils came the pleasant odor of freshly-sawed lumber and the smoky odor of the Gehenna-like fire where the edgings or waste was burning. Winter had set in. The Black River Canal basin had frozen over, but I was impressed by the water pouring over the dam and its tumbling down the boulder-strewn Black River valley.

The village of Forestport, nestled among the foothills of the Adirondacks, was situated at the very head of the Black River Canal (the Black River proper flows through the village's environs). I had been told to expect little more than "a woodpile and a post office." I found much more. Forestport struck me to be a creditable settlement. The appearance was neat and from the activity I thought it an aggressive little village. Forestport was truly a port within a forest.

There was a time, fifty years ago, when one standing in the center of the village would have been surrounded by unbroken forests. Most of the land then was owned by a Dr. Williams. When a site was cleared for homes and mills the original settlement was named Williamsville in honor of the largest property owner. Williamsville was then in the towns of Remsen and Boonville, that part of the village on the east side of River Street being in the town of Remsen and that on the west side in Boonville.

By my arrival in 1892, a half century had elapsed since its founding. The business of ripping logs into building material was going at full blast. Besides the sawmills, there were many supplementary enterprises. The construction of the Black River Canal had increased the value and afforded a market for the vast amount of timber first cut on Blake's hills and tumbled into the new canal basin.

The first mill I saw was Denton and Waterbury's directly on the crown of the hill. Below and across the feeder with its guard lock, on the piece of land jutting out just before the two bridges, was another big mill owned by W. R. Stamburg. Just across the bridges was a yellow-colored two-story wagon and blacksmith shop—a flopping power cable extended along its side next to the river. In a jiffy, with my team of horses at a brisk trot, I was taken across the river's bridges and up the few rods to the "busy corner." On the right was River Street, straight ahead was Woodhull Street lined with mostly residential dwellings. There were also Division, School, and River Streets.

Among the general stores on River Street, the leading one was kept by Harvey Boyce; his daughter, Miss Nellie, oversaw its operation. John Utley and his son, Sam, kept a harness shop, and with the many teams hauling lumber and logs they frequently had several craftsmen working for them. William Clarke and Charles Denslow kept successful liveries. On Woodhull Street among the stores was a hardware store kept by Charles Bingham. It had a skilled sheet metal worker employed constantly, and carried a full line of stoves and hardware. The two principal employers of the village kept general stores. Denton and Waterbury's was next to the post office. Across the street at the corner where a bandstand would be erected was W. R. Stamburg's general store.

During its formative years the village was often dubbed Punkyville, a nickname given it by a party of surveyors for obvious reasons. Then all the mail for the village was received at Alder Creek. Eventually a town meeting was called to decide upon a post office and an official name for the community. The little village, being on a river and at the same time the terminus of a canal feeder, seemed to demand still more dignity. Robert Crandall suggested the name Forestport; it was adopted unanimously. The original post office stood nearly where the current one is. Boxes are rented now but in earlier times the patrons would arrive at a preset time. The postmaster would then call out the names on the envelopes and recipients would step up to the counter to receive their mail.

In 1886 the Town of Forestport was formed from a part of Remsen. Later the west side of River Street was added from Boonville.

"Punkyville" surely had grown from its original two or three houses, a general store, two sawmills, a gristmill, and a butter tub factory. All five early enterprises were erected on the shore of the river and below the dam. Just below the bridge along the state road stood a sawmill owned by William B. Jackson; below the dam was Capt. Clark's feed mill and opposite Clark's was a another lumber mill. The logs for the sawmills were banked on the lower side of Woodhull Street and rolled down as used. About a half mile down the canal was a sawmill that belonged to Dr. Williams, the former owner of what is now the Francis K. Kernan residence on the Alder Creek Road. Behind Boyce's store stood a bark press. Stamburg's tub factory stood on the Alder Creek Road and his gristmill was nearby.

I learned a Dr. Hayden built the first hotel. Almost opposite it was a small, wood-frame two-story school house. The Protestants once held services in the one room downstairs. Currently the Getman House is considered the best hotel; however, there are several fine smaller ones.

In 1857-58 the Episcopal church was built on a site near Beechwood Cemetery. Next in order were the Methodist and Presbyterian churches. The first Catholic church was built about 1851 near the old Catholic cemetery.

In April 1869, the North Lake Dam gave way, taking the state dam here, the bridges, and three mills. A man rode on horseback from Peters Point to bring a warning but in spite of the desperate efforts of the men, evening brought disaster.

During the rebuilding of the bridges Savillian Traffarn ran a ferry across the pond, carrying horses and passengers for a few cents. The boat was attached by ropes and pulleys to a line stretched across the pond and was pulled back and forth by hand.

At Woodhull, on the bank of Big Woodhull Creek, near the present residence of Mr. and Mrs. George Kenyon, stood one of the largest tanneries in the United States. It was owned by Proctor and Hill, owners of several tanneries all over the country. They undoubtedly decided on Woodhull as a good location because of the abundance of hemlock bark.

My driver remarked that there was nothing but the kindest of relations that existed between the employers of the two biggest steam-powered sawmills and their men. There was also a water-powered mill. No pressure was brought to bear on the workers to trade at any of the general stores either.

While this little village was a thriving lumber and sawmill town as well as the site of a number of many single-owner enterprises, the banks of the Black River Canal saw another outfit that had to do with logs, but not their sawing. This was the making of spar and timber "cribs"—rafts of logs from fifty to eighty feet long.

Following the annual late fall closing of the canal, the boat men would dock their packets, prepare them for winter and, with their tow-team, go into the lumber woods to work for the winter. Throughout the winter, typical of Adirondack folks back then, residents lived and worked on top of the snow in contrast to our attempt to tunnel through it nowadays. Throughout the winter, long lines of teams could be seen daily, their sleighs laden with great spars being brought down from the forests to be fastened together into cribs.

Come spring, once the sawmills resumed operation, the canalers would again take to their boats. Some of the men who skidded the timbers to the mill pond, where the cribs were assembled with their distinctive "shanty crib" complete with its arching "shanty poles" on the last raft in each tow (this design allowing the tow-lines of opposite passing boats to pass over the cribs of timber), were the same people to then raft the tows down the dugway to the Erie Canal in Rome, New York, and then on to the New York market via the canal and Hudson River.

Once delivered to the port city, the Adirondack timber was used chiefly as piles in ferry slips. The best, biggest and longest might find its way into a mast of a ship. One spar, so the story goes, was so long and perfect that $100 was offered for one that would match it but was never collected. Logs for the mills were also hauled in and piled in huge stacks along the river until they were sawn into dimension-sized boards. "Black Phil" McGuire had the exclusive part of this lumber business. While he made money, he was no slave driver but rather a kindly, benign Irishman.

My guide into Forestport one day talked at length about the annual spring drives. It was quite a sight to see the basin or little lake literally covered with logs. It was then that the mills started up, for the season's stock was in. The other novel sight I was to look for was that of the canal boats moored to the docks at lumber piles.

*   *   *

Christ Church was a beautiful example of Upjohn design built in 1885 about a mile outside the village then toward Buffalo Head and the railroad station. It was so placed to be equidistant from three sawmill hamlets of which Forestport is the only one left.

By evening I was as fresh as ever when I attended the Senior Warden's Christmas tree service. We had a full ceremony that included an address by me. I shall never forget that experience in catechizing the children that evening, the occasion of the Christmas tree. I had planned to talk to them of how an evergreen tree was a symbol of our happiness over the Savior's birth, the tree ever presenting a cheerful aspect even in bleak winter.

As a young cleric, I was not content to talk from the chancel steps, but ascended the regulation high pulpit, looked down at the fifty to sixty children gathered below me and demanding and commanding their attention said as impressively as I could, as I pointed to the Christmas tree, "Children: attend unto me." With wide eyes and open mouths they immediately obeyed. Then with a broad and flowing gesture that I had practiced beforehand long and diligently in front before my mirror I pointed to the glittering Christmas tree and continued, "Now, my dear children, what kind of a tree is this?"

One hundred shrill voices answered in unison, "Spruce!"

For a second I, too, stood with scopic eyes and open mouth. Then I felt a chill going up my spine. A flash to my brain zapped me with the cold realization that for the first time I had opened my mouth in my church and had been misunderstood by one hundred percent of my congregation. I realized that I was among children who knew trees, which I did not at the time; for I could not have told whether the tree was pine, spruce, or hemlock.

I hastily gathered my wits and, I dare say pleadingly, I asked, "Is it not also called an evergreen?" I met with the silence of the unconvinced that I hastily accepted as a concession and continued my prepared talk to illustrate the ever-brightness and happiness we much cultivate because of the Infant Savior. My unfortunate question was forgotten in the gaiety that followed the service, but I decided then and there to avoid illustrations using trees and woods in the parish until I had learned much more about them. It had been obvious to all I did not know my trees; but the children certainly did.

I recall those ten months in 1892 and 1893, spent as a young deacon-in-charge, with fondness. There in Forestport, on the edge of the great Adirondack Park, I had my first baptism, my first wedding, and prayed with the dying before my first funeral. There I first fished for trout, ate my first venison and bear meat. There, too, I joined the bucket brigade of the local fire department.

One Sunday early in January, while the church bell was tolling, there was a tap on the vestry room door and Mrs. Stamburg came in all a-flutter to tell me that Sol Tardet's last baby was here to be baptized. I acknowledged the glad tidings with many misgivings because I had never held an infant less than two months old in my arms, but our training for such pastoral work was so good that I was carried through and I am proud to say both the baby and I survived the ordeal, although I stammered a bit during the recital of the ritual.

The baptism was administered following the sermon and the last prayers. During the rite I noted a queerness about the eyes of the baby. Upon inquiry I learned that the family was part Indian.

Afterward the women all gathered around to admire and make much of the baby. The women also took particular pains to tell me how beautifully I had conducted the baptismal service—a gesture that puzzled me. I later discovered that my nemesis, a maidenly but aging organist, had passed the word around that the service was as significant to myself as to the baby.

Her remark was meant to get under my skin but I didn't allow it to. However, she was to deliver many other needling assaults. Evidently I did not measure up to the man she would have liked in attendance. We were at sword points during my entire ten-month stay at Forestport. In my mind I called the aging organist an old maid; but she insisted that according to certain fine distinctions involving matrimonial chances she qualified for a rating as a maiden lady. Be that as it may, she acted as though she owned the church and I were an interloper to be tolerated only so long as I recognized her importance.

She made it a point of always being late for services and I never waited for her. About psalm time a certain clumping down the aisle would announce her approach and then the clattering of the organ top would indicate her progress. At about time for "Gloria" she would let out a yelp, for all the world like a dog with its tail caught in the gate, as she took over.

Unfortunately, I boarded with "Auntie," the troublesome lady's aunt. When I insisted upon more promptness and less disturbance she incited her whole family in defense of her position. What chance had I, a mere man, against these embattled women? I fled from Auntie's boarding house and took lodging in the hotel. A short time later the organist retired from her official position and I persuaded Miss Jessie McClusky, a young lady of culture and refinement from Alder Creek, to take her place at the console. She later married the Rev. Manning B. Bennett, my successor at Christ Church. Affairs at the church ran along more smoothly after the change of organists.

I'll always cherish the comment Rev. Bennett made to me years later. He remarked, "Did you ever know that the Forestport congregation thought your sermons were never prepared in advance? They said you did not have to write your preaches; that you just got in the pulpit and talked them off." I hailed this bit of flattering gossip with hearty laughter, as I explained that I had worked hard and had carefully written all my sermons early every week. Then, following a breather from the content, I copied them off on regulation sermon paper, tied them into the proper manila covers and spent hours in sort of soaking them up like blotting paper soaks up ink. I did not memorize them. I delivered the sermons as they appeared in the manuscript. All through my long ministry I followed pretty much this rule and found that it worked. Not once did I ever hear of anyone passing out during the time I was sermonizing.

My first marriage ceremony was without incident and I had almost forgotten it, but on looking through my notes made long ago in my lifetime stack of journals, I find this plaintive, somewhat sophomoric bit of philosophy by way of explanation: "No one is more inconspicuous than the minister at a church wedding."

My first funeral, in contrast, was a series of strange, distracting events. I remember thinking that night, just before I went to sleep, "Can these things really have happened?"

John Glatzabach, an old German sawyer who lived out on one of the back roads, had died. Dr. H. L. Kilbourn attended him in his last illness and as was his custom he discussed the arrangements for the funeral with the family. The widow frankly explained that they were Roman Catholics but they had not worked at it for years and she did not know what the attitude of the priest would be.

Dr. Kilbourn was a loyal Episcopalian and a sympathetic man; he suggested that they might avoid embarrassment and heartaches by having John buried from a "half-Catholic church." Once the widow agreed to the compromise, Dr. Kilbourn and I rounded up the choir and prepared for the full ritual.

First, I went to the Glatzabach home for "House Prayers." The snow was six feet deep on the level. The undertaker had evidently turned the empty casket end up, vertically, and taken it into the house through the woodshed door. With the prayers over and the body now lying in the casket, we realized the casket would have to be taken out differently. Acting on the first suggestion the whole group of mourners picked up axes, pitched in, and began chopping out the side of the woodshed with axes in order to take the deceased outside.

As the door-widening was in progress, I stood up in the rear of a jumper sleigh, reverently holding my prayer book and watching with prescribed "calm dignity" while this curious solution was going on. Suddenly the team hitched to my sleigh gave a start and I pitched head first into the snow bank. The mourners quickly came to my rescue and brushed me off; but as they clawed through the cold, crisp snow to find my spectacles I heard them murmuring certain lurid heresies that I later learned were common in lumber camps but never taken seriously.

When we finally got the body to the church vestibule, Abe Whiter, the undertaker, asked anxiously if I had any particular directions to give him for the funeral. I explained with equal anxiety that this was my first funeral service and I had no intention of deviating in the slightest degree from the ritual.

Whiter's serious-looking face cleared up quickly—he almost grinned as he said, "That's just fine, Reverend. This is my first funeral, too." The rest of the funeral was carried through without a hitch. Abe Whiter and I became a smoothly-working team before I left Forestport. Our "First" had cured us of any qualms about the future.

*   *   *

The Episcopal Church has an aristocratic tradition and it was no different at Forestport. When I arrived I found Christ Church in a healthy, growing condition. The church's register, the *Who's Who of Forestport,* contained names and information that helped me to learn more about the background of my parishioners. Following are vignettes of various people in my congregation. The church records also gave much interesting information about Forestport. In reading between the lines I traced its development from a tiny, upstate frontier settlement to a thriving town that boasted four churches, a half-dozen stores and nine saloons—all striving to satisfy the spiritual and temporal demands of some five hundred natives employed in the two large steam sawmills and the other industries of the town and about double that same number employed in the back country lumber camps getting the logs out and on the canal engaged in getting the lumber to the market.

Christ Church would never have been the same without "Min" Groves. Min was a homespun character who worked long and faithfully to keep the church's interior spic and span—to please God and W. R., her employer.

W. R. Stamburg was my right-hand man. Not only was he the church's senior warden but he was also a pioneer entrepreneur in the lumber industry, owner of sawmills at Meekerville and Forestport. His steam-powered Forestport mill was a showpiece. Stamburg's success didn't stop there, though. Due to his high energy he also owned canal boats, farms, and a village general store as well as a gristmill and butter tub factory. He was a tall man. His head was bald but he had a full flowing beard about the color of Tokay wine. Each and every Sunday W. R. was in his pew with his wife and sweet little adopted daughter. I recall his devout demeanor at services and a custom he had of occasionally licking a thumb to find his place in the prayer book. He employed a number of cousins and nephews in his various enterprises and he herded them all into our church so we had a number of Stamburg families. W. R. had some of the boys at his mill, at my suggestion, make modest, hardwood platforms to raise both the altar and the font about six inches.

W. R. was so devoted to having service begin promptly and without a hitch of inconvenience that he would, on cold Saturday nights, stay by the furnace all night long stoking it with waste log butts he furnished free so that the church would be properly warmed. He always kept a pitcher of water for baptismal purposes sitting on the hot air register so there would be no delay when I needed it at the font. However, at times his ideas of seemliness were rather crude. The swinging oil lamp in the sanctuary developed a slow leak and the oil was making a bad spot on the carpet. I suggested to Min that he fasten something to the bottom of the lamp that would catch the oil. W. R. got an old tin pail and tied it to the base of the lamp with a piece of binder twine. I hesitated to criticize for fear of hurting the good man's feelings, but the women had no such compunctions. The tin pail soon disappeared and in its place a small glass pickle jar was hung in a tiny knitted bag.

This action by the ladies inspired me to make another pious improvement. The font of the church was a beautiful piece of cabinet work, octagonal in shape and seemly in style but the water container was a tawdry piece of cheap graniteware such as was used for a wash basin in kitchen sinks. I was scandalized to administer the sacrament of life from such a mean vessel so, without discussing the matter with anyone, I took the measurements of the font. The next time I went to Utica I hunted in the crockery stores until I found a punch bowl of the right size that I bought and installed. It had never been profaned by liquor and its simple, white luster contrasted nicely with the rest of the font.

W. R. Stamburg's mother-in-law, Mother Hovey, was a woman who had packed much romance and excitement into a long and useful life. In her early years she had been a maid in the household of Baron Herreshoff during his futile attempt to open up the Fulton Chain and she was at the old Manor House at the time of the baron's tragic suicide.

Mrs. Stamburg had rare talent and administrative ability; she directed most of the activities of the inevitable Ladies' Aid of the parish. I remember the church had no proper prayer desk and I had been clamoring for one so much that finally Mrs. J. D. Kernan, a summer member of the church, donated money to buy one. I shall never forget her discreetly presenting the cash and telling me to order the desk but, "Please do it quietly." There was a twinkle of blended mischief and rebuke in her faded blue eyes and to this day I believe this was her kindly, gentle way of telling me to "Take the money, buy my aforesaid desk and shut up about needing it."

Garret Nichols was my Junior Warden; he was also the superintendent of a small pulp mill started by "Black Phil" McGuire to make commercial use of the butts of the saw logs. He was a jolly, amiable man, very devout and loyal to the church. When I fled the castle owned by "Auntie" and my indignant maiden organist, he told me he didn't blame me for leaving the Old Maid's home.

John Kilmer was a great uncle of my organist nemesis. He was over ninety years old. He loved his niece but thought she took herself too seriously. Old John was a fine, upstanding man. For all his age, he took complete care of his own horse and attended church every Sunday. He came around quite often. Before I had a horse and wagon of my own he would drive me about the parish so that I could become more familiar with the home life of my flock. I enjoyed John's company on those trips. During those rides he also filled my head with stories of the old days.

On one of our trips around his beloved Black River Country, old John introduced me to "Uncle Jack" Yeomans. Uncle Jack was not so famous in material success but possessed a charming native shrewdness and ability. Jack was himself so aged that he seemed to linger around the portals of eternity. He was a champion checker player, an accurate and quick mathematician (he was a lumber scaler for a generation) and a capital storyteller. Added to this he had been a close observer of both mankind and of nature, so that he was one of the most interesting personalities of the kind I ever met. He and Alonzo Denton (of Denton & Waterbury) had once killed a bear in the Black River Country with an axe and a club. It was better than any story I ever read to get Uncle Jack to recount the adventure. His comments of people whom he knew or met were always pithy but kind.

Jack's observations of nature, of the habits of trout, of birds, and wild animals were remarkably accurate and extensive. Later in my life I frequently confirmed his dogmatic conclusions from books on nature, or by personal conversations with John Burroughs, whom it was my good fortune to know. Uncle Jack's last job was watching the water flow through the guard lock at the feeder at Forestport—in other words he had little to do. With his matronly daughter for housekeeper, he spent long happy stretches of time playing checkers, telling stories, and smoking his Warnick & Brown, a standard brand of tobacco in the Adirondacks among old-timers.

The land upon which Christ Church stood and the adjacent cemetery was given by Horatio Seymour, who owned large tracts of land around Forestport. Mr. Seymour was the father-in-law of Roscoe Conkling, who ran on the Democratic ticket as a candidate for president of the United States, against Ulysses S. Grant.

Blandina Miller was a vivacious spinster who gained quite a bit of notoriety by how she contracted measles from the Conkling family.

"Ma" Getman operated The Getman House, a small, old hotel. She seldom had any leisure time to devote to outside activities but she always gave generously of her modest means to the church and she had the Ladies' Aid meet frequently in the parlor of the hotel where she served a generous luncheon.

Ma gave the standards for a pair of Eucharist lights in memory of her husband. This last move was very bold at the time since the use of candles tended to confirm any ideas the people had that the Episcopal Church was conforming to the Roman Catholic ritual. I remember dear old Garret Nichols answering that accusation: "It's just the other way around," he said. "The Catholics are somewhat like the Episcopals." Whichever came first is immaterial. The important point is that candles embellished the services and sanctuary at Forestport in 1893.

The Harrigs and the Suypherts were among several high Lutherans affiliated with the Episcopal church. The Harrigs were a rollicking pair of brothers who looked upon the church and religion more as a matter of principle than an appeal to the emotions. Their devotion seemed restricted to fighting at the drop of the hat for Protestantism and Episcopalians and doing their Easter Duty; but they saw to it that their children were baptized and confirmed and left the deeper interests of religion to their wives.

Mrs. Morrall was one of the aged sisters of our congregation and the maternal grandmother of "Skinny" and "Moody" Harrig. She was at the time over ninety years old. She had keen, black eyes and was chipper and lively for one her age. She had been born in Germany and came over to America with her people when she was in her early twenties. She spoke English haltingly because the German language was spoken in her household since she married a German. I spoke German fairly well and she was delighted when I used her native tongue during a pastoral call. I recall her astonishment when I produced my German prayer book. As we prayed together she began to weep as we were repeating the Vater Unser.

I made a startling discovery at that time based on the parish register. Mrs. Morrall had received the rite of confirmation three times! The Lutheran confirmation she received as a girl in Germany. And then, twenty years apart, she had been confirmed twice in our local church. I spoke to Mr. Stamburg about it, but he considered it lightly saying that she had "only received a good strong dose."

Gus Suyphert and his daughter, Lena, were cut out of a different piece of cloth. Gus was an old-fashioned German mystic who delighted in metaphysics; he was my grave digger. Lena was shy and retiring like an old maid. She was her father's constant companion. Not only did she keep house for her father but she even helped him dig graves. The women folks in town looked upon her as odd. The father and daughter team would come to church together, almost holding hands. After the service they would linger and chat with the others, then leave in the same habitual way that they had come. A few people went so far as to make fun of them but I rebuked their callous comments. I held their devotion to each other was something to be commended.

Living at the Getman House afforded me the opportunity to make Charley O'Conner's acquaintance. Charley tended the bar concession at the Getman House and operated a livery stable to boot. In those days, the local community frowned upon a personal friendship between a man-of-the-cloth and a bartender. Sensitive to the community's feelings, I began my alliance quite professionally; however, as the months of seeing each other on a daily basis ticked on, I found Charley and I became the best of friends, which did not surprise me in the least. From our initial meeting I had a feeling Charley and I would hit it off.

Charley had one weakness in life. He liked to swap horses. I call it a weakness advisedly. I remember Charley's horses very well because I used them for my parish calls and funerals. The first one he had was a long-legged, ungainly, irrepressibly independent plug whose bill of sale bore no lesser title than "The Admiral." Charley said he kept him around for laughs. The canal boat captain that he traded with had recommended The Admiral as a good farm horse of no use to him on the boat because he jumped into the canal for a swim whenever he felt like it. The Admiral was not much on looks, but he had one redeeming accomplishment. He was a wizard in the deep snow. He seemed to like to wallow in it. He was rather slow in tough going but, like the good American sea horse he was, the impossible only took him a little longer.

I saw an excellent example of The Admiral's prowess in the snow during my first winter. A mortician from Boonville came to ask me to take the funeral of an Andrew Wells of Well's Mills—then a tiny hamlet on a branch of the Black River about nine miles from Forestport and some five miles back of Hawkinsville. The three Wells brothers were bachelors and some forty years before they had taken up some 1,200 acres of forest land and impounded water and built a sawmill where they sawed and marketed lumber and hauled it to the bank of the canal feeder at Hawkinsville for four dollars a thousand feet and considered this price fair.

Like many of the Episcopalians of that pioneering era they spelled church with a capital "C." The Wells boys also avoided making any contact with "schismatics" such as Presbyterians and Methodists. When they found need of the Church ordinances they summoned an Episcopal cleric to the grounds to serve them. It was the two surviving brothers who told the Boonville mortician to get an Episcopal minister to conduct the funeral, even if he had to go clear to Utica. Since the Boonville parish was without a rector at the time, I was called on.

The time was early April. The roads were almost impassable. I appreciated the offer and company when Charley O'Conner tendered his service to drive me to Well's Mills for the service. We started at nine o'clock in the morning, allowing five hours to complete the eleven-mile trip. The Admiral showed us his stuff, wallowing through everything with gay abandon. We took some shortcuts through fence openings and over fields that were fetlock deep in slippery mud. The winter roads were drifted, the snow punchy and the track uncertain. Where the Black River had overflowed its banks the water was up to the horse's belly. We arrived with an hour to spare. When we put The Admiral into the barn he was a sorry-looking mess.

Following House Prayers there was the seven-mile drive to Boonville where the body was to be put on the train and taken to Holland Patent for the interment. I had to accompany the brothers for the committal service at the grave site. Charley insisted upon driving me properly at the head of the procession to Boonville. I had all I could do to convince him that I appreciated his offer, but it was not necessary. I would just squeeze into one of the other rigs.

John Wells, one of the surviving brothers, gave me a five-dollar honorarium on our return. I tendered the entire amount to Charley O'Conner that night for his services and the use of The Admiral. At my offer Charley went right up in the air and indignantly remarked that if I ever spoke of it again there would be no more hot toddies waiting for me when I came in from a long, cold drive.

Charley's reputation as a horse trader was known far and wide. He was always ready to match wits with all comers. That notoriety made him a marked man among certain gentry who dealt with horseflesh of a shady past. Charley was canny. He could usually take care of himself when deals were conducted in the slow and leisurely custom he preferred. That ploy permitted him time for proper consideration of all the points involved.

One day a stranger drove up to the hotel with a fine looking black mare hooked to a sulky. Her conformation was good and she acted like a fast stepper. Charley's stable at that time consisted mainly of hayburners he let out with his livery rigs, so he didn't pay much attention when the stranger drifted back to the stalls. Even when the stranger broached the matter of a trade he failed to treat him seriously when he told him to look over what he had.

Charley never did tell me what it was that allowed him to be swept up and sucked in but before he realized it the stranger brokered a deal. The dealmaker apparently recognized Charley's weakness in trading. The mare was sweet-looking, the stranger fast-talking. Charley lost his timing and agreed to a hastily conceived arrangement. Before Charley could say "What time did the rooster crow?" the black mare was in a stall and the stranger was driving down the highway with one of Charley's plugs.

From the outset, he should have known she was an outlaw, but it did not take him long to find out her favorite brand of cussedness. The mare not only kicked freely and viciously with her hind legs but she would also rear back on them and strike with her front feet like a stallion so that she had her driver coming and going. If he tied down one end of her she just turned on the forces at the other end and if he tied down both ends she could not travel. So after she had smashed up his buggy and wrecked his harness Charley put her back in the barn and waited for another sucker to some along itching for a trade.

My parish was spread out; many of the calls I knew I would be making would take me into the back country—the more remote parts surrounding Forestport. I knew I was going to need a horse. I was aware of the background of the horse trade that brought the kicking mare to Charley's stable, but I was young and optimistic—at the age when nothing looked impossible. I told Charley about my need to acquire a horse and that I liked the looks of his troublesome mare. He seemed amused at my greenness and warned me to always look past the pretty piece of horse flesh that she seemed to be. I countered his caution. "All she needs is a little more patience than she's ever had, Charley." Looking for a way to pry him to give me a chance I continued, "Besides, she'll get all stocked up and stiff standing in the stable all the time."

With that he consented to let me see what I could do with her. "Go ahead, Reverend," he guffawed, "maybe you can do it. I've tried everything else but I never felt that I could bother the Almighty about a cantankerous female because he wouldn't have time for anything else."

With that he went with me to Utley's harness shop where he purchased a new stock of sicking straps, martingales, curb bits and numerous other mechanical restraints recommended to break horses.

When we were ready we brought the mare out on the barn floor, put the harness and all our new paraphernalia on her and hitched her to the buggy. She did a lot of dancing and prancing but with the help of Ernie, the barn boy, we got everything tight and they jumped back and hollered to me, "Let her go!"

I headed the mare for the Putney place, a good six miles away over a heavy road of loose, mealy sand. I pushed the mare all the way and I drove right on to the barn floor at Putneys'. Stopping by Putneys' in this manner was my way of killing two birds with one stone. From reading the church records, I knew her son had never been baptized. Old Mrs. Putney was rather feeble but seeing me arrive she seemed to come alive and called the entire family in. First we had prayers, then I raised the question of having her strapping son James baptized and confirming him and his grown sister. I felt that the church would—in a way—be responsible if I didn't do all I could to right the derelict responsibilities of the parents.

When we had completed our arrangements James went with me to the barn and held the dancing mare while I got in the buggy and took over. I pressed her over the heavy road back to Forestport. The mare did quite well and was even mannerly when I put her in the stable.

My handling of the outlaw mare appeared so successful that Charley consented to let me use her at the next funeral—providing he could be my driver. Everything went fine until he attempted to obey the undertaker's stop and go signals as the rigs were loaded at the house. The mare would have none of this stop and go business. She was just raring to go and fortunately we were at the head of the procession. Her rearing and plunging created so much excitement that Charley was forced to give her her head and we raced through the village and on to the cemetery with dignity cast to the winds. She stopped at the cemetery fence so we tied her there and waited a half an hour for the rest of the funeral, the solemn half, to arrive.

Abe Whiter, the undertaker, admonished me with ceremonial reproof, "Really, Reverend, I like to have my minister on the alert, but aren't you overdoing it just a little?"

*   *   *

I cannot explain the mysterious forces of Heaven and Earth, but they all came into play the same day I was to conduct the above-described funeral. I was at graveside when Jimmy Duff's relatives found Jimmy dead in a woodlot near the cemetery. Why they picked this particular time I'll never know, but they carried his body onto the cemetery grounds and requested a church service when I finished with the present funeral. Eyebrows went up all around. I nodded my head in the direction of the church next door, gesturing to the small assemblage that indeed was occupied at the moment, but said when I finished I would commit my time to them and the will of the Almighty.

My consent to help brought a strong, "But Reverend . . . ," from

Senior Warden W. R. Stamburg. Stamburg was vaguely pragmatic with a leaning to the conservative. He knew of Jimmy's reputation for benders and did not approve. After the service I lessoned him that, "If there is not room in the church for both saints and sinners, the saints should step out and make room for the sinners since it was for sinners that the Savior founded the church." Mr. Stamburg was as good as his word and poor Jimmy Duff had a proper church funeral.

Jimmy Duff had been a kindly, intelligent old man when he was sober, but all his life he had been a periodic drinker. He was a Civil War veteran and the local correspondent for the Utica and Rome newspapers. His brother was rector of the Episcopal Church at Waterloo, New York.

I recall my brief address that it is my custom to give at a funeral. After carefully rendering the service, I touched briefly on the sad circumstances of Jimmy's death and closed as follows: "Owning his weakness and evil behavior, but leaving with meekness his sins to his Savior." Then I closed with the usual prayer of antiquity: "May his soul, with all the souls of the faithful departed, rest in peace. Amen."

At the "Amen" a sort of holy gasp echoed from all who were congregated in the church. Old Jimmy's body was then taken out to the freshly (and hastily) dug grave. I made it known to all that from then on I would hear no more criticism of church funerals.

*   *   *

The winter of 1892-93 had been severe and long; spring was late. I recall that Easter Sunday, March 25, 1893. The Gospel sleighs, as I called them, drove up on the ice of the basin to the church with their loads of worshippers.

It was when the ice broke up and the spring of '93 freshet was on that I saw for the first time the Black River in all its power and glory. The water at the crown of the dam was all of two feet deep, and tossing, roaring, frothy water came up to within three feet of the bridges. As I watched it, fascinated, and listened to the roar, I coined an expression that I have always remembered: "Better the roaring harmony of Nature than all the artificial clatter of the city."

*   *   *

I remember Forestport in those days as a small town with big aspirations. It was just what its name implies—a port in the forest. Forestport was a woodland community on the Black River Canal. In its heyday, the town was the clearing center for the products of the surrounding forests and they were, in order of importance, lumber ("sticks"), pulpwood, and tan bark. The lumber was sawed from logs that were cut and floated down the Black River in the spring and then held in big booms until the mills were ready to use them. The sawing was done by two large steam-driven mills built on the banks of the canal basin and numerous water-powered mills built along the mountain streams.

Most of the stock logs, floated in the spring drives, came from the Woodhull and North Lake region. When the logs were cut they were skidded to a landing, a wide frozen stillwater on a river. Teams of men worked to place the logs in high piles and marked each end with the code mark of their owners. This was done with the blow of a hand sledge or stamping hammer. All that was left was to await the spring freshets.

Come spring thaw the logs were washed downriver to the mill pond. Once there, river drivers with caulked boots walked among the floating timbers sorting the logs using long pikes to push the softwood inside the various booms that spanned the Forestport basin to await sawing time.

Pulpwood and tan bark were the byproducts of the industry and in those days were considered of minor importance. A man by the name of Hill built a large tannery on Woodhull Creek and handled most of the commercial hides in that section of the country. I only knew of his colorful character by legend. His tannery was abandoned at his death.

There was another tannery on Woodhull that had been abandoned only a year or two before I came to Forestport and I remember looking over the remains of the plant during the summer of 1893. The tannery covered about two acres of ground and the vats, all ten by twenty feet in size, were still filled with the tanning liquor, and the plank walks around the edges of the vats where the workers stood while stirring and turning the animal hides were still in good condition. I also recall two curious steam boilers that were evidently used in some part of the tanning process. They were about four feet in diameter and fourteen feet long. One boiler had three flues about ten inches in diameter but the other had none and they were heated on the same principle as a kettle on a stove. The boilers had been installed some forty years before so I imagine they illustrate early stages in the evolution of tubular boilers. By now, I assume, they have long disappeared as have the vast hemlock forests whose bark they were used to process.

The cream of the exports from Forestport was the "sticks." These were the great spars that were destined to be the masts and timbers of ships and the great columns for the mansions of the rich; but the majority would serve as pilings in New York Harbor and other harbors along the eastern seaboard.

Black Phil McGuire had control of the stick job. He was so nicknamed not because of his race but to distinguish him from his red-headed cousin of the same name. Black Phil was a kindly Irishman, a bluffer, who made a fortune getting the huge spars out of the woods and setting them down in New York's harbor. He educated his daughters at the Academy of Holy Names in Rome, New York.

It was a man-sized job to get those big sticks out of the woods, and to meet that challenge Black Phil always relied on his wild and reckless woods crew. Their badge of fellowship was their full-length beards— the whole lot of them. They cut most of their timbers near Sand Lake. When the snow came they would start hauling them out of the woods to the banks of the Black River canal basin.

Two or three of those sixty to eighty foot spars would make a load for a team. They would load the butts on the forward bob and chain the rear bob to the logs about two thirds of the way back. The bolster on the rear bob was on a kingbolt action the same as that on the front bob and a man seated on the logs steered the rear bob by means of ropes on either side. The arrangement was similar to that used on the long ladder trucks of the fire departments. When the snow was deep, free drivers were warned off the roads in the later afternoons because these sleds never left the road and meeting them meant a long cold wait in the deep snow at the side of the track.

On one occasion, a cold winter's day, not heeding the warning to keep off the North Lake Road in late afternoon, I got caught meeting a flock of teams with the "sticks" and had to pull my mare and cutter off the road into the deep snow and wait a half hour while the teams and loads, stretching back half a mile, went slowly by me. It was a shivery wait for me and the mare.

The commercial development of the Adirondacks was rather a disappointment. Lumbering was done on a grand scale. When the forests were cut over there was nothing to fill the void. Forestport retired into its sylvan seclusion. The canal closed in 1922; its abandonment soon followed. Without the lumber business there was not enough traffic to warrant its maintenance. And besides, everyone at that time was in agreement that the automobile was here to stay and that canals were officially outdated.

*   *   *

When I moved from Auntie's boarding house to the Getman House it seemed like I had entered another world. I became better acquainted with those active in the everyday life of the village and I shed many of the formalities that had shadowed my more cloistered life living in Auntie's.

Ma Getman was a widow and she tried to make her hotel as much like a home as possible. Ma was a square-shooter and an excellent cook. Her services offered no frills but that was made up by her mothering her boarders. We loved her and never let her down.

Right at the start, Ma gave me a sound talking to. "Now look here son," she said, "you have been on ice long enough up in that mausoleum with them old maids. You are young. You should kick up your heels and prance a bit; the good Lord meant that you should have a little fun now and then, but . . . ," she continued more soberly, "don't you go rambling around in them woods without you have somebody with you that knows his way around. We like your preaching and we don't want to have you turn up missing at the Sunday services."

I thanked her for the compliment and advice. A short time later I had cause to remember her timely warning.

*   *   *

A longtime friend, a former schoolmate, David Matthews, came up to visit me for five days. This was the summer when the "Grand Tour" was the current rage in Europe. It seemed every student was taking post-graduate courses in human relations—tramping and boating around Europe—getting a continental polish and seeing the world at the same time. In my effort to try and keep my friend amused I proposed we take our own Grand Tour down the Black River canal feeder to Boonville and back in a rowboat. The journey seemed a simple undertaking, so I did not consider discussing the trip with anyone except to remark that we were going to Boonville for the day.

The canal feeder was nine miles long, winding poetically around the hills from the basin at Forestport to the basin of the canal proper at Boonville. It had a strong current. I knew it would be easy going down and would require extra power returning against the current. I borrowed an extra pair of oars as well as the boat from the lockhouse man.

The trip down was dreamy and hauntingly peaceful. The rower had only to pat the water with the oar blades to steer. We swept along at a good rate and reached Boonville in ample time for a good dinner at the famous Hulbert House. After dinner and a smoke on the upper gallery of the hotel, we took our time and explored this lovely village. We secured the key to the Episcopal church (which was without a rector then), and said a few prayers in the then rather musty temple.

It was mid-afternoon when we went back to our boat and started on our return trip to Forestport. I took the stroke oar, for David Matthews was a strong, athletic fellow and I proposed to set the pace. We speedily got into a rhythmic swing and made fine progress for nearly a half mile of stillwater on the feeder. But when we struck the strong current, we discovered that we were standing still. When we ceased pulling at the oars to discuss the dismaying fact, the boat drifted back toward Boonville. Matthews, who gloried in his physical prowess, took a single pair of oars to pull while I sat in the stem and tried steering. But then we lost ground—or water rather. What to do was a puzzler.

About then a voice boomed out over the water. "Which way are you young fellers going? I say, which way are you young fellers going?" We looked about and noticed the old man shouting to us from the towpath. "You fellers are a-pulling one way and your boat's going the other. You won't get anywhere that way. There's a hell of a bore in that damn feeder every time they open them damn feeder paddles up in Forestport. Folks around here never tries rowing up against it. We gets us a tow if we can't find no other way."

We were in front of the dooryard of a tiny, weather-beaten dwelling on the heel path side of the canal feeder. I espied a clothesline stretched across a corner of the yard and barren of any laundry. I went to the door and rapped. When it was opened by a kindly faced woman, I doffed my hat and asked it I might buy the weathered clothesline, explaining our need for one. The corners of her mouth twitched in a suppressed smile as she observed that we should have a mule to tow the boat. I acknowledged that but said we would have to turn ourselves into mules to get back to Forestport. The good woman ended her brief banter by taking down the clothesline, looping it up, and giving it to me as she said, "Take it and welcome. Hope you make Forestport before dark." She was going to take nothing but I thrust a quarter into her hand, expressed my thanks, and hurried down to Matthews, who was holding the boat against the tug of the current.

We paddled across to the towpath, where we fastened the line to the bow oarlock and started off with vim and determination. But alas, the craft would not steer right without a man at the helm. So we took shifts of half an hour each, one sitting in the stem and steering with an oar as a paddle, the other pounding the gravel of the towpath. Forestport was eight miles away.

On a bend, as I was towing, we met a team towing a barge to Boonville. The helmsman of the barge heard us talking but as yet could not see our tiny craft. He bawled out to his driver, "What's coming?"

"A steamboat," yelled back the driver.

Dan was on the rope when the captain, with a big-bush-of-a-whisker-face, sitting in a rocking chair on the deck of his barge let out a roar of laughter that could be heard for miles.

"Hey, Abergail, come up here quick," he bellowed like a red bull in a dry pasture. A tall, skinny female climbed up on deck from below. She had her scraggily hair wound up in a mangy bun that clung to the side of her head at a rakish angle and she was polishing her specs with her apron as she cocked her head to set the bun on even keel.

"Look yonder, Daughter," the whiskered foghorn continued, "thar is one of them two-legged jackasses I've been warning you against for the last twenty years."

The scarecrow stood without batting an eye until we had almost passed; then she let out with an unearthly piercing screech that sounded like a penny squawker on a sawdust boiler. "You want I should get the shotgun, Paw?" Then she repeated herself in her most blue-ribbon boisterous way. "You want I should run get the shotgun? You want I should, Paw?" This struck me as excruciatingly funny and I fear that I rocked the boat much to my friend's discomfort for when we changed places he grew quite reckless and attempted to pull me into the canal.

Another time, when I was steering and we were passing a large barge, the helmsman observed to me, "Cap'n, I was going to propose you swap mules with me but I see you've cropped the ears of that jackass you've got towing and it's again' the law during fly season. I'll have to report you to the Humane Society."

It was well after dark when we got to the guard lock at Forestport. We returned the borrowed boat and oars with profuse thanks to the lock tender and hustled to the Getman House. Ma Getman, who was becoming anxious about us, got us a good hot supper. On bringing it to us in the dining room, she tarried long enough to chide us for our "wild recklessness." But for all of.her chiding, Ma was a good soul. She came in as we finished supper and told us not to get down to breakfast until nine o'clock, when the dining room closed. She knew we were dead tired. Then just as she turned to leave she asked me to be more careful in the future. I promised. But as she began to trail off she counseled that if I did any more Grand Touring I should take her nephew, Ernie, the barn boy at the hotel. "He isn't any good with the books, but he has a lot of sense. He also could show you the best fishing holes."

The next day, Matthew's last, we took Ma's advice and went off with Ernie. We helped him finish his chores so he could get away earlier, dug worms, and headed off to fish Pine Creek. The creek was so narrow except at the pools, that one could step across it. Ernie assured us the creek was "lousy with trout" in spite of the fact that it might not look as if the prospects for a catch were good. His wisdom proved true. On that trip we caught 125 fish, all of a good size. We threw the smallest back in just to get rid of them. That was in the days before the fish laws were enacted. There were no laws governing the hunting and trapping of bear in those days, either, and the deer hunting season began on August 1, so wild meat was a common dish at the Getman House.

*   *   *

About mid-summer Dr. Kilbourn drafted me as an assistant in his surgery. Doc was the general practitioner of the village and a good country doctor; but in that region where the lumbering industry was so important, much of his practice dealt with injuries in that field of work.

The good doctor was an active member of our church and he often attended Sunday services. During a gathering of the congregation after services he asked me about a rumor he'd heard regarding my novice experience in first aid work. My knowledge was minor, consisting of the practical care of dressing wounds. I thought it quite basic but he told me that there were times when he could use tried-and-true help and that he would like to call on me. So it was that some of my friends came to call me "Doc."

The first case that I was called on to help with was a French Canadian who had cut off a toe with an axe. The man's brother brought him in to the office. As we were washing the wound the brother suddenly remembered something and began digging around in his breast pocket where he kept his loose chewing tobacco. Like a magician who has surprised himself he produced the missing big toe and handed it to the doctor with instructions to sew it back on. Speaking in French, Dr. Kilbourn explained that was impossible and went on with his work. The brother was disgruntled and cursed, saying he was being cheated.

I sterilized the doctor's instruments in a dripping pan on the kitchen stove with boiling water and a shot of carbolic acid. Our patients would come in with their feet swathed in red flannels, gunny sacks, red handkerchiefs, and old rags sometimes wrapped as large as a peck measure. When we had cleared this mess away and washed the foot thoroughly we would put on an elastic bandage from the ankle up to allay the hemorrhage. If the cut was bad and an amputation of a toe was necessary, the patient had to be etherized.

That was my job. I shudder now when I realize the chances I took and how little I knew about this highly technical work. With all the assurances of a specialist, I would roll up a freshly ironed towel in the shape of a cone and put the open end over the patient's nose and pour the ether over the towel. At first I was inclined to be cautious but Dr. Kilbourn would growl, "Don't be afraid of these Canucks, you can't kill the blank blanks." So I would pour and the doctor would be right. One can of ether would just irritate some of them and it would take almost a second can to put them under. Dr. Kilbourn told me that the constant hard work in the woods and hearty eating caused the body to build up a strong resistance against any poisons and it acted in the same way against ether or any of the other medicines he gave them, so he always had to double the dose for a lumberjack to get the desired reaction.

I still remember Dr. Kilbourn's help when he heard that I had visited a home to offer prayers to all the children who had scarlet fever. I had put on a long raincoat as my only precaution against exposure. Following that visitation I aired the coat out but my presence at the quarantined home brought stiff criticism from the community and added to the accumulating dark clouds that gathered over my young head during my stay in Forestport.

The doctor informed me the raincoat had been little protection. I was also told he took up his cudgel in my behalf in barrooms, at the post office and wherever he could get an audience, telling all that he understood I felt my duties were as important as his professional responsibilities and that I should be allowed to pursue my obligations as I saw fit. Thanks to his efforts I weathered another gale of flak.

The patient that I remember best was George Thomas. George ran an axe blade about three inches into the fore part of his foot. The injury required that he have his middle toe amputated. The only effect the ether seemed to have on George was to make him swear harder. The more I poured on the cone the madder he got and the more he swore. George took over two cans of ether, either because of my inept nervousness or his natural cussedness, before he passed out; but the doctor did a neat job on his foot and I remarked at the time that he could probably wear a smaller sized shoe on that foot. We put George to bed on the top floor of Ma Getman's hotel and I took his meals up to him and gave him what little care he needed. We got quite well acquainted during the first week of his recuperation and he treated me much differently when he learned of my profession.

Dr. Kilbourn kept crutches around for the cripples to use and George was up and around in less than a week. Then he became morose and restless lying around doing nothing and he started drinking heavily. By the time the week was out he had discarded his crutch as a "damned nuisance" and was walking around on his heel. He kept out of my way during his extended bender. But when the month the doctor had allotted him was over he sobered up and I went with him to the doctor's office carrying his discarded crutches for his final inspection. I had expected to see that the combination of liquor and carelessness had made a mess of his wound, but he passed with flying colors. The cut had closed nicely and the scar was already bleaching.

Early the next morning there was a knock at my door. It was George. He took off his hat politely and hung it on the end of a fishing rod case that he held in his hand. I invited him in and he sat down on the edge of a chair. With awkwardly repressed profanity he thanked me for all that I had done for him and, more like himself, he boasted that he had bought the best blankity-blank split-bamboo fly rod in Denton and Waterbury's blank, blankity general store for me. He hoped that when I used the blankity-blank rod I would think kindly of George Thomas, blankity-blank old bum. I used the rod many years.

It was while at the surgery that I first heard about the case that seemed to affect me the deepest of any with which I had to deal. It was one of those weird, out-of-this-world cases where only fools rush in. Someone had to go, so I elected myself.

The case was ensnared in ecclesiastical red tape. I held the church somewhat responsible because it involved sloppy record keeping. I was resolved to do whatever I could to prevent any recurrence of the sad condition. My stand was youthful and I remained committed in spite of the attention I brought to it with my bumbling ineptness.

Our church laws forbade the use of the burial office if the deceased had not been baptized. My stand on the case attracted so much public attention that Dr. Kilbourn counseled me to take it easy. But I was young and lacked experience. If I were now faced with the same problem I would approach the situation with the assumption that the sacrament had been administered and use the regular burial service to avoid all the embarrassment that I had to deal with.

The case involved the death of a fifteen-year-old girl from a poor, outlandish family. It came in for so much publicity because the body was kept at the house until decomposition had set in. We did not have sob sisters in those days but the back fence gazettes were just as efficient in spreading the gossip and the Board of Health was forced to act. The board limited their official action to an order to Abe Whiter to go out to the backwoods house, procure the body, and bury it. Abe was a God-fearing man brought up in a Christian family; he took his profession seriously and could not conceive of an interment without the blessing of the church. This is where I entered. Abe did not hesitate to remind me of my Christian obligations. He could have called for help at the Presbyterian church but since he was our grave digger he came to me.

During surgery that morning I had heard about the incident. By the time Abe spoke to me the whole village knew all about the case—including the unalterable fact that the girl had not been baptized. The consensus seemed to be that I was due for a panning whatever I did. I conducted the full service of House Prayers with but one concession: I wore no vestments. Thus I carried out my missionary duties with a mercy and understanding that was acceptable to the various factions in the town. My stand, so pedantic and inconsequential to the casual observer, had a wholesome effect on the village. It was brought forcibly to their attention that one must value and use the Christian Sacraments if one is to have the Christian Ordinance.

As I think back about this case, I believe I suffered the most—not from having to endure the stench of the decaying body during the twenty-minute service, for I would not hurry it—but from the nervous strain the occasion left on me. This condition was brought about from the pressure brought to bear from the local aristocracy of worshippers who were inclined to regard my missionary activities as something foreign and apart from their beliefs since they had all been formally baptized, and by my church's stand on baptism. My youthful religious fervor rebuffed the snobbish attitude and I was irked at the church laws. But in the end I believe I found the best compromise and in the process taught some values. Wrestling to get all the right angles and details involved did cause me stress and I was years trying to throw it off.

* * *

Charley had bought a couple of pigs from a farmer over on the Hawkinsville road. He asked me if I would like to ride over with him and help pick them up. His intention was to fatten them on hotel garbage, then use the meat for his free lunch counter. I seized the opportunity.

Arriving at the farm, we took a wooden crate and placed it in the buckboard. A ramp with slats was placed from the open end of the wagon, where the crate was, to the ground. Charley trapped the first pig, placed a fruit basket over its head and backed the squealing hog up the incline and into the crate. I held the cover down while he went for the second. Just as he was bringing the second noisy pig back to the wagon I released my pressure on the cover of the crate just enough so that the first pig escaped and ran away squealing. "Reverend Byron!" was all the Irishman said before he went about repeating the loading process. I had to let one of those pesky pigs out four times before I could break Charley down. But when he did break he went whole hog, so to speak, and the air was blue with the fumes of pungent Hibernian sulfur. I know, because I can interpret gestures. I understand a little Irish, too. The tale of our misadventure circulated. I could not have been happier. That event marked what was to be the beginning of a long and beautiful friendship.

I could write a book about the conditions that Charley told and showed me. They were raw; the laughs were few and far between for the things he shared spoke of human misery. Charley O'Conner was the hottest pipeline that I ever had but he always made it a point of saying to me, "Now, Father, this is strictly confidential." I never violated Charley's confidences.

*   *   *

So passed the time of my first pastorate at Forestport. I carried on without having any revivals as some churches did. This fact caused one of my new parishioners, an old mill hand, to inform me about what motivated him to join my parish. He clued, "You can join the Episcopal church without getting excited like you've got to git if you join the Methodists or the Presbyterians."

The great social event of that season was the reception given to President Grover Cleveland and his wife, who returned to visit his brother, the Reverend William Cleveland, pastor of the Presbyterian church. (The couple had visited previously on the occasion of their honeymoon in 1886, and Cleveland, as governor, had been to the Bisby

Club in August of 1883.) The reception at the manse rivaled the famed McGuire wedding.

The lion of the occasion was Forestport's own John Kilmer, then a fine upstanding old man of ninety years of age. As he walked toward the President, stooped with age, he presented his hand to shake and with all the self-respect and self-possession that characterized him he stately announced, "I present to you, Mr. President, the hand that shook the hand of Marquis de LaFayette in Utica in 1825." That led to a re-hashing of a story all in attendance had heard before but which President Cleveland seemed to enjoy listening to. The famous LaFayette reception he attended was held in the old Johnson house that stood where the Savings Bank now (1893) stands in the city of Utica.

*   *   *

The other incident occurred when I was a divinity student in Syracuse. Forestport folks called it "The McGuire Affair." It was a romance having to do with Black Phil's daughter, Frances. I never learned just how the romance blossomed but one did with a James K. McGuire (different family with the same last name). James was a big politician and businessman in the "Saline City" of Syracuse, N.Y. At the young age of twenty-four he was elected on the Democratic ticket as the "boy mayor of the city." When I arrived in Forestport I came to know the family of Phillip McGuire.

*   *   *

My own social life during those happy months had a background of stirring romance. My first love was Jessie, the organist from Alder Creek; but when I moved to Ma Getman's I came under the influence of her beautiful sixteen-year-old daughter—actually I fell head over heels. I was so serious that I talked over the prospects of marriage with Ma. She took the more sensible attitude assuring me that my romantic feeling would pass. She knew I intended to leave Forestport to pursue advanced work. She was right. Several years later both of my Forestport sweethearts married, but we remained friends the rest of our lives.

Realizing I was too young to continue in the work of my sacred profession without more institutional experience and study, I left Forestport and the Black River in the autumn of 1893 for post-graduate work in our General Seminary in New York.

The Road to Atwell

If a notion prompts you to seek a much-needed break from polished life, turn toward North Lake. The last miles from Reed's old mill pond trace the arduous route once made by horse and wagon. It is the sole back country road leading to the headwaters of the Black River country.

Byron-Curtiss: "Since I have been coming to the region I have seen few changes save for the slight changes lumbering makes. The only other change is the method of getting in. The first motor car negotiated the entire stretch in 1907. When I first came, automobiles could not have gotten in had they existed. Teams of horses negotiated the rough-and-tumble narrow, stony, soft wagon trail well, though the buckboard they pulled pitched so much passengers often got out and walked. A trip from Forestport Station to the foot of the lake (North Lake) often took eight to ten hours."

Something strange happens from Louse Hill to the Timber Line. One minute you're wide open on a sand plain. The next minute you enter the forest-dark, inviting and timeless. Whiskey Spring comes into view just before the notch in Mulchi Hill. Peeks of Mink Lake flicker between the trees. Reed's Mill Pond is opposite the track to North Wilmurt. Horses ascending wet rocks gave Slip Rock Hill its name. At so-called "Pop Sherers" the pavement ends. Pop and his sheep are long gone. Railroad Hills is next, so formidable a challenge a rail line never left the drawing board. North Lake lies six miles beyond.

Old-time resident: "It's a twisting, rough dirt track and it keeps out the riffraff a permanent resident declared seventy years ago. That person was dead serious. There is still only a handful of year-round residents."

Barren tree branches of winter. Slick stretches during mud season. Summer's greenery or autumn's lush, gracious colors. The roadway returns the traveler from his modern-day haste to simpler times. Yesterday in the Adirondacks. Atwell, New York.

Tall Stories of Atwell Martin

"Old Atwell Martin was a noted Adirondack guide and hunter."

This caption appeared on the back of a faded photograph of Bart Matteson's that his wife, Ola, owned, reported E. A. Spears in the Utica Observer Dispatch *newspaper article he penned entitled "Hermit of North Creek: His Romance Shattered, Recluse Took to Woods." Reclusive? Atwell was, to a point, but he had earned enough respect as a guide to have been listed in the 1870* Guide of the Adirondack Wilderness.

He lived in an A-frame wigwam-type shack almost twenty miles from the nearest town and he liked to keep his distance from women. His appearance could be called wild or unkempt and he certainly had a bushelful of odd habits. He worked hard at not doing too much, preferring to labor just enough to make whatever money he really needed to get by on.

But Atwell Martin had an inventive talent of telling tall tales to the fishermen and hunters who were his clients. What made stories by and about Old Atwell so popular? Rev. Byron-Curtiss preferred not to explain but rather to inform and "add to the harmless gaiety of the readers." I'll let you be the judge of Atwell Martin, hermit of North Lake.

*　　*　　*

Even with Babe, his blue ox, Paul Bunyan was a piker beside Old Atwell, who came to the headwaters of the Black River a decade before the state surveyors arrived in 1850 and lived in a clearing by a brook that still bears his name. Our post office is also named Atwell. He made his impression, not only on the wilderness, but also on the minds of his contemporaries who passed on the legends we have of him. It is said he could shoot around a corner. He was hunting a fox on Grindstone Mountain when the cunning animal dodged around a ledge. Without hesitation Atwell bent the barrel of his trusty old gun across his knee, shot around the ledge, and got the fox.

One time, as he got on the eastern shore of Mud Lake, he espied a magnificent buck standing out across the little glacial body of water. Taking careful aim at so long a distance, Atwell fired.

When the smudge from the black powder had settled, he was surprised to see the buck still standing across the lake. He reloaded as quickly as possible and fired again. Again, when the smoke cleared, the buck was standing in relatively the same position. Quickly reloading, he elevated his sights and aimed carefully for the discharge. This time he did not wait for the powder to clear, but began ramming home a charge in the muzzle-loader at once. Well, he shot five times at each end of Mud Lake and it took Old Atwell an hour to detour and get to where the buck had been, when to his amazement there were five bucks heaped on top of each other. It was in November; the winter closed down about then. Old Atwell did not have to rustle much for meat that winter.

*   *   *

In the following text taken from Spears' *Observer-Dispatch* article he continues telling what he learned from spending countless hours talking to Byron Cool, who knew Atwell best.

"Then young Atwell fell head-over-heels in love with a girl which decided she didn't like him." That stunned Atwell.

"Most young men would have picked up another girl and forgotten their broken hearts, but not Atwell. He was different. It drove him to the tall timber where he landed at North Lake.

"Atwell wanted to build a shack to live in, so Byron Cool hauled several logs from the foot of the lake to Reed's Mill a few miles down the tote road toward Forestport, and when the logs had been sawed, he nailed together his little board wigwam in which he lived for many years.

"Atwell Martin wasn't much of a hunter, trapper, or guide. In the summer he sat out in front of his wigwam and played his fiddle, probably mournful things in memory of that girl, and in the winter with his wigwam covered, sometimes with as much as six feet of snow, he also played his fiddle. He sought every newspaper he could get hold of and read its every word.

"He nailed over his door a dried up weasel to keep the witches away. He thought it was also bad luck to stick stove wood through the griddle in the top of the stove. He insisted on loading up the stove through the door at the end of the firebox."

It was those oddities that first gave rise to rumors about the reclusive Atwell, that he "took things easy—except for that girl," and once he took on a bit of guiding and had a hand in other odd jobs "making just enough to live on," word of the jilted hermit spread like warm butter on a hot summer's day.

*   *   *

There were many stories told about the hermits of the North Woods who seemed to find the solitude of the Adirondacks strangely congenial. There was nothing to do and plenty of time to do it. North Lake had an abundance of solitude so it was an ideal place for a hermit to live.

Atwell cared little about ambition and without that character strength he viewed village life as distasteful. He escaped the distractions work required; he left behind women who, if a relationship was made, could "break one's heart"; and he left behind contact with his fellow man and embraced instead a life of solitude in a truly primeval wilderness. The headwaters' ample rugged bosom, he felt, would receive him kindly; its territory would afford sufficient scope for his attitude toward avoiding work (other than what was necessary for survival) of making a living and all without the tug and struggle of society. He could deal with the poverty of nature with only necessities: tools to build a cabin, steel traps for procuring fur-bearing animals, a rifle and ammunition for hunting. In a small clearing alongside a little stream, that is now colloquially known as Atwell's Brook, that emptied into Lake Sophia less than a half mile away, Atwell had found his home.

Stern necessity demanded he explore his new-found surroundings beyond the environs of his cabin to provide his larder with game and fish and to put out trap lines. The success of those lines would be what he would depend on to secure cash needed to purchase flour, tea, beans, and other staples not to be found in the wilds.

By reason of his timid nature he adopted a unique way to make his initial explorations and not get lost. Armed with an axe and his dog in leash he would blaze his way as far as he desired in a given direction. Then if he wished to investigate or explore at an angle from this line he would tie his dog to the last blazed tree and cautiously advance into the forest and continue as long as he could hear the dog's bark in answer to his calls. In this manner he became familiar with the vast trackless territory. By his second year he knew all the valleys and had blazed trails to ponds and lakes where deer came to drink and fish abounded. Some of those bodies of water—Horn, Canachagala, Hardscrabble, and Little Woodhull Lakes—still have trails leading to them that were originally blazed by Atwell Martin.

To Atwell belongs the dubious honor of trapping the last wolves around the Black River headwaters. This was authenticated by an incident that occurred since my own days in the region.

Richard Camp was driving a team over a tote road on the top of a mountain on the eastern shore of North Lake, a log chain trailing behind the wagon. Into the muffled steps of the horses there sounded, for an instant, the sharp click of metal. Camp stopped the team, thinking a horse had cast a shoe; however, both horses had their iron shoes intact. Typical of an experienced woodsman he did not forget the matter but continued to investigate for the cause of the clicking. Tangled in the leaves and debris over which the log chain had dragged, he found a rusty iron ring. As he picked it up Camp found a rusty chain was attached. Further digging uncovered an old wolf trap. Word of such an unusual find traveled quickly by the grapevine. Charles Cunningham, an aged North Wilmurt hunter-trapper, on hearing of it, visited Camp. Upon inspection he identified the trap as having been one that Atwell used forty years earlier. Hearing Cunningham's belief, Camp wanted verification, so decided to take the trap to Atwell's sister, Mary Hall, who still lived, at that time, in Forestport, and who agreed it had belonged to Atwell. That height is now known as Wolf Mountain.

*   *   *

The only gainful labor fitting the dignity of a hermit was "goyding" eager gentlemen who blossomed out once a year with guns and fishing rods but were innocent of the knowledge about where and how to use them. Since the conversational value of a fishing or hunting trip in the wide open spaces was a topic of conversation between city sports during the rest of the year, the guide would strive to be highly entertaining to his charges. If he acted in this way he would be richly rewarded. Atwell was well aware of this and he seldom disappointed his patrons.

Atwell had lived in the woods near Lake Sophia ten years before a surveying party came to plan for the building of several dams creating reservoirs for water storage along the Black River Canal. Once North and South Lake reservoirs were completed a few hardy sportsmen began to filter in over the original North Lake road. (The old route left the train depot at Buffalo Head and went east to Bellingertown and Enos. There it crossed the Black River and continued northeast to Farrtown, crossed Twin Lakes Creek and headed north to Reed's Mill. From Reed's it continued northeast to the head of North Lake.) Atwell built comfortable campsites for the sportsmen he guided along the new shoreline of the impounded water. Easy money (it didn't require hard physical labor) was to be gained by sharing his total knowledge about the locality.

Atwell's chief contribution to the construction enterprise was in the preliminary information he offered to the surveyors as to the nature and character of the area they were to cover. His chief glory was the dogged persistence with which he stuck to his little clearing, in spite of his taciturnity and indifference, becoming the pioneer and valued guide to sportsmen who, though never especially welcome to him, he served faithfully and acceptably for many years.

His services were particularly appreciated for he had mastered the secrets of his wilderness and knew how and where to secure game and fish. His eccentricities and peculiarities were numerous, which emphasized the worthiness of his virtues as a pioneer. His virtues were not submerged but survived in spite of his oddities. No better proof of his strong and superior personality is the fact that another recluse, Owen Jones, who settled on the tract with the advent of sportsmen and who was a contemporary of Atwell's for twenty-five years, has left behind but two or three stories of himself while those of Atwell are many. I will write of those fanciful and true stories I have verified by talking to old and reliable people who personally knew Atwell Martin.

As the headwaters of the Black River increased in popularity, notable people who were wilderness enthusiasts arrived by buckboard. Atwell guided them all at one time or another. Among the most notable were Judge Northrop of Syracuse and the Honorable James S. Sherman of Utica, later vice-president of the United States. There were professional men not only from the Mohawk Valley but from as far away as Albany, the state's capital.

Among the annual visitors were Captain A. B. Gardner, John Roberts, and two brothers, Harry and Joe Beach. Gardner worked at the photography firm of Gardner and Frey of Utica. The captain would boast that he always managed to get to his camp over the rough roads without breaking a camera or a single glass plate. Once he induced Atwell to sit for his picture. From that still life, Frazier, a notable portrait painter from Utica, painted a striking oil on canvas portrait of this old-time guide. It showed a tall, angular man with stooped shoulders similar in some respects to President Abraham Lincoln. He appeared rather stiff in a store-bought suit, a semi-hard bowler hat, and a knotty stick for a cane. His feet were encased in homemade moccasins of deer leather. The face, in repose, is kindly but firm and gives a hint of his character. People who saw the painting and knew Atwell said it was a good likeness. The last I ever saw the portrait it was hanging on the wall of the Atwell post office. I would imagine it would be a prize if it has survived to this day.

*   *   *

"Atwell Martin had been highly recommended to me as a guide," Harry Beach of the Rome Beach Lumber Company family told me. He had a long, lean, mangy appearance. "That was discouraging," Beach recalled with a hoot, "but if you backed off a little and took in his profile you could see a reflection of the 'light' that was hidden under his bushel of tonsorial neglect."

"When I inquired among the natives to get the local slant on him I found that he was a guide with a breezy line of chatter who knew his way around in the woods. The men liked him as a person and respected his woodcraft skills. The women? Well, they considered him a mite careless about the truth and other peoples' victuals. At first I thought this might be due to a natural feminine prejudice against men cooks but there was irrefutable evidence.

"He was easy to deal with so we made arrangements. One of my specific understandings was that I was to do the cooking. Atwell was agreeable but it did not set well with him. In fact he became a mite moody, he didn't seem to live up to the advance notice I had of him being a raconteur. I was later to learn otherwise!"

*   *   *

Reports of Old Atwell's ability to eat enormous quantities of food are persistent, some fanciful and legendary. He was noted for his sincere yet quaint and humorous expressions related to food. Those lines would often make an even larger impression than that made by the quantity he could put away. Mrs. Putney used to be the cook at Perry's Number Two logging camp. Later, Ed Klock's wife hired her as cook and domestic helper at the State House. Atwell was fond of her cooking and always stood by her when she was putting up the lunches for parties he was hired to guide for, watching, hoping, and often asking in his high falsetto voice if she was going to be packing this or that into the tin lunch pails.

Harry Beach told me the following story and he swears it's true. On tramping out to Forestport for supplies over the old North Lake Road by way of "Pony Bob's," Atwell used to sometimes stop overnight with "Wash" Brunson and "Lib," his wife. One evening he and Wash began playing cards at the kitchen table. Lib had just taken a batch of bread out of the oven and piled it up on the far end of the table opposite Atwell and Wash. Then she covered the loaves with towels to let them cool. When it came along bedtime, Lib noticed Atwell was nibbling a piece of bread crust but thought nothing of it, supposing he had reached under the cloth and broken off a side crust from a loaf, such as sometimes form on homemade bread.

When Lib arose at five in the morning, as was her custom, to start the fire and get breakfast for Wash after his chores were done, she came downstairs and, to her surprise, found the men playing seven-up and Atwell still nibbling. Lib quickly noted the cloth she had placed over the bread now lay flat on the table's surface except for a slight rise at one end. Atwell Martin was eating the remains of her last loaf; he had obviously eaten the entire batch of five loaves during the night.

*   *   *

One fall Art Bellinger, of Bellingertown, took Atwell a grain sack of apples, knowing the old hermit's fondness for the fruit. They visited in his wigwam cabin until late in the evening, Atwell munching the apples. At last Art lay down in the bunk and went to sleep. When he awoke in the morning Atwell was still munching apples and was almost down to the bottom of the grain sack.

*   *   *

When Gideon Perry was getting out lumber in the Little Woodhull country Atwell worked for him one season scaling logs. He boarded with the men in the frame house at Reed's Mills. Mrs. Roselle Putney of Forestport did the cooking. She always put up an extra big lunch for Atwell, in a pack basket, practically filled. One morning she had hot

soda biscuits for breakfast. As the men were going out to their job, Atwell picked up his pack basket lunch, hefted it, and said plaintively to
Mrs. Putney: "Miss Putney, you ain't got any of them soda biscuits left
have you, to put in for chinking?"

*   *   *

"I should have taken the hint when I heard Atwell mention a 'blind
deer' when he told me about the time he was hard up for fresh meat,"
reminisced Harry Beach during one of our talks, "and how he never felt
very well when he did not have plenty of fresh meat to eat."

The old man's story continued in this way. It seems during one of
his famine spells Atwell managed to crawl out to a favorite deer runway back of his camp about a mile, toward Little Woodhull Lake. He
used to secure two or three deer a year here, so he eased himself down
on a stump and patiently watched for several hours. Eventually he saw
two deer coming down the trail moving slowly and carefully. He
cocked his gun and waited for them to get in position for a solid line
shot. Odd as it seems, he noticed the deer in the rear had the tail of the
front deer in his mouth; the forward-most deer seemed to be leading
the other. He soon saw by their course that the second deer was blind.

This was a situation filled with possibilities. Atwell took careful
aim and shot the tail of the leader off close to its rump. It jumped and
made a speedy getaway jumping into the woods at once. The blind deer
stood on the runway shaking and bewildered with the tail of his companion dangling from its mouth. Slipping up quietly, Atwell took the
end of the gory tail in his hand and led the deer to his cabin's clearing
where he butchered it properly. Being blind and so not able to get ac-
tively around the forest, it was big, fat, and in prime condition. And so
the old hermit managed to satisfy not only his gnawing hunger but to
perform the work with the least amount of labor.

Another tale the Beaches heard revolved around Atwell shooting a
large black bear at Little Woodhull Lake that proved too heavy for him
to tote to camp. It was circulated that he solved that problem by starting a fire, roasting, and eating a sufficient quantity of the meat to make
his load light enough for him to carry.

*   *   *

Harry Beach made it a point to tell me that his party had such good
luck on their first trip out with Atwell that they returned several more

times, but that as successful as they were that first season it was not without an incident that underscored the guide's reputation.

"Atwell filled his part of the bargain. He showed us plenty of game but he was not putting his soul into his work. Something was missing. The old man was holding out on us and he was being subtle about it. We primed him to little avail until the last day of the trip. Then we decided to give our reluctant guide the works and see it he could take it."

Beach continued reminiscing. "We had spent our week hunting in Township 5 first near the Indian River and later around Horn Lake. While Atwell knew the region well and was good at pack-carrying, making camp, chopping wood and the like, he was a bit untidy and careless in washing up. So Ben and myself did the cooking for the party. All week it seemed impossible to fill Old Atwell up; he was always scraping his plate and asking for more. So on the morning of our return trip to North Lake, knowing if we broke camp early and left we would arrive at North Lake and our boats by noon, my brothers and I plotted since we had time to kill.

"After breakfast Joe said, 'Atwell, we better have our lunch now. It might be easier and save the bother of stopping to set up our cooking pots at noon if we eat our lunch now.' The old hermit answered: 'Just as you say, Mr. Beach. Lunch naturally comes after breakfast anyways so why wait. Fetch on the grub.' So we mixed another pail of flapjack batter, fried another pan of salt pork and boiled another pot of coffee and shoved it at him. He ate it all to our astonishment.

"Just for deviltry as Atwell was chewing the last pork rind and wiping his tin plate with a slice of bread, I quizzed him. 'Atwell, you might have your supper now? We could then push right through till nightfall.' At that suggestion he didn't even blink when he assented saying, 'As a matter of course, supper came after lunch; why wait on formalities?' Atwell propped himself against the butt of a tree and looked like he was ready and willing to consume more food! If he had any hint of our little plot he never let on. So the boys set to making another huge batch of flapjacks, another pot of coffee, and frying their last hunk of salt pork. Atwell did that full justice putting down that feed to the last crumb.

"As he filled his pipe for a smoke, the party washed the soiled dishes and stowed them in the pack. Joe then directed, 'Come on now, Atwell, we are late and we must hit the trail.' But to our surprise he looked up from his comfortable post and calmly informed us he never worked after supper. Our deep plot was not working out right. Giving Atwell the works was like putting the cat in the cage with the canary. A contented smile began to move across his face. He belched and beamed on us to show his appreciation of our kindred spirits. Atwell was sitting pretty. All was well with his world. It was obvious he was not about to budge. He forgave us for our misunderstanding the proper succession of his daily routine and began to converse affably about this and that until he locked into a mellow reminiscence.

'Well, boys, the luckiest shot I ever had was when I was paddling the dugout a bit beyond Joe Tanner's point in the second wide waters of North Lake in the vicinity of Split Rock Bay. A buck was swimming along easy like. He wasn't in any more of a hurry than I was. At that time I was fresh out of meat so I put the paddle down and picked up my gun, aimed at its neck just at the water line, and fired. The bullet went through its neck, severing the spinal cord and killing it instantly but then it exited the deer and skipped on the water twice. On the first skip it went smack-dab through a thirty-two-inch trout that had just at that moment jumped into the air for a fly. It kilt that trout deader than a hop pole. The second skip took that bullet from the surface of the water in Split Rock Bay into the forest where there was a lot of trees and underbrush. You see a bullet on the loose like that does funny things and it makes me curious.

'That is why I always like to look around when one gets raring that way. I was naturally grateful for this windfall of game and fish but I weren't done. I scooped up the big trout, eased the big buck to the boat, tied my boot lace around its antlers and made it fast to the wooden boat. Then I paddled to shore to take a look-see. And would you believe it, boys! When I began to investigate around I seen that single bullet had blazed trees for a mile. I had no trouble following the course of the bullet; it went clear up Split Rock Valley.

'The pathway led to a black birch where it had entered the trunk exactly in the center. It was hollow and proved to be a bee tree, for honey was running out of the bullet hole. I got some on my finger and licked the sweet gook and thought how grand 'twould be on me flapjacks. I planned to plug the hole with grass and leaves until I could get a pail or kettle up there to put the honey in after I had returned to camp, dressed out the deer and cleaned the fish. But when I reached down to grab a fistful of grass a rabbit grabbed my hand and hung on. He must have smelt that honey cause he was there in an instant. It kind of startled me; I twisted its neck smart like and it fell into the bushes. As I picked up the rabbit I saw that skipping bullet had also knocked off two partridges and broke the wing of another. If it hadn't been for the fluttering of the crippled bird I chased up the line in another two hundred years I wouldn't have noted another windfall in a shag bark maple.

'The speed of the bullet was nearly spent by the time it lodged in the plates of bark on that tree which was acting peculiar swelling and contracting like the tree was blowing a bellows. I went around the tree to see if the bullet had gone completely through, which it hadn't. About then I noticed a queer thing. I wouldn't have seen it either had it not been for the ragged ends of the bark. I spit on my hands, drew out my belt axe and chopped into the tree to investigate what was the cause of that peculiar acting tree. Now, boys, you can believe me or not but in that tree was the nicest nest of 'coons I had seen in many a year. I suspect they'd found the tree hollow and had gone in there to hibernate for the winter. 'Twas their combined breathing that made the tree swell and shrink so.

'Well, now, I took the 'coons, the partridges, the rabbit, the salmon trout, and the deer back to my cabin, then started back for the bee tree with a washtub. I got the honey all right but I had to kill a bear and its cub who had gotten there ahead of me and were ready to put up an argument. I had to use an extra bullet on them but it still might be considered a profitable venture even if it was in reality my luckiest two shots. I got enough out of the pelts to buy my supply of flour, tea, and whatnot for the entire winter, too.'

"Having thus delivered himself," concluded Harry, "Atwell proceeded to unroll his blanket and prepare for sleep. We reminded him that we had had all of our meals and were ready for a day of hunting unhampered by any stops for culinary operations before returning to Cool's Mountain House for the evening. Atwell was low in tone but quite firm. 'Sleep ALWAYS followed supper. We've et so now we should lay down to sleep.' Humbly we asked if he would be ready to start out if we cooked up some breakfast. 'Well, I always like a good breakfast,' he rejoined, 'before I start a day's work. What are we waiting for?'"

*   *   *

Later on, the Beach boys told me that Atwell told them about a hairy experience up on what we now call Wolf Mountain. It was one of the many times his quick wit helped him squeeze out of a tight situation. While following his trap line a pack of wolves got wind of him and started a chase. Soon they were breathing down his neck and he wasn't doing so good. Hard pressed for a solution he was just thinking that his next of kin were about due for some sad news when he saw a big friendly tree in front of him. Atwell kicked off his snowshoes, dropped his rifle, grabbed the lowest limb, swung his leg up pulling himself up many more feet by shinnying to the next large branch that provided safety. The wolves formed a circle around the tree, first pacing, later sitting on their haunches as they licked their chops and howled. Late in the afternoon when the shadows were getting long on the snow two of the wolves went off in the direction of Bull Moose Creek. There they picked up two beavers from the colony at the dam and returned with them to the tree Atwell was roosted in.

The wolves had enlisted the help of the beaver to cut down the tree. Perhaps it was their revenge for his trapping their clan members. When the tree came crashing down it caused so much confusion within the wolf pack that Atwell was able to take on the wolves one at a time choking them to death with his bare hands. Atwell said he got enough bounty out of their hides to pay for his trouble.

This choking to death of wild animals who threatened him was a common thing with Atwell. Panther Bay on North Lake gets it name from the fact that he choked a panther to death there once. And it is said that one winter when he was short of provisions (having had no powder or bullets) he secured meat by the simple process of walking up to a deer that was floundering helplessly in deep snow and secured it by shutting off its wind with his strong hands.

*   *   *

One March day Atwell was making his way from South Branch Outlet to North Lake, through the gap between Wilmurt and Cool Mountains. He had been out looking for a brace of spruce partridges, so had no bullets in his pouch.

It was one of those sub-zero days of which we usually have two or three in March, as a sort of parting shot of old winter. On the ridge of the gap, Atwell spied a good-sized black bear only a couple of rods away and foolishly let drive at it with the charge of shot in his gun.

Enraged, the bear took after him, and then for a quarter of an hour it was a case of sprinting on the part of Atwell and galloping on the part of the bear. Finally nearly winded, Atwell scrambled up onto a big rock and began to get his wind back. The old bear lumbered up to within a few yards where Atwell was perched, stood up, growled, and bristled its fur, its wicked little eyes gleaming fiercely.

Old Atwell did not know what to do. His shot had only irritated the bear and he had no bullets for his gun. But a bright idea occurred to him. Although it was a dreadfully cold day, because of his running the perspiration had oozed freely out over his person. His face and forehead were festooned with frozen pellets of sweat. He quickly rammed home a charge of powder and a wad, clawed off a handful of frozen lumps on his face, rammed them home, and fired. The shot was fatal to the bear. The friction on the barrel of the gun as they were discharging melted the lumps of frozen sweat into water, and the water when it struck the fearfully cold atmosphere instantly froze into a stick of ice about six inches long. This icicle took the bear between the eyes and the poor beast died of water on the brain!

This unusual experience gave Atwell a unique idea for securing bears without having to tote their carcasses weary distances through the woods. He had Avery, the gunsmith of Salisbury, build him a special double-barreled gun with one barrel on top of the other. The lower barrel was a smooth bore for shot, the upper one was rifled properly for bullets. Armed with this gun, Atwell, whenever he ran across a bear anywhere within a mile or two of this camp, would fire the lower barrel of shot into the bear, and it would take after him. Then Atwell would turn and leg it for his camp, keeping just ahead of the bear. Arriving at the clearing, he would turn and give the bear a mortal wound with the bullet from the upper barrel. By this method, as he once explained to Ed Klock, he was able to get the bear to camp under its own power, thus avoiding the necessity of toting its carcass.

*   *   *

There is a huge rock at the inlet of Twin Lakes that was so shivered during the glacial period that on the lake side it had a sharp edge with tiny recesses or hollows on each side of it. Atwell espied a fox curled up and asleep in one of the hollows. He pulled up his gun to shoot it, and as he aimed he noted another fox curled up, asleep in the other hollow. He shifted the muzzle of his gun slightly, so as to hit the sharp edge on the rock, and fired. The bullet was split into halves on the sharp edge and killed both foxes.

*   *   *

There is a balanced rock on the top of Cool Mountain that, as Atwell discovered in a peculiar way, revolves with the sun once in twenty-four hours.

He was hunting on the mountain when, being tired, he sat down and leaned against a large rock to rest. He fell asleep and did not wake up until sundown when he discovered his shirt was worn off his back.

Studying the strange freak of nature he noted that the balanced rock was resting on the face of another rock just flush with the ground. He thereupon hit on the novel idea of utilizing this contraption of nature to grind his corn meal. He would buy corn by the bag, pack it to the balanced rock, and between sunrise and sunset his corn was ground into a good quality of Johnny-cake cornmeal.

A bare spot on the shoulder of this mountain facing westward toward Boonville is a clearing Atwell made for the purpose of winnowing his meal aided by mountain breezes. He made sure he ate enough grits and always boiled a morsel of salt pork with the gruel. It was one of his standard meals for years.

*   *   *

It was commonly assumed that Atwell hated women. That blanket assumption was far from the truth. In reality, women just made him feel uncomfortable when he was in their presence. To escape embarrassment he kept away from them as much as possible, yet possessed an innate sense of propriety as the following event will show.

When Ed Klock took the job as custodian of the North Lake Dam, he established his residence in the original log structure, the State House, where Atwell also lived during the years he served as the lake's first dam tender. Klock wasn't there but a short time when he got a message in February telling him to skedaddle out to Boonville without delay—some important legal papers awaited his signature. It was midwinter and the snow was deep. No road had been broken out since winter set in early in December. There was nothing for Klock to do but to buckle on his snowshoes and hike outside to a farmhouse outside the timberline where he could secure a horse and cutter to complete his journey it being twelve or fifteen miles before he would get to a road opened in the winter's snow.

He told his wife and her woman companion (Mrs. Putney) that he would tell "that man Martin" whom as yet he did not know very well, to come over each day and do any needed chores. But he took the precaution to heap up the wood boxes with fuel, to get water from the spring and other devices to aid and comfort them in his absence. On his way out he stopped at Atwell's cabin, explained the situation and asked the old hermit to go over to the cabin daily to see how the women got on. Atwell was taciturn and noncommittal.

Klock arrived back on the fourth day. There had been no storms and the women had gotten along very well, but they had seen nothing of Atwell. The next time Klock saw him, he took him to task in a kindly way for not getting over for possible services to the two women, adding he would have paid him for his trouble. Not getting any answer, Klock pressed the recluse for an answer as to why he had not gone over. After some squirming and writhing of his shoulders, Atwell blurted out: "Well you see, Mr. Klock, I didn't want to do anything to make the neighbors talk." The nearest neighbors were the Reeds at Reed's Mills, seven miles away, with five feet of snow on the ground and nothing but a snow shoe track between North Lake and the Mills!

*   *   *

The code of the wilderness is very strict regarding hospitality. The woodshed is always open to the weary traveler if darkness overtakes him. But the code is indefinite about women travelers—especially un-attended ones. Thus, Atwell was strictly on his own when Lib Brunson and her sister entered the recluse's world one evening and announced they were going to stay the night—a situation he felt required delicate handling. Atwell's precautionary courtesy exercised toward Lib Brunson and her sister on an occasion of a visit to North Lake is hilarious in retrospect.

Atwell considered women an ill omen of sorts, "bringing only catastrophe." He did hold his tongue and never commented much about them beyond the brief statement that, "They were females and there was a law on them," reserved only for a male audience. In the presence of women he was quiet, indifferent, notably uncomfortable, and almost always lacked a proper greeting because of his uneasiness.

The occasion of Old Atwell's paying cautious courtesy to Mrs. Brunson and her sister was on a visit they paid him at North Lake one summer. Lib wished to see her husband, Wash, who was working in Perry's lumber camp and they also purposed to pick some berries while in the area. Both women were familiar with the simplicities of woods etiquette, so since they planned to sleep in Atwell's woodshed, a bark affair in one corner of his clearing in the forest, they had brought along some blankets for their comfort. Atwell's welcome to them was restrained; though he consented that they prepare their supper on his stove he did not enthuse over their plan to sleep in his woodshed but was noncommittal. He consented to eat supper with them but was silent and taciturn during the meal.

While the women were washing up the soiled dishes he busied himself at three small tasks, forerunners of the strange course he was soon to follow. He relaid the blankets in his bunk, whittled kindling for the morning's fire, and got a pail of fresh water from the brook.

When Lib went outside with the dishpan to throw the water away, Atwell was standing outside the door. As she re-entered the cabin he closed the door swiftly and they heard the rattle and snap of a padlock, as he slipped it through the staple of the hasp and locked it. Naturally both women were astonished; but before they had time to express it, Old Atwell said in his high-pitched voice, "Miss Brunson, be you all right?" She spoke up and said "Why, yes Atwell, we are all right, but what . . . what's got into you?" He interrupted her by saying firmly, "Stop your yarnmerin' and let the other woman speak for herself, Miss." Whereat, Lib's sister said rather dubiously, "Why, yes, Mr. Martin, we're all right." Then he proceeded to explain his strange action. "Folks about will talk," he said. "Now you wimmen, you've got wood and fresh water and the bed's made, the best I can." Lib snorted with indignation and replied, "Nonsense, Atwell. The closest neighbors are the half dozen people in the reservoir tender's family nearly a half mile away through the forest, the men at a lumber camp a full two miles away, and that old codger that lives three miles down the lake, and he's deafer than a hemlock stump."

Atwell stopped in his tracks like he was thinking things over but Lib said she was certain he was going to be unwavering in his resolve, first because of the terse look on his face and secondly for what he said demurely. "Yes, Miss Brunson but that old coot's got good eyes and he shore can talk, so you just keep still and everything will be all right."

"Unlock this door," Lib continued. She was not at all happy with his decision to lock them in. "Where'd you get all them foolish notions, Atwell? You know me and my sister. We ain't got no designs on you."

Atwell felt safe, though, and because he did hold the upper hand he conceded a point. "Maybe you ain't up to no monkey business but you know how they like to put in the papers about them rendezvouses and clandestine assignations. I don't want no reputation like that." The hermit was not about to take a chance for a local scandal to begin and Lib realized the conversation was getting too involved so she switched over to the obvious question, "How be we going to get out of here?"

Atwell hedged. That question was a poser for a bit. "I ain't come to that yet. You women just keep quiet until I get this thunk out."

He puttered around, Lib recalled—she told me this story many times. "He seemed to be worrying for fear he had not done everything proper." His mind did not lay in coping with romantic situations. "He seemed to be truly wracking his brain to think of something that he had forgotten that might trip him up later on," Lib resumed. "At last he had it. He marched resolutely back to the woodshed door, cleared his throat and quizzed, 'Be you women all right?'"

"Yes, we be all right. What chance have we got to be any other ways?" Lib ended. Satisfied, Atwell stooped and slid the key under the door concluding with these instructions. "Now, Miss Brunson, here's the key. Take it. Indeed I's locked you both in but you says you're fine and you got everything you need. In the morning I'll come and you can give me the key and I'll let you out, and the neighbors can't say but what everything is all right and proper." He ended with, "And besides, you never know what neighbors will say if'n you give them something to talk about."

*   *   *

I submit here an illustration for the reader's consideration. I feel it illustrates Old Atwell's cynical outlook toward the world and its "blemishes" (the things Atwell found distasteful about civilization). The example is illustrated by his retort to John A. Roberts, a dry goods merchant of Utica, when he introduced his wife to the hermit. Mr. Roberts had sent for Atwell to come to the State House to arrange for a fishing trip the next day and introduced his wife by saying, "Atwell, this is my wife." The old fellow did not bow or offer to shake hands, but half turning away, said, "Yes, yes, like enough, like enough."

Mr. Roberts and Old Atwell became good friends for all of this raw retort when he was introduced to Mr. Robert's wife, and he guided for the Utica merchant for many years, even to the second generation. Hobart V. Roberts, the famous photographer of wild game, with a camp at South Lake, is a son of merchant Roberts.

*   *   *

Ed Klock said he saw Owen "Kettle" Jones in 1895. "He was living in a camp which had probably been built all of a score of years before. The building was of hewed and squared logs about fourteen feet by eighteen feet. I called to see him; he was seated in front of his cabin; considerably crippled by dropsical legs, badly swollen. He gave me and my companion tobacco for our pipes grown in his clearing. 'Twas too much for us.

"Kettle wasn't such a bad neighbor as neighbors go. He was a quiet man and liked to putter about. There were rumors that he wasn't even a real hermit. Some said he was a refugee fleeing from the nagging of a termagant wife. Others said that he had been mixed up with the wrong people and he was hiding out. Neither were true, as some of the old-timers came to learn having sat on a split log stool and sipped the juices of wild fruits after they had fermented in his homemade still, for his nickname many of us felt also represented his love of alchemy and the experimenting he would do. He had a stock of brandies that was not recognized in bonded circles, but that did not detract from their potency or bouquet, that being a fact to which I can personally testify.

"In spite of his hobby, Kettle was always a moderate drinker; he preferred his home brew as a dressing for his food. Every meal was a ritual where he and his pet 'coon would sit dunking their foodstuffs as sober as two judges—content and satisfied with their lot in life. This particular pet raccoon came to play a role that was to distinguish Kettle in the eyes of North Lakers. At first, folks considered him to be a harmless old codger, but that was before he got mixed up in the 'coon dealing—only then did folks come to the conclusion that Kettle Jones had more savvy than it appeared.

Raccoons are common in the woods and many hunters have tried to make pets of them only to find the animals cannot be trusted unless they are chained or kept in cages; so when it was reported that Kettle had them running freely around inside his cabin like cats it stirred up quite a bit of interest. Several hunters, lumberjacks and camp owners approached Kettle to purchase "pet" 'coons. Kettle began to traffic, it seemed, in a fair number of the forest critters but only to summer camp owners. Soon a problem developed. A buyer often returned their newly purchased raccoon for it would not eat well. Other campers found theirs ran away. These problems attracted attention. "How remarkable," the natives thought as they listened to a number of past customers talking. "Everyone has the same problems." Before you knew it the North Lake grapevine buzzed with flim-flam tales of trickery. Kettle acted innocent to it all while others thought the situation was at least a remarkable co-incidence. Kettle was asked for his opinion but he had no idea. The old boy had to have a secret and it was the locals who quickly figured it out for they knew him the best.

Kettle was sharing his brandy with the animals—letting them sop their food in it. This was a natural thing for 'coons since they prefer to dunk food before eating it, and it accounted for their docile behavior in his cabin. That was an easy mystery to solve. But the fact that clinched Kettle's reputation with his neighbors was that there had never been but one 'coon and all he had done was to wait until it came back before selling it to the next customer.

Atwell was not attracted to Kettle Jones because of his brandy but he tolerated him. During the first winter of Kettle's tenure Atwell closely observed the lake's newest move-in but ignored the man. Kettle didn't bother Martin's trap line. That made him a pretty decent fellow. They went their own ways, minding their own business, until spring. Atwell tired of talking to pine stumps. Over the winter he had developed a new batch of yarns—the sort of tales the old hermit had become famous for. Surely Kettle would be more appreciative of Atwell's sto-ries than the stumps. As it turned out Kettle was a very good listener and a social life developed between the two men.

Kettle announced at one of their infrequent meetings that he liked the area and intended to stay around a while. Kettle then went into his plan about building a dugout canoe to use for fishing and jack lighting deer. Old Atwell had come to have a respect for the way Kettle handled an axe and knives so when the newcomer came right out and asked him if he would not give him a hand he at first remained noncommittal, as was Atwell's custom toward anything but an offer of food. Kettle of-fered a bit of brandy toward their partnership. Until this point Atwell remained misanthropic toward any advance toward friendship. Finding it difficult to deny a request for help in the wilds and after savoring some of the brandy he grudgingly agreed concluding there was some personal benefit to the dug-out plan. So it was their joint effort in building the crude watercraft that brought them together.

There was a small stand of virgin pine on the Indian River above Horn Lake in Township 5. Although it was a considerable distance from North Lake that stand would provide the best material for a dug-out. Atwell suggested they go there, pick out a likely tree and cut it down. The first tree felled turned out to be a perfect log. Both men did their share in working it into a serviceable boat. After first trying it out in Horn Lake whereafter they made a few modifications the men worked the log boat back to North Lake. The partnership worked passably well until fall approached and hibernating time grew close. It was then that the partners became irritable and had several minor flare-ups. The final split came one night when they were out on the lake shining for deer.

Atwell was in the stern paddling, Kettle was in the middle with his gun primed, ready to shoot. The jack lantern hung on a jack staff up on the prow of the canoe. In due time a deer was spotted swimming across the lake. Atwell started paddling to put them in position for a killing shot but a quartering breeze made the dug-out awkward to handle. Kettle got nervous and started some back-seat driving. "Steady now," he whispered. "Hold her steady, just as she is."

Atwell swung his paddle viciously and growled at him to mind his own housework and shoot the buck. Kettle's old flintlock blazed away and the lake plunged into darkness. He had shot the jack staff clean off. The light, which Atwell owned, sank to the bottom of the lake. The night was black and the cool air was filled with rank sulfur. Atwell became enraged. Charges and countercharges were hurled back and forth under a dark, moonless sky. Kettle alleged Atwell was to blame because he did not know how to paddle a dug-out. Atwell declared that any person who claimed to be a woodsman that could not shoot around a jack staff ought to go back to hell and stay there. Their arguing continued until they located their beach; what friendship there was ended. The next day they sawed the dug-out precisely into two halves, plugged up the open end with pine block shakes and caulked the cracks with a compound of bacon grease and spruce gum. Each used his half-boat for several years.

Atwell once nearly drowned coming down the lake in his queer craft. A gale of wind in the third wide waters upset his tub and it speedily sank in the forty feet of water there, but good fortune was his. He had saved a cud of pure spruce gum to chew. At the time of his upset he had this lump well worked up in his mouth so that it was full of water when he went down. As he came to the surface he slowly blew out a great bubble of saliva, bound together with the adhesive juice of the spruce gum. The bubble kept Atwell afloat and he drifted to the shore.

*   *   *

Between North and South Lakes on the Bull Moose Stream, about a mile from the highway, there is an opening or clearing in the forest, of about three acres. I always supposed it was an old beaver meadow, until John Bellinger of Forestport put me right.

John said: "Why that is no beaver meadow, Reverend," whereupon I asked what made the clearing. He then explained that when both Old Atwell and Paul Bunyan were in their prime, Bunyan made the trip from Wisconsin to North Lake to see Old Atwell, he had heard so much about him. Atwell received his fellow woodsman heartily and they got along fine for a fortnight. But one day when they were hunting on the Bull Moose Stream, they got to quarreling over something and had an awful fight. Finally Paul and Old Atwell got to tearing the trees up by the roots to lambaste each other, and that is how they made the clearing I thought was a beaver meadow.

I asked John, 'Who won?' So John said, 'Old Atwell beat the life out of Paul Bunyan. The latter's body is buried here under the dam.' So it appears that we of North Lake can claim that the headwaters of the Black River is the last resting place of the famous Paul Bunyan, slain in a fight with Atwell Martin, the Hermit of North Lake, by spruce trees snatched from the primeval forest.

* * *

The circumstances of Atwell's passing were sad, but before I get to that I best catch Atwell's life up-to-date. Following the flood that carried away the earth and timber dam at North Lake the state thought the reservoir should have a gate-tender stationed to regulate the flow of water for the Black River Canal. Atwell Martin was the area's sole year round resident at the time. The role pleased him. He had slowed down in his wanderings and tending dam gates didn't interfere much with his "settin'," which had become quite a pastime.

Moreover the state offered to pay him. [Author's note: It's been reported he earned from $600 to $1,800 per year. I have not been able to find the official amount.] Whatever the figure, it was a terrific job that came with an official log shanty to live in and the wage was stupendous for a man who had little ambition.

He held that job for four years and he might have stayed on in that position—living was easy—but the job eventually was viewed as a political plum and Atwell was not tied into the political patronage web. When he retired he had saved his entire salary. To that sum of several thousand he added another $1,100 earned from guiding services and trapping. He planned to keep the money in a safe place—in a sock hidden in his cabin—using it only when he could no longer be active and easily care for himself. But, alas, he was too trusting, a simple and honest man. Thinking others were like him, when people came to borrow money he gave it. One scalawag who professed to be a friend convinced him to turn his entire savings over to him for safe-keeping (he was reportedly going to invest it). Atwell never got his money back.

I'll let Eldridge A. Spears who got the lowdown from my old friend Byron Cool tell the rest. "Time passed on and one day at Cool's State House someone asked Atwell how old he was. 'Well, as a matter of course, I ain't 80 and I ain't 90, but I'm some old, however.'

"Then one day late in the century Dr. Wiggins of Remsen was at North Lake and they asked him to have a look at Martin. He looked and said: 'Boys, you'd better get this old man out of here.' Billy Mulchi, who drove the stage for years between Forestport and North Lake, took Atwell to the County Home at Middleville."

Martin died there in 1894.

Two years following his passing North Lakers succeeded in getting a post office. Byron Cool thought enough mail arrived at the lake to warrant a post office. Since Atwell Martin had been its chief landmark for decades, Cool originally wanted the post office to be named "Martin" but the Post Office Department felt there were several other "Martins" so they decided on Atwell. The tiny post office remained the lake's chief landmark for decades.

While Atwell Martin doesn't have a monument in stone, there is a pile of rocks in his honor. All that remains at the site of his bark wigwam shanty today is a cairn of stones at the end of a short trail along Atwell Creek. Atop the pile has been placed a rusty circular saw blade from an old mill with a faded inscription written in paint identifying that as the site of the North Lake's hermit's home.

A Mystery of the Wilderness

A.L. Byron-Curtiss had personally known the eccentric "Dingle Dangle" Jones, having met him between 1894 and 1896. When Thomas C. O'Donnell, one of the Adirondacks' best writers, met the reverend, one of the North Woods' best teller of tales, it resulted in a remarkable recording of the history and folklore of the Black River headwaters. O'Donnell included many of Byron-Curtiss's tales, including this one, in his book, Birth of a River, *and while he was faithful to the reverend's style and brought the stories to the general public, Byron-Curtiss did have his own voice, which we can hear in this account.*

Among our peculiar characters of the Black River Country was a John R. Jones—"Dingle Dangle" to those who knew him well, because of his custom of heading for a place in the forest in an aimless manner, often beginning in the wrong direction. For some odd reason he scorned the use of a compass. He was one of those fellows who just bang through the woods, lying down on a blanket, sleeping through the night, and the next morning continuing on and eventually coming out all right. He was a great walker if that is any kind of an accomplishment.

I probably knew him about as well as anyone else around North Lake did. I first met him in Byron E. Cool's Mountain House, a place of rest and refreshment at North Lake. I recall thinking he must be very shy. He had a reluctant, self-conscious manner during the conventional greetings we exchanged as Mr. Cool introduced us. Rather short in stature, with a drooping walrus mustache, he had eyes that were as blue as the limpid sky, yet bore withal an expression of a dog who had been beaten in a fair fight and was now reconciled to a slinking semi-existence.

Dingle Dangle was an odd Welshman all around. Not at all talkative, once levered into conversation he would express himself in the characteristic Welsh brogue of a rising inflection of voice, giving his opinions pointedly and unhesitatingly, and sticking to them, though they might be of wide divergence with the commonly accepted views or circumstances.

One hunting season, during a heavy fall of snow that was building great clumps on the boughs of evergreens and rendering it impossible to see much beyond the end of one's gun, making successful hunting difficult, I ran across Dingle Dangle in the forest. I expressed my disgust at the conditions, but he declared, "But, Reverend, its fine. This way you can see the blood." In vain I argued that we could not see a deer in the maze of the white mantle prevailing let alone fire and draw blood. But he only reiterated his dependence on "tracking 'em by the blood."

There was talk of a romance in his life that had kept him a bachelor, undoubtedly contributing to his eccentricities and driving him to the wilderness as a semi-recluse. Such legends frequently arise in connection with an odd character, but there was no basis of fact to believe this about John, just rumor. He gave credence to the rumor when Cool questioned him once. While his answer might not seem life altering, the experience was a personal tragedy and drove him into a woods life. He had courted a girl in Steuben Valley, a Welsh settlement, proposed and been accepted. He furnished a home, complete from a cook stove to a piano. But when he pressed his intended to "name the day" she jilted him and married another. Thereafter, until his mysterious disappearance from our life, he spent most of his time in North Lake country wilderness.

By trade Dingle Dangle was a painter and paperhanger, excelling in his craft. He would work sporadically at this occupation, earning sufficiently to purchase supplies, and come to North Lake and live his solitary life, first in a tent and then in a small frame camp of his own. After several seasons living in a tent, he had accumulated sufficient lumber, mostly salvaged from abandoned logging camps, to build a small, comfortable (by his standards) shanty and barn on a site in the Split Rock Bay area of the lake. That site was across from Panther Bay Inlet, the location of my first cabin. He built it during my first year of ownership of the Nat Foster Lodge.

I took much interest in him and delighted in his company. During the summer I loaned him tools and oftentimes lent a hand in the work. I have always been proud that after its erection Dingle Dangle came to my camp, signed my log book of guests on July 11, 1901, and we celebrated the whole affair. He became most neighborly and voluble, showing me with pride the little furniture he had accumulated. An old cook stove, a card table, and some hard bottom chairs, a few dishes, a cot bed, and the like. He had even gotten a used boat somewhere, one of those clinker-built, patent affairs in two sections for easy transportation. It was bolted together in the center, and the oar locks were hinged to enable shipping the oars at a decent width over the narrow shell. It was rather leaky and the bolts and the holes were worn, but it would carry two men in a pinch. We profanely called it "Dingle Dangle's lemon-squeezer."

Unfortunately, he was not destined to enjoy his snug camp for very long. The third season, while he was off fishing, somehow his camp got afire and burned to the ground. Some of us got over in a hurry to rescue what we could, but were held back until a fusillade of ammunition from his gun shelf subsided; lead from exploding bullets was going everywhere. We were only able to drag out his cot bed and a chair. Those and his lemon-squeezer were all he had left.

After this disaster Dingle Dangle led a still more precarious existence. How he did get on was a puzzle to all of us. Sometimes a cottager would let him occupy his place as a caretaker, but he was as likely as not obliged to vacate when the owner or tenant came in. We suspected he just lived most anywhere, a hollow stump, a brush shelter, and, of course, in any one of the outlying camps. Then he would depart up the lake in his lemon-squeezer, to no-one-knew-where. We suspected he had a little brush-and-bark shack in some remote place in the wilds. Secrecy was strong with him; probably from a natural bent but with the gloom intensified by his disappointment in love, the fire, and the solitary life he lived afterward.

Like Chauncy Smith, an old guide at Number 4 who once claimed to find a nugget of gold not far from Mt. Marcy (but he could never locate the place again), Dingle Dangle also claimed to have discovered a vein of gold and silver beyond the head of North Lake near Ice Cave Mountain or some other rocky outcrop or near the second stillwater, we always figured. Fred Owens, a painter and paperhanger from Barneveld, New York, and an old friend of his, said he knew he packed in some sticks of dynamite to open the granite of the hills and aid him in his prospecting. No one knew exactly where the dig was located; the indifference of the people to its location indicates their estimate of John and his claims.

Jones owned an old wreck of a Winchester rifle, which from its proclivity to go off at odd times increased people's desire not to have him around. By the simple process of smartly working the plunger to throw a shell from the magazine to the breech of the gun, the cartridge would explode. Once it exploded in this manner when he was in a boarding house camp and the bullet went through a bed in the sleeping loft overhead. Fortunately no one was in the bed; but naturally John's stubborn refusal to part with the gun or at least leave it behind when visiting did not increase his popularity.

Eventually Jones devoted all his time to trapping. He would prepare his camp and map out his trapping line in November, picking up his traps and going out with his catch in March. He probably made no great amount of money, as he was an indifferent woodsman anyway, in spite of his many years as a recluse. But it was the day of small things, living was cheap, and once he got his supplies to his base camp he could exist.

Early one November he appeared at North Lake with big plans for the winter. He was to use an outlying camp (probably O. L. Snyder's) on Snyder Lake, one of those little glacial bodies of water far in the wilderness. Snyder was a founding member of the Adirondack League Club and built a log cabin at the lake as a base camp for fishing trips to Horn Lake and Indian River. The region was favorable for trapping and by setting out several lines of traps and with reasonable diligence he should have been well rewarded.

Dingle Dangle spent the night with John Redmond, keeper of the State House at North Lake. As usual Jones' possessions were pitifully meager: a pack basket and an old-fashioned telescope case containing all his duffel for the winter. Also, as usual, his clothes were poor and threadbare. The Redmonds, kind-hearted Irish people, pressed some extra clothing upon him. Mr. Redmond, too, crowded a few additional supplies into his too-full pack basket; some salt pork, coffee, and tinned milk. He also phoned out to Van Scouten's at the lodge at Honnedaga and found the caretaker had extra flour if Dingle Dangle wanted to stop on by.

Borrowing a boat from Redmond he set off early the next morning, rowed to the head of North Lake and reached Snyder before evening. At the camp he found two hunters, but they were going out the next day to Honnedaga with a deer they had shot. John offered to help, knowing there would be flour enough for him to last through to March. This seemed like the best time to go out and procure it. Starting early and using the Adirondack League Club trail, Jones covered the four to five miles reaching Honnedaga Lake before noon. There he took dinner with Van Scouten, the solitary caretaker of the league property at the lake. He gave John the large supply of flour he'd promised and accompanied him in a boat to the trail on the north shore near the head of the lake where Dingle would return over to reach Snyder Lake. But John started out blind; he raced blithely into the brush. Van Scouten told him he was not headed right, the slashed trail to Snyder Lake being off to the right, but John shouted back cheerfully, "Oh, I'll hit him when I get over the ridge."

Whether John ever "hit him" (the Snyder Lake trail) will never be known. Van Scouten was the last person ever to see him. Since he was a bachelor with no close kin, no one became alarmed. March came and went. John did not appear at the outside village as he normally did when not in the mountains. April was well along when some of his friends took note of his nonappearance among them. After communicating by telegraph with Jack Redmond at North Lake they ascertained John had not been seen all winter, and with commendable zeal they organized a searching party at once and started for the wilderness.

Arriving at Snyder Lake, they found John had never reached the camp, from his trip after flour. His telescope case had not been unpacked, and the provisions only partially removed from the pack basket. Only a package of his favorite Warnick & Brown tobacco on the tiny table indicated the brevity of his shift over night. They spent several days examining the trails from the lake and region around. But anyone of experience knows this is a difficult and always incomplete task in the tangled thickets of a mountain wilderness like the Adirondacks. Many million square feet of Mother Earth there are in total upon which the human eye has never rested.

Clarence Davis speculated that Fred Owens figured Burt Lindsay killed Dingle Dangle for the presumed gold, but I wouldn't want to accuse someone of a terrible crime like that without proof. At last they gave up their search (any thought about Lindsay's possible involvement) and the fate of John R. "Dingle Dangle" Jones remains a mystery.

Whether he lost his way and became mired in a bog, or whether a limb or tree fell on him or he broke a leg—these are all permissible conjectures. One of the above catastrophes probably overtook him, for John had been accustomed for years to banging in a floundering fashion, through the forests, independent of a trail. He was not of a temperament to lose his head if lost, but to camp for the night and at daylight to resume his progress to "somewhere," always arriving. He must have been incapacitated in some manner. I had thought when lumbering of the region began a few years after his disappearance, some trace of him might been found, and I asked the bosses of the logging camps to tell the men to be on the lookout, but nothing was ever found. Mice, foxes, and other valets of the forest will eat the bones of a dead animal. I have seen deer carcasses completely disappear after two years. The annual falling of the leaves of the hardwoods, too, will completely cover an object in two or three years. The cutting over of the tract of its commercial trees where he disappeared has been completed now some years. Nature alone will hold sway there for a generation. The knowledge of John's fate has been sealed.

Editor's note: The following is a quote from the December 25, 1894 Boonville Herald *newspaper story entitled "Dingle Dangle Jones' Gold/Silver Find."*

"A man named Jones who has been in the Adirondack forests forty-eight years has been out recently to consult a lawyer as to his right to a small gore (a deep, narrow pass between steep heights) of land which he claimed. He was informed that he could not claim the land, and he went back to the woods satisfied.

"He claims to have discovered a gold mine or gold vein a little beyond North Lake. Some of the find has been sent to Newark, New Jersey to be assayed and it was found to contain $12.00 of gold to the ton. Thus Mr. Jones claims would not pay, but he believes it can be found in paying quantities and intends to keep at work until he finds out. There is also some silver mixed in with it."

The Bellinger Clan

As the crow flies some eleven miles southwest from North Lake, half a century ago there was a quiet little village popularly known as Bellingertown. This forest community had a general store and a post office referred to as Enos, the name of one of its first pioneer families. Bellingertown was not the official name. Local reference in the speech of the people thereabouts, however, was always Bellingertown. Representatives of this family were still living in Forestport a decade after I was a young deacon-in-charge of the Episcopal church there. Between 1892 and 1893 I made pastoral calls in the hamlet where we had a few communicants. In this I was but following in the footsteps of the founder of the parish, Rev. Dr. Edward H. Jewett, whom I came to know when I was a student of his at Holy Cross Monastery in West Park, New York. He was professor of Homiletics then, very dignified and somewhat prosey, and it was not easy for me to imagine him doing the strenuous work of planting our church in the Black River country of the southwestern Adirondack Mountains. Yet the dear old professor told me of how he had once "had to go to a little village of Bell— something for a funeral." The virgin forest had not as yet been cleared off, the day was hot and muggy, and bloodthirsty mosquitoes got after the young cleric with a vengeance.

I chuckle now as I recall his telling of it in the elegant study of his residence at the seminary. To hear him tell it the little demons of the air got after him so savagely that he nearly perished; he only saved his life by having the driver of the buckboard stop for him to cut off some branches of shrubs and trees with his pen knife that he waved, wielded, and swung around his head to shoo the pests away. As he told it one would believe that he wore out a whole armful of the leafy sprays in his continuous vaudeville stunts going to and returning from Bellingertown.

The name Bellingertown is from a family of pioneer settlers transplanted from the Mohawk Valley. Patriots of our embryonic nation, representatives of the family participated in the Battle of Oriskany;

their names cast in bronze are affixed to the Oriskany Monument. The Black River clan of this family sprang from a lively romance, a near homicide, and as sturdy, virile, and picturesque a group of descendants as I have encountered in my somewhat varied and long life.

Over a hundred years ago a young Jonathan Bellinger left the Mohawk Valley and wandered down into Otsego County looking for work. He secured a job with a wealthy farmer by the name of Pitts. Honest, upright, good-looking, and a strong, willing worker, he made a good impression on his employer by his fidelity to his work as a hired man. He also made a favorable impression on the young Sally Pitts. A "sparking" followed. They fell in love and secretly became engaged. Now while a farmer's hired man has often fallen in love with his daughter it seldom leads to a near homicide as it did in Jonathan's case. When young Bellinger asked Sally's father for permission to get married the elder man roared "No!" and ordered the young man to gather his possessions and "be on your way within the hour." Instead, Sally and Jonathan eloped. Before sunrise the following morning they were married by an accommodating parson in Cherry Valley. Alas, when they returned to the bride's home with the parson's marriage certificate as the presumed passport to peace and reconciliation, Sally's father threatened Jonathan with a shotgun.

As one of Jonathan Bellinger's grandsons recalls this part of his family's history, "Grandfather saw the tall timber of the North Woods real fast. And skedaddling they did go." Eventually the young couple's flight brought them to a site near Enos, a speck of a settlement, long abandoned, located along the present North Lake road. Through hunting and trapping, Jonathan had previously familiarized himself with the area. He also had made a mental note of a particular location along the Black River that was naturally suited to putting up a dam in the future. His homestead site came to be known as Bellingertown; however, the locally approved pronunciation was "Bellnertown." The men who would come to be born and live in Bellingertown were some of the most colorful guides and lumbermen ever to be found in this region.

The evolution of the frontier village began with the coming of young Jonathan. He had a keen eye for its present and future opportunities. The forest abounded with game, the Black River and its contributory streams had, so claimed grandson Dell Bellinger, "so many trout that the fish had to jump in the air to get by each other and were so avariciously hungry fishermen had to take the precaution and bait their hooks behind trees to avoid any trout that would jump into the air, snatch the worms right from the fishermen's hands and flop back into the stream again." The river also provided a site for impounding water and building a sawmill. A bend of the river, the contour of the land, the banks and the current all combined to make just the spot to construct a dam across the river to secure hydraulic power.

Jonathan built a log cabin first, then tackled the dam. It was composed chiefly of hewed logs strung zigzag across the stream, weighted down using stones and earth, and grouted in clay. Evidence of the dam was still there when I visited "Bellnertown" for a pastoral call in May of 1893.

Living alone in the Adirondack wilderness, Jonathan and Sally got by in the primitive standard of surviving similar to other pioneer homesteaders in the mountains of New York. The little ready cash needed to buy flour, sugar, salt, tea, and such came from a cash crop available every month of the year, provided by Nature and well-scattered throughout the wilderness. It was the wolf population that abounded in the region.

Jonathan had settled in the Town of Forestport, Oneida County, about a mile from the boundary line for Herkimer County. The number of wolves in Herkimer far exceeded that straggling few in neighboring Oneida. But Herkimer County offered no bounty; the only bounty collectable for wolves was the five dollars per hide the state offered. This resulted in the majority of the Mohawk Valley trappers putting out no wolf traps, resulting in an increase in the wolf packs. As settlements continued to develop in the Valley in the decades following the Revolutionary War and the War of 1812, the wolves retreated farther into the North Woods of upstate New York as farmers systematically killed them in an effort to protect their cattle and sheep and rid the countryside of a menace to man.

Surrounded by a trackless forest abounding in game, Jonathan realized he must depend largely on the wilds for cash. Daily he heard the long, drawn-out howl of the wolf outside the log cabin he and Sally kept. While tending his trap line he would often note the telltale tracks in the snow or see a wolf slinking off into the woods. Numerous packs thrived in his neighborhood just waiting his attention. Shrewdly he studied the economics. If wolves were killed in Oneida County, a twenty-five-dollar bounty could be collected—ten dollars from the county, ten from the Town of Forestport for ridding country land of the pests, and an additional five dollars from the state.

It did not take him long to evolve a system to take advantage of the supply-side economics and still be legal in a strict application of the bounty law. When a varmint wolf in closely neighboring Herkimer County was caught in his heavy steel traps it was not immediately executed. Instead, Jonathan would work a burlap grain sack over its head with the help of a pole, hog-tie the legs, toss the live animal into his buckboard, and start for home. As soon as he crossed into Oneida County he would pause, shoot the wolf, remove the hide, discard the carcass and continue on his way. Thus, when asked by the town clerk to swear that he had indeed shot the wolf within the Township of Forestport, Oneida County, he could truthfully swear he had.

How hunter-trapper Bellinger worked out trapping the leery animals became legendary, for he certainly gave the animals a run for their money. With his success also grew myths of interesting adventures associated with early North Lake folk.

*   *   *

I divert a bit from the Bellinger history because Dell was a wonderful teller of tales. "I always felt privileged," Dell Bellinger would tell me, "to have been brought up in a close household as the Bellinger clan was." As a young lad, Dell was always asking his grandpa, his pa, or his brothers to tell him about living in the olden days. His pressing them for their recollections lead to many an unexpected yarn. And yarns they were. He knew this for a fact because many of his family members worked as guides for "Dut" Barber at Jock's Lake (renamed Honnedaga Lake by the ALC) and later for the Adirondack League Club itself. A guide's mystique to city-bred gents who vacationed in the wilderness was made up of the native's expert knowledge of the woods and waters, his resourcefulness, and local color.

Dell accepted some stories as truth, or at least with a grain of truth, for instance the story regarding how a mettlesome black bear was caught at Honnedaga Lake. Evidently a large bruin that had been raiding Forest Lodge and neighboring camps for several years evaded all standard attempts to capture it. His activities became storied. As the bruin's raids continued unchecked so grew among the club's guides a respect for the animal's cleverness. Not wishing it any harm, if you can believe the yarn, a mixture of black-strap molasses and high-class moonshine whiskey were mixed in an old maple syrup evaporator pan and set out for his lapping. By accident a guide stomping around in the woods came upon the drunken, but happy-as-a-lark, critter. He placed a noose around its neck and led him off league property. After hearing a stern lecture that if he ever again failed to observe the warnings put on the enameled posted signs, the next time he would be shot, the bear shook its head as if it might have understood and ambled off into the woods behind Perry's #1 lumber camp, snorting as it lumbered along swinging its head to and fro as if cussing back but realizing it had been given a second chance. He was never to be seen again.

*   *   *

That story was half believable; however, Dell had others, many more, and the following one centered on his grandfather. It evolved from the days when Grandad Jonathan trapped wolves. Dell never reckoned there was a grain of truth to it but he pointed out versions of the tale survive and are still popular in the lumbering shanties. The tale went like this:

One winter during Jonathan Bellinger's days of wolf trapping would never be forgotten. As Jonathan was carefully making his way down what's now called Mink Lake Hill with his team pulling a homemade jumper, he caught the howl of wolves coming from behind him. The sound indicated a rather large pack, and he found it odd that they would be so near. Relinquishing any control on the reins he allowed the work horses a free head. The animals responded and enlivened their pace sometimes recklessly picking up speed down the boulder-strewn slopes. The howling grew in intensity as the pack drew closer.

In the last fleeting rays of light of twilight Jonathan caught a glimpse of what was fast approaching. A pack of wolves it was but not the typical number. There were tens or maybe hundreds. At that point it didn't matter. Regardless, they were no match for him. But what to do? The sage hunter could think of nothing but to quickly throw a bearskin wrap over himself and drop prostrate onto the jumper as the horses bolted forward. It wasn't long before the large pack caught up and one by one he could feel their muscular weighty bodies as they first leaped on to the jumper from behind and made their way over the top of the duffel, always howling, as wolves, sled, Jonathan, and the team moved along. The woodsman wondered if this was the animals' revenge for all his trapping, for he had sworn at the top of his lungs he would rid his part of the county of all the wild demons.

Eventually the howl of the wolves ceased and the pace of the steeds slowed. Lifting a corner of the black, furry hide he ventured a peek and much to his surprise he saw a light in a distant window. Crawling out he gathered the leather reins and coaxed a bit more speed to further him toward the light—his cabin, he presumed, since the animals had stayed the course and remained on the narrow open pathway that was laid out from North Lake.

When he pulled up to the tiny log cabin the illumination from the source of light shining from the window reflected on the snow to reveal a pair of wolves in the harness. Imagine his surprise. The wolves had devoured the horses, eating their way into the harness. Dell said his grandfather thought he might try driving them around for a while but thinking better of it he ended up killing them. Why? Well it was obvious. Wolves were quite vicious, they were too hard to keep because they didn't eat hay and, besides, he needed the money!

*   *   *

Jonathan Bellinger was married three times. During Sally and Jonathan's first ten years of marriage they had acquired over one thousand acres of timberland. Sally bore three children named Jon, David, and Ann. Sally saw the erection of the sawmill following the building of their log cabin home and listened to the screech, the rumble, and the groans of the gang saws. The sawmill remained in operation until the marketable timber was cut off and the lumber operation drifted deeper into the forest.

Bellingertown's population also de-creased. Without the stands of timber there was no other industry the settlers could engage in. An agricultural enterprise was out of the question. The residents claimed the soil was "too poor to even raise hell." Pioneer life was strenuous and Sally died at a young age. Jonathan, like many of the sturdy pioneers, grieved at his wife's passing. However, he was also realistic. He faced poverty and constant battles against Nature and there was the necessity of a home to keep, children to raise, and the need of feminine efficiency that impelled him to seek another helpmate from among the girls of other mountain-living families.

Following Sally's death he married a Merville girl by whom he had six more children, five sons, and a daughter: Lige, Will, Arthur, Henry, Fred, and Jane. Following the death of his second wife he took a third, the widow Skelton, who bore him no children but who did bring to the union three children by her first marriage. Jonathan raised them as his own. The girl grew up and married a Farley. They were the parents of a boy, Cyrus Farley, who became an outstanding and valued character of the Black River country. Known to one and all as "Cy" he had a keen mind and was droll and "quick on the trigger in retorts and backfire."

Once when Cy, with a party from Rome he was guiding, was sitting around the evening campfire, the members got to discussing matrimony and the object and purpose of marriage. On their appealing to Cy for his opinion he gave it solemnly as "mostly for discipline." Jonathan brought up all his children—natural and adopted—to be a close family unit. Their fraternity and fellowship were as warm and cordial as though all were of the same blood.

As the natural sons of Jonathan all grew to maturity, two remained in the Black River headwaters throughout their lifetimes. In common with most of the men of the southwestern fringe of the Adirondacks, the Bellingers became guides for the members of the aristocratic clubs and others like former Lieutenant Governor of New York Timothy Woodruff, who settled at Kamp Kill Kare. Arthur "Archie" and Fred also guided for the Adirondack League Club, as did their sons. In his old age Archie used to crow about all the famous men he had guided for. To my surprise and delight he would say, "everyone from President Grover Cleveland to the Reverend Byron-Curtiss."

Archie was more of a phlegmatic type than Fred, who oozed humor on any and every occasion that permitted it—which, with his savvy good sense, made him a reliable and remarkable state employee in the eyes of his superiors in Albany, after he pressed charges against his own son for accidentally shooting a doe. Although he would not even spare his own family in pursuit of his duty he failed to report that the sixty-dollar fine was waived.

Fred's state position made him well-known to the folks who lived and frequented the North Lake country he was responsible for patrolling. As a game warden he also demonstrated many rather original ideas about the duties of his office. As a native and warden he held that the growing list of restrictive game laws were put in place by "silk stocking" sportsmen and as such they and only they should be forced to obey them. He would ask friend and stranger alike to show their hunting or fishing license. It was his custom to note the number and person's name in his own pocket book of record. The one thing he would NEVER do was look in a sportsman's fish creel or frisk their clothing for possible birds. Nor would he sneak after a hunter who was making his way through the woods. In other words Fred was not looking for trouble. With such a course and method, hunters and fishermen in the region cooperated with Fred, even assisting him by bringing game law violators to his attention.

Otto Horner used to tell about the time he ran into Fred as he was hiking out of Sand Lake with a basket full of black bass. Fred pawed over the catch until he turned up a fourteen-inch trout—it was out of season. "Beauty ain't it?" he said looking Otto in the eye. Then he shook his head in mock sympathy, "Otto, you're getting color blind; you better go over to Boonville and see a doctor."

The surly, threatening. and generally offensive manner of many game wardens, both private and state, is my sole criticism of their ways. Meeting a man on a trail they will impudently demand, "Where are you going?" and "What are your doing here?" I've also experienced them sneaking, squatting, and skulking after me. Everyone they meet on a trail is to them a potential victim because they happen to be in hunting and fishing country. Fred was unlike any other I ever knew and yet he also could throw his weight around if need be.

Dr. Kilbourn was Forestport's health officer. During one of the dog quarantines in the woods, Doc caught Fred's hunting dog Spot and went to his home to report the incident. Fred listened to Kilbourn, then told him to wait a minute while he went into the house to get a piece of rope for a leash. When he came back out instead of the rope he was holding his shotgun in a position that said, "I'm ready for action." He gave the doctor a meaningful look, then said quietly, "Spot ain't going hunting with you today, Doc. Better try somewhere else."

Fred, as state game warden, was a frequent visitor to North Lake. While his territory was all of a quarter of a million acres, he covered it conscientiously via trails, tote roads, and an old abandoned highway that connected North, Sand and Big Woodhull Lakes. He was a very determined man when he set his mind on solving a case. When some of the members at the Sand Lake Club, whose names have been lost to history, dynamited Mud Lake and killed most of the trout he worked on the case for a month before finally winning a conviction. Later he arrested some of the same scoundrels for slaughtering does, cutting out the saddles, and leaving the rest of the meat on the ground to spoil.

Once he ran up against an embarrassing snag when he caught some Boonville men red-handedly dressing out a doe. As Justice Seth Lyon was about to fine them, one of the guilty members asked to speak to the judge privately. That brief conversation lead to another hurried con-sultation in the kitchen between Lyons and his son-in-law, Warden

Bellinger. On returning to the bench the judge announced the fine might have been seventy-five dollars apiece to the men but he was reducing the fine to ten dollars net. The rest of the story not spoken in public? The man threatened the judge that he would report him for selling a buck two weeks earlier. Judge Lyons quickly made arrangements including the offering of a ten-dollar "loan."

*   *   *

The patrol route between Sand Lake and Big Woodhull entered North Lake just back of my original camp, so Fred would always stop and have a visit with me. Sometimes he would borrow one of my boats to get to the foot of the lake and back to his home at Bellingertown. When I was away from camp Fred would help himself to one of my boats but always left a note stuck under one of the siding shingles by the door explaining he had borrowed one. He never failed to close every note with "Thank you in advance for the favor, Reverend."

Once when he was staying for several days at Charley Brown's State House hotel he suggested that we go to Hardscrabble Lake fishing. As it was on the private preserve of the Adirondack League Club and as the guest ticket Mr. Thomas R. Proctor of Utica had applied for me had not come yet, I demurred. Fred's comeback was, "But, Reverend, I'm entitled to a guide, so you come along, and if the club gets nasty about it, why, I'll explain you went along as my guide." Needless to say I demurred no longer but went back into my camp and assembled my fishing outfit for the trip the next day. From past experience and with and without a proper pass, I knew that if the day was cloudy and the trout were feeding Hardscrabble would yield an enormous mess of fish.

When Fred and I arrived at the little glacial lake the next morning the raft from which the fishing must be done from was near the inlet across the lake from where we entered. There was nothing for us to do but to make our way along the shoreline in order to commandeer the Great Eastern for our foray on the trout. There was a quite a pool of water at the inlet a couple of feet deep and maybe eight to ten feet wide. Across it lay a small spruce log bridging the expanse. The shortcut of a dozen feet appealed to me. Just as I had stepped on to the log Fred exclaimed, "Oh, Dominie, just look at the trout fry in that pool! There must be thousands." At that moment my feet slipped from under me and I landed kersplash in the pool along with the thousands of fry. 'Twas then Fred's humor took possession of him and found its outlet in his amazed explanation of, "Why, Reverend, I did not tell you to go in after them," and then he laughed long and loud as he graciously waded in to give me a hand out.

It was on this occasion that I learned from Fred how to quickly start a fire even from wood that had been soaked the night before from a hard rain. I knew all about birch bark curls as kindling but Fred showed me another resource. It was to hack off, with my belt axe, the dead and dried up tiny limbs at the bottom of a small spruce tree. Those twigs are full of pitch and gum and will burn fiercely when ignited by the flash fire from a mass of birch curls. We soon had a husky fire going and after I had stood around it and steamed myself warm we made slight repairs to the old raft, got on it, paddled over to the deep water, and fished successfully for several hours.

It is remarkable what an intelligent man will do and undergo for a mess of trout. My steaming myself dry was no figure of speech. It was really so. Fishermen have that kind of devotion. I've fallen into other lakes, stumbled down into streams where my clothing has become water-soaked. My teeth have chattered from the cold but the inconveniences never turned me from my goal. To fish was all that mattered.

*   *   *

But to get back to the Bellinger clan and some more of its distinguished members. I have introduced you to its patriarch, Jonathan, his wife, Sally, and two of their sons: Fred, the game warden, and Archie, who once declared he had guided for me before I was born. Fred had one son who had the misfortune to lose an arm in an explosion from a gun, a most unfortunate hunting accident. Notwithstanding his handicap, he continued hunting the remainder of his life. He was the son whom Fred impelled to go to the local justice of the peace and "confess judgment" to inadvertently shooting a doe and to pay the fine.

Archie had two sons, John and Dell. Like some of the earlier Bellingers they carried on the tradition of staying and working in the woods. Within their circle of acquaintances both were distinguished, although Dell was more of a character with a capital "C." John was quiet and demonstrative. Reliable but taciturn. Not to be imposed upon too far—like his father—while Dell was the opposite, talkative, witty, and very picturesque. He was original in his speech and would drop aphorisms and proverbs that were worthy of preserving. Dell was also the only one who would cast the sole Socialist vote in the Town of Forestport year after year. Being a Socialist myself, I asked Dell, "How come?" His explanation was typically brief, laconic, and pithy. He said he voted Socialist because he believed in it. His neighbors told him he was throwing his vote away but he would answer, "A man might better vote for something he wants and not get it than to vote for something he don't want and get it."

Both John and Dell worked for the League Club as guides for many years. John, known for being a man of few words, was never imposed on for very long by any thoughtless or inconsiderate members he guided for. It is a fact that oftentimes people of wealth somehow do not understand that their servants are human beings exactly like themselves in the realm of sensitivity and self-respect. Or if they knew it once, they have forgotten it. It remained to John to put one of these small groups right in this regard on an occasion they probably will always remember. And, it was all done in John's determined and effective manner.

This all came about on a day that John was guiding a party of young people from Honnedaga Lake to Bisby. The journey was of about a dozen miles and required crossing a few lakes including the head of North Lake.

John's party assembled on the verandah of Forest Lodge. Manager Bion H. Kent was making suggestions to the young people and giving John some final instructions. The pack basket John had slung on his back was well-loaded and quite heavy but several of the teenagers added items. One placed a camera, another a book and a bundle of magazines and just as they were about to embark, a girl, a lovely "butterfly," added a package of maple sugar candy. At that John spoke, "Mr. Kent, you have forgotten the most important item of our trip." Impatiently Mr. Kent inquired what that might be. John retorted, "My oars," turned and walked down the steps to the boat landing.

This would probably have closed this incident of thoughtless imposition were it not for some of the members continuing to crowd more items into his pack—items they deemed unnecessary for them to cart. There were more books and magazines, a belt axe a boy told him "didn't hang from my belt properly," and a canteen of iced coffee after they had drunk its contents. John endured it all silently.

About half way. on the foot trail between North Lake and Canachagala Lake was a spring of sweet water. Rustic wooden seats had been placed there for weary club travelers to rest. John's party stopped. John, as guide, walked a few feet farther to a nearby log, eased himself down and worked the heavy pack off his back. He then emptied all the items that had been added to his basket since the party left Forest Lodge. The additional items comprised a sizable pile on the forest floor. When one of the members asked what he was doing he explained he was going to leave the belongings on the log saying, "I have carried your hand junk on the trail as far as I am going to." Sheepishly each of them stepped forward and retrieved their property. As John told it afterward, "They were as quiet as h_ _ _ the rest of the way." Despite this outburst of quiet anger John was not discharged. In fact the youngsters either never brought up the matter to their parents, or if they had nothing more was ever said. Such situations occasionally arise and are due, I think, principally to an absence of mutual understanding between employer and employee.

*   *   *

Dell Bellinger owned a little camp at South Lake two miles beyond North Lake. There he and his wife spent many happy weeks in the summers of their declining years. During his first few retirement years he claimed to come down with the "quinsy" as soon as cold weather set in. Using his unscientific mind he set about to track down a cure for the re-occurring affliction. I found the diagnosis amusing and was never sure just what the symptoms were. I did enjoy Dell's illogical cure though. "I'll grow whiskers," he exclaimed one day. "Yes sir, that'll be what I'll do." It was as simple as that. Every fall from that time on he grew a full beard and the "quinsy" never bothered him again.

Once when I was waiting at the Atwell post office for my mail who should come in trailing the mail car but Dell and his wife in their little Model-T runabout. I had heard that he had been laid up for some weeks with rheumatism, an affliction we both shared. I greeted both with real joy and anxiously inquired about his health. He explained that he had had a bout with it but was "fair to middlin', thank you, Reverend." I was pleased and expressed so by saying, "Dell, you can't keep a good man down." Quick as a flash he answered, "No, nor a squirrel on the ground, either."

This would be a fair index of Dell's character. He was, like many of the North Lake folks of the Black River country, lacking in a formal education beyond what he gained from his common school learning. Yet his depth of mind showed to me he as well as other backwoods natives maintained good judgment within their area or zone. Dell did keep his mind alert by reading magazines. Two of his favorites were the *National Geographic* and *Audubon*. His wife was a district school teacher who shared his interest in reading. I wonder, too, if a more formal education would not have spoiled them.

Dell's wife, Jesimine (Jasmine), a.k.a. "Minnie," was a Black River girl born in Boonville. Her maiden name was Lawrence. Her father, Abner, acquired area fame as the founder of the Moose River Hotel. He enjoyed the confidence of his neighbors and was repeatedly elected constable of his town. Jesimine taught school in Steuben and at other district schools in neighboring towns. Following her marriage to Dell she taught in Forestport, the old Linday district in the township of Wilmurt, the schoolhouse in Bellingertown, as well as in districts no longer in the memory of most people living today.

Sophisticated people may smile and cynics would sneer at such tiny seats of learning today, but I can testify that the children who attended those small outposts of learning in the mountains of rural upstate New York were well prepared. Children learned the fundamentals of knowledge with a keen relish for reading good literature equal to those educated in village or city schools. It was my privilege for many years to plan and carry out an idea I had thought of for distributing good literature to these country schools as well as to men working in the lumber camps.

At one camp I found an intelligent and interested young bookkeeper who cooperated with me in getting books and magazines passed on to the remote camps in the West Canada Creek and South Branch of the Moose River areas. Naturally I did not neglect distributing old prayer books. The aforesaid bookkeeper got interested in a copy I had given him and eventually asked me to baptize and confirm him.

Not until I came to know Mrs. Bellinger did I come to fully appreciate the worth of the teachers of our old district schools and their important place in our unfolding American culture. To be sure it might have been practically unrecognized by the general public (and scarcely realized by the devoted young women who labored so faithfully in the one-room buildings). This realization came to me in a flash one day when I was speaking appreciatively to Mrs. Bellinger of a couple of young men from Bellingertown who had helped me build the chimney and fireplace in my camp. As she listened to my praise of them her quiet face lighted up and she commented, "I knew they would grow up to be fine men long ago when they came to school as little boys."

It was then I saw the teacher's work as somewhat similar to my own as a pastor. We were both preparing children for the future: mentally, spiritually, and socially. Since then I have classified school teachers on the highest level of social servants. I admire their attitude toward life. It is one of a participant, not of a spectator, and includes an active interest in continuing personal mental development throughout their lifetime.

One of the jobs that Dell had for a score of summers that helped keep him alert to the realities and fundamentals of life was that of guide and general factotum to Hobert V. Roberts of Utica and South Lake. Roberts had won international fame as a photographer of wild game. And, as a point in North Lake's history, Roberts began his career of taking flashlight pictures of wildlife at Little Woodhull Lake. In one issue of the *London Illustrated News* I recognized the exact spot where the flash pictures of deer, heron, and raccoon had been taken—all only five miles from my camp. One of the pictures I noted must have been made by an additional flash from another boat. I detected this, with some glee, from a form in the picture showing two startled deer on the shore. I was positive I saw Dell in a boat touching off the flash powder in a pan from the top of the bow staff.

The next time I was down the lake for mail I took the magazine with me. I had planned to show Dell, who I expected would also be at the post office. Of course he was. "See here, Dell. What do you think? I am sure that just the other day King George was looking at these pictures in Buckingham Place. In fact he might have been so impressed with your work in the use of magnesia for taking pictures that he wants to know who you are." Dell had not seen the current issue of the magazine. He stared at the picture of himself crouched in the boat for about a minute and then offered, "Hell, Reverend, the old boy don't realize how honored he and his old woman are to have my picture in his castle." And that was that for Dell Bellinger.

Over the years nighttime pioneer-photographer Roberts lost his edge to the competition. He was getting along in years and was too old for the careful, cautious work necessary: enduring the chill of the night time mountain air, the dampness, and late hours. He presented me with prints of some rare and novel pictures, autographing them at my request. I hung them in the main room of my Nat Foster Lodge. My favorites were of three hawks soaring in the air with fleecy clouds as a background. The other was of a baby loon riding on its mother's back.

Robert's abandonment of his picture taking left Dell without any definite seasonal work, so he registered as a guide with the Adirondack League Club's southeastern base at Honnedaga Lake.

Dell did have the misfortune of a one day's experience with a club member that did leave a bitter taste in his mouth. A ready epithet dripped from his tongue whenever the incident was brought up. He had been assigned to accompany a club member on a trail tramp from Honnedaga to Bisby Lake. This particular individual was evidently one of those parsimonious persons found in all walks of life.

The weather was sparkling cool and invigorating. The two moved along the lovely trails with agility and pep so that they arrived at Bisby before one p.m.—in time for dinner, whereas if Dell had loitered or craftily taken his time in manning the row boats kept at each landing they would have arrived at their destination in the late afternoon instead. The thoughtless man whom he was accompanying and whose duffel he had packed docked him half a day's pay. Added to this slap in the face there was no club member at Big Bisby desiring to hike to Honnedaga Lake. Dell had to make his way back to his base on his own time the next day. No wonder Dell felt aggrieved.

This one incident solidified his opinion of the unthinking and inconsiderate club members, of which there were a number. "Why that spit-on and pounded-down s.o.b. was so stingy he'd chase a louse through hell barefooted to get his tallow, by God," he'd spout. I covered my mouth with my hand the first time I heard him tell of this. I didn't want him to see my grin as I said, "Dell, maybe its true, but why the perfumed language in telling me about it?" Dell looked at me and smiled. He took my mild rebuke in good part and apologized for his strong language. However, I learned long before I came to know him that a man's use of profanity does not necessarily indicate depravity of character. Rather, it is just a vulgar and disagreeably bad habit with many. I have known men possessed of fine Christian principles who would scorn to do a low-down thing, even possessed of a fine culture, who on occasion could swear like pirates.

*   *   *

With the harvesting of the lumber crop that took a couple of centuries to grow, Bellingertown, in common with all the sawmill hamlets on the southwestern slopes of the Adirondacks, got slowly whittled down to near zero as good people left to seek other places where they could earn their bread and butter. Eventually there came to be but three people living at the site of what once had been the scene of frontier activity. Dell and his wife lived in the only original commercial building left from the fifty or more domiciles that once came to be in that mountain hamlet. The general store had been a fair-sized frame building. The other building was the summer cottage of a fine Polish priest, Rev. Joseph Jankowski, pastor of St. Stanislaus Church in Utica. The old Utica Consolidated Water Company had been buying up land along the region of the upper Black River region to safeguard the watershed of its reservoirs. My cousin, Frank C. Hopkins, was president. He thought it would be a good idea as a public gesture to give the pastor a deed to a lot. I told my cousin that it would be a good ecclesiastical gesture, too. So Father Joe, as he was affectionately called, built his cottage across the river about an eighth of a mile from Dell's home in the store. Father Joe, Dell, and his wife became good friends.

Misfortune, however, seemed to hover over Father Joe's activities in providing this little retreat from parochial cares in the city. One or two distressing accidents befell parishioners who went up to work on the seasonal cottage. It eventually burned. The last time I was to see Dell and his wife, the ruins of the cleric's summer home were still visible. Now with both Dell and his wife passed on there are no people living at what was once a busy place in the forest.

The river flows on unimpeded by a dam, just wheel tracks mark the turnpike road and the sand from a long sand hill over which part of the road ran slides still farther downhill creating a trench-like scar on the landscape. The only substantial item there now is the iron bridge over the river, replacing the wooden bridge that first spanned the stream when I used the road in the early days of my going to North Lake.

In closing my chapter on the Bellingers the following incident occurs to me. A party of us were going in to North Lake about 1896 or '97. We had taken the only train available from Utica at 1:45 a.m. and had a buckboard and team awaiting us when we got to the Forestport Station about 3 a.m. Daylight began to appear as we got to this wooden bridge at Bellingertown. In the party were Rev. Gotlieb Meisenhelder, a Lutheran pastor of Rome and a close friend of mine, and Rev. James J. Burd, rector of Holy Cross church in Utica. Also accompanying us were a couple of laymen from each of our parishes.

As we were crossing the bridge someone espied some set lines. We told the driver to stop. Dismounting we hauled up all three lines that had long and wiggling eels on each. The eels were killed quickly by the simple process of banging their heads on the iron rim of the wagon wheel. It was a lively operation. I can still vividly see Rev. Burd with his Irish dander up swinging an eel about in the air and bringing its head down with a bang on the felly of a wheel. Someone produced a jackknife and the lines were cut off close to the dead eels heads. The lines were then tossed back into the water and the eels were crowded under a seat with our duffel. We had them for supper.

This was not the end of the affair, though. Twenty years later I was telling about it in Charley O'Conner's place at Forestport. I had not noticed Dell was sitting in there and listening in. All of a sudden he stood up and exclaimed, "Well I'll be goldarned, Reverend; 'twas that your bunch that cut those lines? I remember all about it. I'd set the fish lines the night before putting eels on for bait. Then, I got up at an early hour to see what I'd gotten only to discover I only had lines. I knew darn well someone had cut the lines and would have reported it to Uncle Fred (the game warden) only what I was doing was outlawed by that time."

I smoothed things over saying, "Those were the days, Dell. Those were the days."

Dell quieted for a moment, then offered a peace. "I'll forgive you, Reverend, if you'll tell me once again how you stood off that loafer, League Club protector Hopson, when he wanted to look in your fish basket."

"Gladly," I replied to him, and to all who were then listening I explained I had firmly told Hopson that "as a private protector he had no right of search." With a broad grin, Dell approved, "And so you sent him off with his tail feathers dragging. Yes sir, those were the days."

A moment of hush came between us, then from Dell, "By the way, Reverend. Did you ever find out who glued the pages together in that religious almanac of yours. You know the one you tried to use the time you married that canal boat captain and that cook from Boonville?"

I appreciate a good joke on myself but I prefer that it does not become too personal in a public place but Dell went right on about it in a heightened voice. "And the bride wanted to go to Rome after that for the ceremony, but you had already swapped off the sack of potatoes the groom had given you in payment for some Warnick and Brown smoking tobacco."

I did what I could do to hush him but Dell was irrepressible. "Haw, haw, haw," he roared, slapping my back unmercifully. "Them were the days. Reverend, I'm your friend for life."

And so he was.

The Reeds

If you go for a drive through the woods six miles southwest(ward) on the dirt roadway leading out from North Lake, by and by you'll wind through thirteen curves that twist like a corkscrew over Railroad Hills. Stop at the end of the last snake, kitty corner from an inviting sheet of placid water and just before the original North Lake road intersects from Farrtown—in former times North Wilmurt—you'll come across an overgrown field on a rise overlooking the road. Climb up and walk in the tall grass and bramble clearing. Poke around. Sooner or later you'll come on to an old cellar hole. One hundred-forty some odd years ago the pioneering Dawson family cleared that area, excavated a hole in the bony earth and laid a well-crafted stone foundation from the multitude of rocks picked off the land and hauled to the building site. Whatever else the pre-Civil War family did here, the shrubby greenwood forgot long ago. But the pit remains.

There once was a thirty-acre plot with a log cabin that stood on a knoll and a frame house and barn built in the hollow. Both buildings were small and unpretentious. In addition to the residences there was a small sawmill that received its power in days of old from a large pond created by damming Otter Brook's outlet.

There, since the late 1860s, lived a family comprised of Mrs. Hull, a widow originally named Reed but since remarried and widowed a second time, and her daughter and three sons.

About 1869, the Hulls arrived in the Black River's headwaters, purchased the Dawson place, a thousand-acre tract of forest land, and settled at this junction now known as Reed's Mill. In the days when I first began going to North Lake, the family was the only inhabitant of this little settlement. I never heard a single word or a whine of regret from either Mrs. Hull or her children despite the fact that she and her two husbands had come from prominent downstate families, yet chose to move to a tract of forest utterly without experience in the ways of

76

the woods. Had she held on to her Brooklyn property the twice-widowed mother and brood might have continued to enjoy a higher standard of living than what they put up with in the mountains. Why then did parents prominent in downstate social circles relocate to the wilds of upstate New York? For the sake of their children's future? No.

At an early age Addison, the second youngest of three sons, contracted infantile paralysis—polio. The disease left him paralyzed from his knees down to his toes. His parents were ashamed to have their friends see their crippled "Addie," as everyone called him. He was weakened and shriveled when I knew him. His legs were useless but his thighs were normal. Mrs. Hull sadly told me of her son coming down with the childhood illness and always referred to it as "Addie's crippled condition."

Addie and Henry's stepfather visited weekends and whenever he could absent himself from his business responsibilities in Brooklyn. Henry, a Civil War veteran, eventually replaced his stepfather as head of the family when he died and successfully ran the lumbering operations and sawmill.

Addie was no real help to his older brother in the day-to-day lumber business, but he was a crack shot and managed to press himself through the woods to trap, hunt, and fish. His ability to propel himself around was truly remarkable. His method for getting from here to there was by crawling. I recall a small pair of crutches leaning against a wall in the house but I never saw him use them in all the years I knew Addie. Instead he just wormed about with remarkable agility on his hands and knees or upright on his knees, which were protected either with leather pads or a pair of hip boots cut off at the feet (so the toes would not catch on roots and rocks).

With his double-barreled shotgun slung beneath his chest he would crawl on all fours like an animal to a favorite deer run to watch and wait. Because of his infirmity, balance was a problem. To prevent being toppled over from the "kick" of the gun, he would sit with his back against a tree. After bagging his deer, he would crawl back home to get help to retrieve the carcass.

Once he killed a black bear. It was a wonder to us all that he was not mistaken by another hunter and shot during one of his trips through the woods. By 1932 he boasted twenty-eight notches cut on the inside groove of the forepiece of his shotgun, each one representing a deer he had killed.

By 1907, Addie, then an adult, had been caring for his aged and

ailing mother for some time. That summer Walter Hasting's grandfather, Matthew, summered in a camp at North Wilmurt at the point
where Twin Lakes stream makes a sharp bend and flows under the
bridge on the original stagecoach road from Forestport to North Lake.
His parents and a registered nurse in their employment were staying at
the family camp while his father recuperated from typhoid fever. Mrs.
Hull took a turn for the worse in the middle of the night and Addie,
knowing the Hastings had a nurse with them, wanted the nurse to come
to Reed's Mill so she could aid his mother until a doctor could be summoned. It's been lost to the passage of time whether Addie sent someone or crawled the two miles, but the latter has always been the belief.

Henry never forgot his service and position as a veteran of the
Civil War. On the back road (old North Lake Road) six or eight miles
beyond the Reed's place lived two aged bachelor brothers, Scots in
ethnic background, named Taylor. Archie Taylor was a Civil War
veteran. Before his death he had asked to be buried by a huge boulder
overlooking the Black River. His request was honored, and as long as
Henry lived he often hiked over to the old Taylor Place on Memorial
Day and placed a fresh American flag by Archie's grave. From the road
I have seen it fluttering by the great boulder many times. By now
Archie's grave has surely been forgotten.

Henry and Addie lived on for years following their mother's death.
Both men were literate, good companions, and valued by all who knew
them. I especially enjoyed talking with them about the old days and
often passed idle hours target-shooting. I never failed to call on them
when going into camp.

In 1915 the new North Lake Road was improved. The highway
crew made Reed's Mill their headquarters. The road work that year
infused a diversion in the old men's rather dull routine. Before the
project was completed, Will Ano, superintendent of the highway
project, tacked a sign at each end of the Reed's property line where the
road ran through. The sign read: "North Lake, 5 miles. Please close the
gates and slow down to 75 miles an hour." It was a joke, of course, for
the "Railroad Hills" that extended beyond for five miles could never be
driven at breakneck speeds.

Both of the Reed boys had their eccentricities. The original
telephone line into the State House was a special line installed by the
old Canal Board. A phone was installed in the Reed home for the
convenience of anyone traveling over the road who might need it. No
charge was made for it to the Reeds. Both Henry and Addie were

instructed about the ring signals, but Henry did not readily absorb the information. Besides, he was suspicious of the contraption anyway. One day while I was visiting there came a long ring. Henry took down the receiver from the wall case and as instructed said, "Hello." No response followed. He repeated his greeting several times but did not get results. It was obvious he was vexed. Finally he yelled into it, "Hello? Hell!!" and never again picked up the phone. Unless Addie was around the ring was always ignored. Old people are often instinctively conservative. This avoidance helped Henry escape a lot of irritation. The continual unanswered ringing did annoy visitors but it was also a source of amusement.

Addie's eccentricity was chiefly in over-valuation of old items. He and his brothers were avid readers. Following their mother's death they continued her subscription to the *Brooklyn Eagle*. They saved all the issues until the mass of back copies filled a fair-sized space in one of the rooms. One day when I stopped by to see Addison, he seemed overly serious and asked me to go upstairs with him. I was thinking "a family mystery" as we climbed, but my suspicions were stopped short when I was shown the stacks of old newspaper. He then asked me how he could sell them for what they were worth. I asked for more enlightenment; he explained, "As how I was a minister, he could trust me and he knew he could sell the old copies of the Brooklyn paper for a big sum." I had to tell him tactfully that if he could get them outside, he would probably get more for the paper as junk than as newspapers. The state and many public libraries surely had complete files. I inquired as to how he got the idea of their being worth so much. His reply: "Why, Henry Ford is buying at big prices all the old stuff he can get." This had an element of truth in it. I understand that Ford's mania for old stuff even put up the price of old privies.

Henry died first and was buried outside the Adirondack Park's "blue line" beside the body of his mother. Addie continued living alone until he became too feeble to get about, eventually moving to the Herkimer County Home where he was sort of an honored guest.

Before he moved to the home for the aged and poor, he arranged for the sale of the Reed's one thousand acres to the State of New York. He wanted the forest land, pond, and home site to become part of the Adirondack Forest Preserve. Addie was severely criticized for this deed by some of his mountain neighbors. He had even been offered a greater profit had he sold it to an individual. But he was insistent that the tract of land should remain "forever wild." He had lived in the forest since childhood and the land had touched his soul.

An interesting incident occurred at the time of Walter Hastings' grandfather's death in New York Mills. Addie had a friend bring him to the calling hours that were held in one's home in those days. His friend lifted him from the car onto the porch and he crawled into the house. His rubber gloves and his hat he took off as he entered the house and set them on the floor by the door. His dress was impeccable. Shirt and tie, suitcoat, and felt hat. And to protect his trousers, his footless boots. He crawled to the casket and asked Walter's dad and uncle to lift him up so he could review the remains. When he was ready they put him down and he went to the door, donned his hat and gloves, crawled out to his waiting friend's car and headed for home. A lesson to any and all who ever complain about a minor ache or pain.

With the passing of the Reed's homesite to the state, all buildings were torn down, gasoline-fueled earth-moving equipment have pared down the steep grade of the worn track that ascended Reeds' Hill. The clearing that has been passed by thousands of travelers since the days of the buckboard shows the work of Nature's regenerative hand. The reverend noted over the years that reforesting of a clearing by natural agents alone is very slow-paced. Somehow the seeds of both hard and softwood trees do not germinate readily in Reed's pasture, which was cleared of virgin woods.

Other river valleys have ruins of great civilizations. The Black River valley has overgrown stone slabs to forgotten yeomen settlers, loggers, tannery and charcoal laborers and miners. The falling-down stone walls, worn millstones, rubble piles of former dams, and crumbling foundations cite no names, but whisper silently of the ones who had been. Nameless. Obscure. Lost to the passage of time. They didn't go down in history but that doesn't really matter just as long as we all recognize that hard-working hands once worked the land.

The Wendovers

Here's to the Wendovers, the sneaking devils
Outlaws, trespassers — never on the level.
Eat your cereal and do your chores
Or in a week, they'll be at the door!

As long as people have raised children, parents have labored over what to do with finicky eaters. North Lake folks' remedy was to threaten a visit from the local devil's delegates—the Wendovers—or curse eternal damnation in hell if meals were not finished.

So notorious was the Adirondack mountain clan that the mention of their name put back-fence gossip to shame. Whether the family named Wendover deserved this distinction is arguable. I suspect their reputation as outlaws, drinkers, and fighters far exceeded their deeds.

Here in the primal forest surrounding Forestport—once the stamping ground of pioneer trappers and meat hunters Nat Foster, Jonathan Wright, and Nick Stoner—George Wendover was born in 1849.

Settlers relied on hunting and trapping, not as hobbies, but to put food on the table, clothing on their backs, and money in their pockets. The quality of their lives was measured by how successful they were afield. George had to be one of the most outstanding men back in the deep end of the gene pool where hunting genius appeared. Word spread among the sporting parties that came by train to the Forestport station, most often arriving in the wee hours of the morning, that George Wendover had woods savvy. He hunted smart. The man outclassed the average guide.

City-bred deer hunters steeped themselves in hunting lore. They had acquired a formal education; George was uneducated. They were refined; George was rough around the edges. They were novices and usually knew it; George was a student of the woods, water, and mountains. A hunter or fisherman arriving at the edge of the woods had two choices: Be lucky during deer or fishing season, or toss luck aside and go with a sure bet—hire George Wendover.

George met his clients at the depot across from the Buffalo Head Hotel and Saloon. A buckboard would transport them to North Wilmurt and thence by foot over a rough trail to a fishing or hunting camp. Year after year he would guide the same parties. The sports found George to be a gentleman. He took care of his charges, and they in return showed their gratitude in word and payment for his dependability.

In his youth he was a lanky, lean pioneer-like man. Rugged, with leathery skin, he was a scrappy woodsman who moved with ease through the woods, and he was an expert marksman with a rifle. When I came to know him well he was still wiry and little but his skin was shriveled, seemingly dried of any moisture. He was an old patriarch by then. He and his son Lon were passionate operatives, highly skilled in all tasks involving woodcraft. They could construct a temporary brush shelter or a weathertight cabin all with just basic hand tools.

George lived and raised his family of thirteen children in a small, weather-beaten house in Wheelertown, on the north side of Hinckley Reservoir. The Wendovers were known as a wild and reckless lot, but in my day they had begun to feel the inevitable encroachments of civilization. They still adhered to their clannish traditions and their informal code of ethics, but they slowly adjusted themselves to certain obligations that they found too difficult to avoid.

I recall the day when North Lake gatekeeper Charley Brown saved Lon Wendover's life. Lon was a shifty, stocky, quick-witted rascal and the apple of the old man's eye. One cold night in the woods Lon fortified himself with a little too much moonshine liquor. When he did not wake up in the morning his kinfolk became worried. Lon had a lifeless look. They fashioned a crude carrying device and brought him into Charley's State House. Charley phoned for a doctor in Boonville but figured by the time the physician arrived he would only find Lon dead—and that's if he wasn't already. Lon showed no pulse, his color was a pasty ghostlike pall.

When the doctor arrived he tried the prescribed therapies, but they had no effect. Unable to suggest any other alternatives, he advised them Lon was probably as good as dead and left for another case.

Charley had been watching every move without saying a word. Lon's kinfolk seemed dumbstruck, confused at the tragedy their brother faced. Cautiously, so as not to offend the assembled clan, Charley suggested that maybe he could help. Heck, if what the doctor said was true, it wouldn't do Lon any harm.

George charged Charley to go ahead if he had any ideas. So Charley Brown got out a bottle of spirits of ammonia and a spoon and started pouring the pungent liquid into Lon's mouth. Within minutes Lon sputtered and belched, then with a wild frantic look in his eyes he reared to his feet and staggered to the door. When Lon came back, clutching his stomach, visibly sick but revived, he made a comic remark about downing another quart of pumpkin whiskey and gettin' rip-roarin' drunk and raisin' hell—if he had the stomach for it. All eyes then moved to Charlie, who downplayed his assistance quite casually. He explained he had learned that medical trick from old Doc Kilbourn. Doc had told him years ago that he found lumberjacks usually had a natural resistance to medication. Lon was as hearty as any two lumberjacks. The young doctor who called had not taken that into consideration. From that time forward the Wendovers were beholden to Charley Brown.

Byron Cool

Byron E. Cool was born in Forestport in 1859, and received his early education in schools in Forestport and Little Falls. As a young man he worked as typesetter on the Palmyra *Courier* and the Utica *Republican*. Following a breakdown in health, Cool changed his plans to continue to pursue a career in printing and moved to North Lake where he became caretaker of the camp at the end of the North Lake dam. He later purchased the rather insignificant looking building and turned it into a North Lake establishment complete with an eight by ten foot barroom. He named this snuggery Cool's Mountain Home.

Somewhere during the sixteen years Cool operated the Mountain Home he sought membership in the Masonic Lodge. He found his application was denied because he "sought to ease the thirst of his customers at Cool's Mountain House with beverages containing alcoholic flavoring." When he divested himself of this practice he was admitted.

Cool was the first to develop and maintain several attractions for the fishermen, hunters, and summer guests who came to enjoy both his hospitality, which was a special characteristic of his mountain retreat, and the peaceful surrounding environment. Customers at his home and his North Lake neighbors were entertained by his interesting stories based on his long experiences of living within the wilds of the Black River headwaters.

His best-known accomplishments at the lake were a lookout platform built in a tree and a large flat rock on top of Cool Mountain and a groomed trail to North Lake's natural wonder, a large area that contained many glacial erratics, which he dubbed Monument Park. He even built a wooden box that contained a book for visitors to record their visit and comments.

In 1883, Cool married Frances A. Burt of Forestport. Frances joined him at North Lake soon afterward, sharing the experiences of the woods and mountains for over sixty years.

It was through Cool's efforts that a post office named Atwell was established at the lake. He became its first postmaster.

Byron was an outstanding woodsman and guide, an entertaining host and a Christian gentleman. He was also one of the Adirondacks' first naturalists, speaking up for the conservation of the natural resources and the preservation of the land when it was an unpopular subject.

His great love for the woods and the water, and for the rich variety of wildlife and plant life that lived in them, led to a vast body of literary work written in defense of a protected Adirondack Park. He wrote editorials and columns, was a lecturer and statewide advocate. He often expressed his ideas and appreciation for the Adirondacks in poetic form. He was also an amateur photographer; he preserved many interesting scenes of the wilderness in a fine collection of pictures that he bound with great care and taste.

Raymond S. Spears knew Cool well. Spears wrote about his long-time friend the year after he died in an article entitled "Byron E. Cool's Good Work" that appeared in the March 1944 edition of the *Lumber Camp News*. Excerpts of that article follow.

Byron E. Cool has passed on, but we can thank the memory of Cool's good works for the supply of wild meat that New York State has today.

Byron Cool was one of the first Adirondack woodsmen to see the need of conservation of wildlife and forest cover. When he was in his hotel at North Lake and before that he said, "Let us protect the deer!" At that time the kill of deer in New York state was perhaps 2,000 in a year—and deer were jacked in summer, crusted in winter, and meat hunters often killed as many as a hundred in an autumn, even after the first of our rationing was begun and the limit per hunter was put at three deer an autumn.

Cool became a conservationist. He said, "Let's save the deer, partridges, rabbits (northern hare), bear, and other game." He wanted fur animals protected when their pelts were not prime—in the days when ignorant sports and stupid interests called mink, foxes, marten, fisher and other beautiful, valuable fur-producers "vermin" and where wildlife gangsters destroyed everything in sight—even poisoning game.

Byron Cool recognized the wildlife meat season as chiefly in the autumn months "after the leaves turn." He saw that fur caught in December and January was worth several times as much as the same skins taken in September and October, "blue

hides," and in March and April—"fades and sheds." He argued
the matter with us woodsmen. He urged obedience even for the
faulty laws of the 1890s and early 1900s.

The great campaign for conservation that Cool and a handful of sensible woodsmen and sportsmen waged from 1890 on
came to a head in 1910. The violators changed to law-honest.
Public sentiment, urged by Cool and his fellow conservation-
ists, turned to preservation of the forests, of wildlife, of the
state's waterpower, and to stopping the killers who destroyed
not only their own share but the share of hundreds of others.
Thus rationing came in the bag limits of ducks, grouse, wood-
cock, deer, beaver (which Forest, Fish & Game Commissioners
reintroduced into the Adirondacks) and other wildlife. It was
protected against destruction till plenty was restored. Pheasants
were introduced. The state legislature that appropriated
$10,000 for restoration of beaver also gave $10,000 for planting forests of spruce, pine, and other trees. All this magnificent
program Byron Cool not only supported, but helped introduce.

There were only half a dozen or so active, open advocates
of conservation when Byron E. Cool took up the thankless and
brave cause of wildlife conservation, protection of the public
rights in water power, over wild lands, to adequate forest cover
in the Adirondacks. He saw cleared lands that never had paid
wages or produced profits for farmers and dairymen restored to
priceless wilderness across Central New York. He saw the wildlife restored to the new, second growth a few miles from upstate cities, and thousands have their share of sports, of wild
meat, or furs, of fish rationed among them where before only a
few hundred had obtained meager returns "killing everything in
sight."

Our mountain people, our professional and amateur wild-
crafters, our sportsmen and our Nature lovers have been richly
rewarded because there were philosophers and right-thinkers
like Byron E. Cool to figure through the real needs. He could
have been a mere guide, a mere hotel keeper, a mere woodsman, thinking only of himself, working for his own pocket all
the time. Instead he choose to work for the common good.

When the habit was to boast of wildlife outlawry, to brag
the cheating of the state, of the public out of its land, Byron
Cool stood against the sorry spectacle of the day. He lived to

see the right prevail more and more. He would not claim for his own efforts. He was, perhaps, too modest to realize his own good works. The good that he did was state-wide. It reached into the fundamental opinions of the public, of politics, of the benefit to the many.

The deer that range the new forests of central and upstate New York, the sport of the nature lovers, the thousands of families who have fish they catch and game they kill to eat, the youngsters who catch prime fur and trade it for books and clothes and other necessities—here we see that the good men do is not interred with their bones, but it remains, as Byron E. Cool's conservation work stands forth.

All that evil period of notions, of wastes, of grabbing lands, water power, getting public values first and personally, passes on. Where the farms that never paid profit nor wages, were abandoned, there grow up forests, there come wildlife, there is profit—springs have been restored, brooks long dried up flow again. Thanks, Byron E. Cool.

After the sale of Cool's Mountain Home, Frances and Byron Cool managed summer hotels and private camps at Lake Kora, Nehasane, and Twitchell Lakes. They also had charge of the Masonic Home at Round Lake for several years.

When they retired from active service they moved back to their native village of Forestport where they contributed much to the life of the community.

The Adirondack League Club

The Adirondack League Club's private preserve, according to Byron-Curtiss, was analogous to the European aristocratic system for royalty and nobility. A "rendezvous" for "American nabobs . . . where business and pleasure could be most agreeably combined."

"The charter of the [Adirondack League] Club declared its purpose was the preservation of the forest for the pleasure and recreation of its members," vented Byron-Curtiss in his original typescript, "but somehow or other they never could pass up an opportunity to pick up a quick dollar in the lumber or investment market."

The Reverend A. L. Byron-Curtiss was a man of the cloth, but compared to the stereotype of how clergymen were supposed to behave, Byron-Curtiss was a tad off the mark. The reverend would turn his head the other way when minor illegal activities were engaged in by his North Lake neighbors. His justification? Simply that his sentiments lay with them and against the ALC's "disturbing moves."

"With Byron-Curtiss at the focal point, the reader is apt to conclude it was a black and white situation. It wasn't," concluded ALC historian Edward Comstock Jr.

Author Thomas O' Donnell called on Byron-Curtiss, a witness to and participant in the doings around North Lake, for help when writing Birth of a River, An Informal History of the Black River Headwaters.

For his part, O'Donnell relied on the reverend's body of informal material, accepted the offer of unrestrained use—crediting and thanking Byron-Curtiss throughout the book, interviewed other people and then made his own interpretations.

Some incidents Byron-Curtiss participated in involved the activities of the "Dirty Dozen," a select group of the reverend's cronies who O'Donnell held were "dedicated to the promotion of minor irritations, insofar as these might discourage attempts at over-zealous enforcement of the trespass laws. . . . The more enthusiastic of the Dozen's efforts were directed against the Adirondack League Club's game keepers, but beyond the destruction of a few [posted] signs and scaring the living

88

daylights out of one or two officials its activities could be classified pretty much as horse-play."

The following adventures of the ALC and the Dozen (who believed that if they left no evidence there would be no case against them) is the reverend's. I have tweaked the occurrence from Byron-Curtiss' original manuscript and camp diaries.

Byron-Curtiss' attitude toward poaching and trespass on ALC property, as well as land the club leased from the Gould Paper Company, was not atypical. On the other hand, it should be noted that all Adirondack natives did not behave like the "Renegade Reverend,"— my tongue-in-cheek descriptive label for Rev. Byron-Curtiss because he choose to bend some laws.

I see mirrored in many of Byron-Curtiss' tales a turn-of-the-century opinion held by many Adirondack natives who opposed outside influence, whether it be newly imposed game laws outlawing deer hounding and jacking or the limits put on trapping and the taking of game. Locals resented government intervention in their long-standing freedoms. And wealthy private preserves like the league, which by 1896 had legally posted eighty miles of boundary line with enameled tin signs, also did not set well.

It was stated in the 1896 club's yearbook, "The Club's compliance with the terms of the law making poaching on private preserves a misdemeanor has just been tested and confirmed by the conviction of two gentlemen who doubted, trespassed and attained conviction, fine and repentance." It was in 1896 that the "Dirty Dozen" idea was hatched. In Byron-Curtiss' camp diaries, the reverend makes light sport of his trespass and poaching on and using the ALC's posted land. In one incident he disguised himself as a millionaire member accompanied by his personal "guide" and without being detected used league facilities right under the eyes of Club Superintendent H. Dwight Grant.

In 1899 J. W. Pond, chief fish and game protector of the state, traveled throughout the Adirondacks to learn firsthand how the laws were being enforced. He learned the laws for the most part were being upheld but found that the further one got back in the woods the less the laws were observed.

According to Charles Sperry, "Everyone knew the tall, lithe Seth Lyons who lived ten miles out from Forestport Station. Once one broke over Mulchi Hill on the North Lake road, Lyons' residence was the first past the Oneida-Herkimer County line marker before one came to Timberline, where the woods began." Sperry remembers that his grandfather "usually stopped at Seth Lyons' just to say hello and give the horses a little rest."

Lyons was known not only for his convenient stopping place along the wilderness roadway to North Lake but for his work as a local justice of the peace. His appearance was memorable as he often handed down fiery decisions that outsiders speculated favored his locality. What a character he must have projected with his long, bushy, white hair growing out sideways from underneath a hat he was seldom seen without. Add to that his long, white, bushy beard and you had an imposing figure of a man.

Times were changing. What was allowed yesterday could not be allowed to continue. Local sympathy had to be reversed. One play Chief Pond employed was to order game protectors to points deep in the woods. They would go to areas on patrol disguised as sportsmen under assumed names. When they caught violators red-handed or suspected a violation the protectors were to secure enough evidence to lead to a conviction, then escort the lawbreakers to an adjoining county where they would receive an impartial hearing and a just fine. In this way the state's game laws became generally obeyed and the minor violations of the laws were overlooked for the bigger picture.

The organization of the Adirondack League Club in 1890 was an important occurrence to the natives living in the Black River and Fulton Chain country because it constituted the first serious encroachment upon the assumed freedoms they had always enjoyed. In 1894 the club absorbed the Bisby Club founded by some Utica, New York, sportsmen in the 1878s among whom were Thomas R. Proctor and General R. U. Sherman. The Bisby Club made no pretensions of interfering with the local customs and traditions, so they were tolerated by the natives as a fertile source of cash and amusement. The Adirondack League Club was a different matter. Their membership took up many pages in the *Who's Who* of that day.

A group of Western New Yorkers assumed the Bisby Club (it was a merger and not a one hundred percent amicable one) and 329 acres of forest land it owned around the first Bisby Lake, then purchased some 150,000 acres of woodland at about four dollars an acre. Their territory took in Jock's Lake (renamed Honnedaga), the Bisby Chain (only upon purchase of part of the Wagner tract), Little Moose Lake, and a number of smaller lakes. They built impressive lodges and individual camps on the shores of three lakes and in their heyday they employed a large staff of managers, game protectors, guides, and foresters.

The woodsmen paid little attention to the club until it posted its land and thereby declared the territory a preserve for the exclusive use of its members. The club controlled at one time between 150,000 to 200,000 acres by ownership, lease or other arrangement, some of which was considered very good hunting and fishing grounds in the region; so it would have been strange indeed if this did not stir up antagonisms.

According to the law on private parks dating back to 1871, private preserves must be posted every forty rods and defaced signs must be renewed each year. It needs only the imagination to recognize how simple it was for an irate group of hunters to wreck these signs. The club started out by using very durable signs of heavy tin that were highly enameled. They were quickly appropriated by the woodsmen and adopted to all sorts of uses from reflectors on lanterns used in jack-lighting deer to roofing sheds, and with sardonic humor they added a bizarre touch to the open-air plumbing in use at the turn of the century. With the disappearance of the expensive porcelain enameled iron signs, cheaper ones made of cloth were used but the hunters seemed to find as many uses for cloth as they did for tin.

The local courts were inclined to discourage trespass charges whenever they were able and pettifoggers in cooperation with the justices of the peace stretched the laws into weird and fantastic dimensions. There was no open rebellion beyond the frank expression of mutual contempt; but there was a loosely organized vigilante committee composed of several wiseacres who disguised themselves under the title of the "Dirty Dozen." They directed the general sabotage and intimidation used against the club game wardens and anything connected with the trespass restraints. Outside of the destruction of the signs they seldom went beyond a rather vivid brand of horseplay and hair-raising tricks to discourage the enforcement of the trespass regulations.

The Dirty Dozen started as a gang in 1897 when the Adirondack League Club put its first game protector, George Davis of Boonville, at the head of North Lake. Some of the locals got together to find some ways to keep him from getting "lonesome" on his job. The men viewed their wild pranks as basically harmless so long as no victim was physically hurt. In their eyes their actions did not make them wrongdoers.

Byron (Cool) tipped off Davis that some poachers were at work out on the Horn Lake trail. He started up the trail with his coattails flying to keep up with him. A mile or two up he found a fresh deer hide stretched across the trail with this sign on it, "This is from the Dirty Dozen; you will be next."

Davis sat down to consider the matter.

A rifle bullet clipped the bark from a tree near his head. Davis jumped up and another bullet kicked up the dirt at his feet. Davis decided not to wait any longer. He started off full tilt for the foot of the lake, talking to himself. There he telephoned John Commerford, the manager of the club at Bisby Lake. Commerford came over with him the next day wearing a bowler hat and he and Davis went up the Horn Lake trail to look over the situation. They got back a little before dark and Commerford's stiff bowler hat had a hole right through the top. One of the women asked him, "Why Mr. Commerford, what happened to your nice new hat?" Commerford shrugged her off with the remark, "Oh, that's nothing. I tripped and ran a stub through it. I should have known better than wear a derby hat on the trail." The little lady slipped him a sly wink just to let him know that she knew he wasn't telling nothing but the truth.

Davis quit that night. I saw him at the Hulburt House in Boonville the next year and asked him why he had left us so soon. He explained that he had only taken the job for his health and it wasn't as healthy as he had thought it would be. I remarked that perchance he had quit for his health; but he let the matter drop.

It was a year before the ALC could get another man to work at the head of North Lake. Then a tenderfoot from Cooperstown by the name of Dexter, who did not know black flies from punkies, took the job and the Dirty Dozen swung into action once again.

Across the club trail to Canachagala Lake they stretched a strong, black linen set line and fixed a trigger on a yellow birch sapling that they bent down close to the trail. Dexter's foot tripped the line and the sapling flew up and caught him in the head. He was badly scratched about the face and both eyes were blackened, but there were no permanent injuries. He explained to Ed Klock that he had been walking along the Bisby trail in the dark and when he came to the ledge he had become confused and fallen off the cliff. Klock was all sympathy and he gave him a box of salve to put on his cuts and cautioned him about going over the trail at night when it was dark. Dexter resigned the next day.

The Dirty Dozen reportedly included Byron Cool, the genial tavern keeper; Ed Klock, the kindly dignified State Custodian of Reservoirs;

Art; Fred and Dell Bellinger; Mort Mayhew and six others lent their moral support. Mort Mayhew held a sharpshooter's badge, won on the outdoor range at Deerfield as a member of the old Citizen's Corps, N.G.S. New York It was he who reportedly shot around George Davis on the Horn Lake trail and later punctured Commerford's derby hat.

Ed Klock and Fred Bellinger set the yellow birch trap for Dexter on the Canachagala Lake trail. They claimed that if Dexter had known his business and been on the alert he would have detected the bent-over sapling and avoided it. They had done nothing but save him from some more serious accident that his carelessness and ignorance might lead him into.

A few years later Fred Bellinger, an uncle of Dell's, took over the job of state game warden and patrolled the whole district including Woodhull, Sand, North, and South Lakes, Reed's Mills and Forestport. He followed a strategy that he believed included the best interests of all concerned. He kept on excellent terms with the locals, let it be known he would run down each and every poacher in the locality, but was less rigid when it came to minor infractions. Game Warden Bellinger did not look for trouble, but he kept track of the hunting permits and inspected the fishing creels and packbaskets in such a way that violations were reduced to a minimum and little or no trouble was involved.

Death in the Mountains

The setting is a 9' x 12' white clapboard building originally used as an engineer's office but since converted into one of the smallest post offices in the United States. A small sign neatly lettered in red against a white background announced the building as the Atwell Post Office, named after Atwell Martin, the hermit who was the first settler in the remote northern Herkimer County wilderness.

Located on the east side of the State House, the tiny office was a stone's throw from the picturesque shoreline of North Lake with Ice Cave and Sugarloaf Mountains towering in the background. There were no hours posted. Local residents, men at the lumber camps nearby, camp dwellers, and vacationers just knew the mail could be picked up between noon and one p.m. following mail carrier Amo LaFountain's arrival. Amo also delivered grocery orders along with the "road mail." He once boasted he "carries more milk than the milkman."

If Charlie Brown, Atwell's postmaster, happened to be busy with some of his other duties (there were many, as he operated the State House, took in boarders and tended the reservoir gates which regulated the flow of water in Black River), his assistant attended to the postal work. While the distribution time always remained the same, the days varied over the course of a year—alternate days between May 15 and July 1; July 2 to September 15 saw daily pickup. By September 16 the post office schedule was back to alternate days. During winter and through spring's "mud season" (November 3 to May 14), mail was received and dispatched only when Brown called at the Forestport Post Office for it or sent out for it.

Since 1896, the first year Atwell, N.Y., was granted a post office, the site had always been a popular stage for local society to meet. Full-time and summer residents would gather, sitting on the wooden slat bench that stood on the narrow porch or congregating on the sandy front yard. The early decades of the nineteen hundreds witnessed an influx of lumbermen representing a broad mix of ethnic groups from eastern and western Europe who immigrated to the Adirondack Moun-

tains for work and the opportunity to raise their standard of living.

A small ledge along one interior wall of the post office provided a place for writing. Business was conducted at one window through a grilled opening surrounded by glassed-in pigeon-holes which could be rented and from which one received letters. A sorting table was behind the counter. Tacked on the walls were a variety of advertising posters that pointed out the superiority of air mail, informed patrons what stamps were for sale and how to register a letter and insure parcels, and urged them to "Join the Marines." The only thing not squarely governmental was a small glass case just to the right inside the door.

There Charlie Brown sold, as a sideline, chocolate bars and hard candy, chawin' and eatin' tobacco, small sacks of Bull Durham for rolling cigarettes, and picture post cards of North Lake and vicinity photographed by Hobard V. Roberts, who won international fame as a photographer of wild game.

On this particular day Rev. Byron-Curtiss was at the tail end of his philosophizing. The subject was retirement. He was counseling, "The first effect of unaccustomed leisure I have noted in my long life is demoralizing to the average man. But after a period, men have found themselves and begin to use their leisure intelligently and for their betterment." As he concluded the academic confab, he ended with his characteristic wide smile that exhibited a great array of gold teeth. It was meant to express his satisfaction with what he had just voiced and also served to greet his friend, Dell Bellinger, an Adirondack League Club guide out of the Honnedaga Lake country who had just driven up to the mail service.

I often used to meet Dell when he drove over to the Atwell Post Office in his old Model-T Ford runabout from his camp two miles distant on South Lake. The mail usually was dropped off by twelve noon. Anticipating its arrival most of the patrons of our little community would gather around the post office building gossiping and bantering with each other while we waited for the mail to be sorted.

Wilkes Dodge, superintendent of repairs on canals, had a camp at Atwell Bay on North Lake. On this day he was feeling pretty big-headed about the thirty-six-inch land-locked salmon he was showing off to the gathering. He claimed he had caught it in South Lake. I guess he might have—I gave him the benefit of the doubt—but according to the local custom of dealing with braggarts, no one acted as if they believed him. Instead there seemed to be a general air of understanding (it might have been the truth in this case) that Dell Bellinger had actually caught the salmon and sold it to Dodge. Dell might have been able to settle the question, but he was in a haste to return to Honnedaga and fleet-footedly scurried past the crowd, waving in his neighborly way, picked up his bundle of mail and skedaddled, leaving the small crowd to work over Dodge. Pointing to Dell, who by that time was climbing into his motorcar, Dodge swore he could prove his claim contending, "Dell will verify the accuracy."

The following day prior to mail time everyone was on hand to see the fun they anticipated based on yesterday's performance. Dodge showed up early with a bottle of bitters in his vest pocket. When Dell drove up, Wilkes sidled up to him and offered him a swig. Dell wasn't a man to pass up free whiskey; he took a good long swallow. Then Dodge cleared his throat and got down to business. "By the way, Dell," he said, "didn't I catch that prize salmon off Trout Point in South Lake the other day? These people seem to doubt my word."

Dell scanned the crowd. His facial expression took on a fake bewilderment. First he looked off toward the head of North Lake in casual speculation, then directed his glance back to the bottle Dodge had returned to his pocket. He noted the superintendent pat the pocket holding the bottle. By then several onlookers were unable to repress snickers. Dodge spun toward them and glared as he lifted the bottle from his jacket and handed it to Dell and restated his question with impatient emphasis on each word, "DIDN'T I CATCH IT WITH MY OWN HOOK AND LINE, DELL?" The question was almost beseeching. Dell was going to take his time responding; that part was obvious to all. He lifted the bottle to his lips several more times. Each gulp was followed by a pensive facial expression. Time was needed to consider the matter. Then in a drawl he replied, "Well, Dodge, come to think about it, I didn't see you catch it any other way."

And with that he placed the bottle into his pocket and stepped into the post office.

*   *   *

One morning a short time following this incident Dell rowed up to my camp. I could tell by his manner that something out of the ordinary was on his mind. He came right to the point, which wasn't like Dell.

"Reverend, we got trouble over at South Lake. You've got to come over with me right away." Dell's eyes did not show their usual gleam. "Jerry Shaw has 'kicked the bucket' sudden like and you and I are about the only ones around here able to take care of things."

"I'll be ready in just a moment," I returned. "Just let me put on my clericals. I'll be right with you."

As I changed clothing I quizzed him for some of the particulars. I was not well acquainted with the deceased. "Well, Reverend," the sage guide informed me, "I reckon the little green devils with the curly tails and little straw dunce caps got the best of old Jerry."

I felt my eyebrows automatically rise; bending my elbow I made a motion as I moved my hand to my mouth. "Yeah," Dell nodded. "They spell it with two O's like in booze."

Dell's wife joined us before we went up to the Shaw camp. I spoke a few simple words of sympathy to the widow to strengthen her faith in the mercy of Divine providence; then we asked the women to move over to the porch of a neighboring unoccupied camp while we got Jerry's body ready for the undertaker.

Jerry Shaw had lost more than a weekend worth of weight. He was pale and emaciated. His body wasn't a pretty sight. When alcohol's poison digs in it doesn't take long to make an awful mess. The sour stench of liquor was everywhere. We both felt the need to fortify ourselves for the task, but despite our making a thorough search of the place, not a drop of alcohol could be found.

We got the body washed and cleaned up; then we ripped the door off the woodshed and laid it across two chairs, covering the weathered planks with a clean sheet. Next we laid Jerry's body on top and tore strips from another sheet for homemade binder strips. When we got the body in shape we covered it with another sheet. Soap and witch hazel had accomplished wonders, but we could have done with a few peppermint lozenges.

When we were finished we made another search for Jerry's stash of liquor but met again with disappointing luck. Not one to give up Dell said to me, "Hell, Reverend, that booze is around here somewhere. We definitely need a drink after this; I'm going to ask Jerry's old girl where she's got the booze hid." We went out of the camp. I waited in a lawn chair while Dell went over to talk with the women.

When he came back he gave me a wink and a nod. I got up and followed him out back and over the trail to a spring. There, behind an old log was a stone jug about half full of liquor. We brought it back to the camp planning to wash our throats clear and rest a mite before making the next move. Dell reached in through an open window for some tumblers he eyed sitting on the table. Filling both we lifted the glasses and drank to the last journey of his late lamented friend. The brew definitely made both of us feel much better.

By the time we had finished belting down a couple of drinks Dell looked up at the sun and estimated it was about time for the undertaker to arrive at the other end of the lake. "Reverend, I reckon it's time to get going," he announced as he stood. The women had joined us by then, and as we started walking Dell's wife questioned him as to why he had picked up the liquor-filled jug and felt it was necessary to carry it along. Dell countered that he was only going to take it as far as Mulchi's Spring because that vein was so much colder. We would leave it there, borrow Mulchi's boat and continue on to the foot of the lake where Yeomans, the mortician from Forestport, would be waiting for us.

We arrived at the landing a bit ahead of Yeomans, but not long after we had smoked a bowl of tobacco he arrived. We exchanged friendly greetings, then rowed back to Mulchi's dock and spring. It was our intention to first prepare ourselves properly with some more bub-a-lub (as, we conjured, Shaw would have approved) before continuing with the final duties to the old boy.

When we considered ourselves to be in the proper spirit for the solemn undertaking, we placed the body in the litter, carried it to the dock and ever so carefully loaded it into Mulchi's boat. Balancing the undertaker's basket had not been a problem on the trip over. In fact we had arrived without a hitch, but the sleek guide boat was not going to respond as flawlessly on our return. That was made clearly obvious from the onslaught, for once we loaded the corpse in the moored boat we had problems. Charon could never have had more trouble crossing the river Styx than we did navigating that lake.

No one needed to tell us loading the mortician's basket with its burden crossways was a bad idea. It was obvious from the moment we set it down across the gunwales that we needed to find the balance point. Our original intent was to carefully balance our load over the middle seat then secure the entire burden using cord wrapped around the seat and the bucket snug-like to keep everything from shifting. That idea would allow two of the three of us to sit in the bow and stern seats while the third member would lie prostrate under Shaw's body and steady the load. Experimentation proved that plan to be the wrong move.

Next we positioned the body-basket lengthwise over the middle seat but it would act as a fulcrum point, we surmised, since any movement would cause one end to tip up and the other down. Subsequently we rested the burden across the middle and front seats. That allowed me to sit on the stern seat to steer while Dell and Yoemans had to straddle the basket and paddle.

Naturally, the additional weight and our positions caused trouble with the watercraft's balance. It was mutually decided to take along the stone jug. We'd use it as additional ballast. In retrospect, I am positive we looked to all the world a comic sight. Steadying the boat was not our only problem.

Our own equilibrium was also questionable. It and the boat's balance was made worse each time we lifted the stone jug ballast to our lips. Knowing our own equilibrium had progressed to a point that it was noticeably inferior we had a pow-wow about our situation. We looked back toward the shore from where we had departed. It wasn't all that far away. Then we looked toward the far horizon trying to focus on our destination in hopes it would remind us that our skill at navigating the guideboat while intoxication began to set in could get us into some trouble.

Foolishly we ventured further out on the lake. We were invincible. About the time we reached the middle of South Lake the wind came up, got in behind us, and swung the craft around so we were in the trough of the waves. Dell was the first to realize the gravity of the situation we were in. "Bring her around, Reverend!" he called. "Bring her around into the wind. It'll be a hell of a note to lose Jerry now that we've got him so well started for the outside."

Yoemans, up in the bow, was not only scared but he had a touch of sea sickness. He took turns heaving his insides to the windward as he dipped the oar into the water and pleaded with us not to lose his stiff. As a confession "in extremis," he admitted Jerry Shaw was the first customer he had had in two months. As a result, business was poor. If he lost Shaw he might just as well jump into the lake and follow him to the bottom, the way he was feeling.

For all our trouble, we reached the end of the lake safely. The mortician had his corpse; Dell had the remainder of the jug, and I rejoiced in the joy of living in a dry skin. We each took a final swig to celebrate our timely escape from the dangers of Poseidon's deep; then, with the wagon loaded, Dell and I stood and watched the buckboard move down the forest road. Dell held the jug up to his ear and gave it a deft shake. "Well," he said, "it's knocked off one man and damned near drowned three others but there's still a few sips left for the women." With that we rowed back to Shaw's landing and killed the old stone jug.

Dell and his wife arranged to take the widow out of the woods. And while I hiked the two miles back to my camp on North Lake I pondered the frailties of mankind.

Buckboard along the North Lake Road on the way to Atwell

"Mud Hole" at headwaters of the North branch of the Black River

Dirt road over the North Lake dam. Byron-Curtiss' mountain house and saloon, established in the 1880s, can be seen on the right

City sportsmen were often drawn to the wilds of North Lake

Early log cabin on North Lake

The McCluskey party at North Lake camp near Jock's Brook Outlet

Perry's sluiceway dam on the Black River

Atwell Martin's North Lake hermitage

Atwell Martin, hermit of North
Lake. Photo by Gardner & Frey

Rock cairn Rev. Byron-Curtiss helped construct marking the
location of Atwell Martin's hermitage

Dell Bellinger at home with
his pet chipmunk on his lap.

The Reed homestead on Reed Hill, c. 1890.

Reed's mill pond at the headwaters of the Black River

Hunting expedition led by George Wendover (second from right), c. 1900

Wendover's Gooseneck
Creek cabin

Courtesy of Edward Blankman

George Wendover

Courtesy of Dorothy Mooney

Mulchi's Hotel, Forestport

Hunters and guides

Hunters and guides at Buffalo Head railroad station, Forestport. Guide Jim Dalton, second from left, with pack basket.

Giles Becraft (second from left), one of the more famous Adirondack guides

Adirondack League Club game protector's cabin on North Lake

Amaziah Dutton (Dut) Barber spent many of his
years at Jock's Lake (Honnedaga Lake today)

Sans Souci camp, South Lake

Members of the
Sans Souci camp
at South Lake

Fishing party on the Black River

Canachagala Lake and diversion canal to North Lake, c. 1890s

Adirondack sports
and guides

Courtesy of North Elba Historical Society

Fisherman with the day's catch

Courtesy of John Chamberlain

The trail to Little Woodhull Lake.
Note the long crosscut saw left
hanging a century ago by a lumberman.

Photo from author's collection

North Star Camp, Horn Lake (1890s-1910)

Fred "Adirondack" Hodges

Louis Seymour, known as
"Adirondack French Louie"

Courtesy of Edward Blankman

Courtesy of Edward Blankman
"French Louie"

Courtesy of Edward Blankman
Withers place in North Wilmurt along the Twin Lakes stream

Burt Conklin,
Wilmurt woodsman
at Rustic Inn

Courtesy of Edward Blankman

Photo from author's collection
Composite of images of John Burroughs and *North Country Life* magazine

Linn tractor pulling into Gould Paper Company's Camp 7, 1922

Camp 7 bunk room and mess hall at Ice Cave Mountain, c. 1920s

Lumber camp
cooks at Camp 7

Courtesy of George Shaughnessy

Mrs. John B. Todd
at Camp 7

Courtesy of Dorothy Payton

Little Deer Lake. Photo by Grotus Reising, 1897.

Hunters' reward at North Lake

Winter scene at Nat Foster Lodge

Little Woodhull Lake in winter

Photo from author's collection

State House at North Lake

A Near Homicide

None of the Black River headwaters settlements had a burying ground. A lack of cemeteries didn't mean North Lakers lived forever; bodies were taken outside for interment. One either went southwest to Forestport to find a burying plot or headed southeast and crossed West Canada Creek where a meager, stingy affair of about an acre was located along the main wagon road.

I knew of only two deaths from natural causes at the North and South Lake settlements in the fifty years I lived there. To be sure there were deaths, but the causes were from logging accidents, accidental shootings, and drownings. Natives lived to be a great age, often spending their final years outside with relatives or in the Herkimer County poor house as North Lake's famous hermit, Atwell Martin, did.

I have always contended longevity was a consequence of the healthfulness of the mountain region and its immunity from crime. I credit the people of great age that I knew, for in great part my accumulation of history and lore has come from the older residents.

"Uncle" John Van Dyke was in his seventies when I first met him. When I last talked with him in 1915 he was 87. I witnessed him in action. His physical strength had yet to be sapped. He was still able to cut blocks from logs with a two-man drag saw, split and pile his own winter's wood, shoot game without the use of eyeglasses and he could even heft and carry a pack I estimated at forty to fifty pounds. His only impairment was his almost total deafness. Folks used to say Uncle John was so deaf that he would have to wear lightning rods on his ears just to hear it thunder.

I know for a fact that he was unable to hear the rumbling of an approaching storm because while I was at his place a storm began to build in the far distance. The approaching front presumably caused the fish to stop biting so I stopped fishing, left the dock, walked up to his place, and placed my fishing gear under the verandah and went inside to visit. "Why'd you stop fishin', Byron?" he questioned. "'Taint like you to come in so soon." By dint of shouting I made him understand.

Uncle John was born in 1828 in the little town of Westernville, a village north of Rome. He was considered "delicate" as a youth, not destined to live very long. To help sway the balance of life in his favor, his parents moved north into the Adirondacks where the thin, slight boy grew to adulthood. Growing up in the mountains benefited his health perhaps in some of the same ways tubercular patients improved in the balsam-scented mountain air. He was wiry, with arms like spindles, but physically tough. Uncle John could, if needed, raise a much larger-framed man off his feet with a good blow, but the gentle-natured man was seldom provoked to that level of anger.

Folks around always remarked that he was so physically tough that even in old age he could hold his own in physical labor and endurance, for a while at least, against men much younger. Keen, alert, with a clever sense of humor, he was clean in life and habits (Van Dyke did not use tobacco products or drink). He trapped when there was money to be made in that activity but successive years of living alone for months were not to his liking. He was never a solitary individual. The post-Civil war years brought prosperity to the Fulton Chain region (Old Forge). He grew up a skilled woodsman and found skills he had always relied on to survive could be used to make money by guiding. That career brought him to the Woodhull country where he eventually set up his own fishing and hunting camp, beginning his last career at Big Woodhull reservoir. The near homicide of this story was the closest to willful human slaughter that tract had ever seen, and John, who got his sobriquet of "Uncle" with age, was the center of the affair.

Uncle John had a good constituency of summer people who frequented his small refuge at Big Woodhull, a guest house of sorts but lacking the condiments of glamour. Yet he still attracted lawyers, judges, doctors, and their families chiefly from Rome, Utica, and Herkimer. Among his annual visitors was Judge Defendorf of Herkimer. John's lodging was famous for his delicious pancakes. It became a tradition among his clientele and friends to ask him for the recipe. He always ended the directions with a twinkle in his eye, "And don't forget to stir the batter with the sun to get the best results." Once in a great while the flapjacks were of poor quality. When that happened he would say he had neglected this or that. The excuses ranged from the quality of the flour to him dipping water from the wrong corner of the spring box.

But it was not his pancakes nor the good fishing at the lake that he became best known for—rather it had to do with his set-to with the

Adirondack League Club during the early days of its organization in the 1890s. The affair was quite irregular in character for Uncle John Van Dyke.

In talking with club members, I know that it would be agreed by now that in the early years of its organization the ALC carried matters with too high a hand and did some things without due process of the law. This is not surprising. The territory the club took in was almost a complete wilderness, the M&M railroad had not yet been built through the Adirondacks, justices of the peace were many miles outside, and the few game laws there were not observed by natives.

The earliest survey that accompanied the Adirondack League Club purchase showed Uncle John's camp to be on league land. There used to be a state road that ran in back of my original camp. It followed a route that began at White Lake Corners (Woodgate today) running easterly through the woods from the White Lake Station (today's Bear Creek Road). The eleven mile roadway aided in the construction of the reservoirs at Chubb, North, Sand, and Woodhull Lakes. The roadway was eventually abandoned. In my day sections of the access road from North Lake were in bad shape. I can see where a buckboard ride along that route would not make for a merry journey. It was an adequate foot trail, however, and was the route of choice when hiking to Sand Lake and Wolf Lake Landing, the western terminus on Woodhull Lake. The Van Dyke abode was near Brook Trout Point on the shore of the original Woodhull, an easy row from Wolf Lake Landing. Wolf Lake and Woodhull Lakes were separate bodies of water until the dam on Woodhull Lake flooded the channel between Remsen and Brook Trout points. Following the creation of the reservoir, the entire expanded body of water is referred to as Woodhull Lake.

Van Dyke's dwelling was small; it could accommodate about a half dozen guests. It wasn't much of a place: a log structure with a wood stove, beds, chairs, tables, dishes, of course, and the necessary tools to get by in the forest. The boats were probably the most expensive possessions.

A persistent rumor filtered through to John that club people were going to send a team and buckboard in and take his chattels, remove him from the premises and burn the camp. Van Dyke sought the advice of Joseph I. Sayles, a lawyer in Rome who had been his boyhood friend in Westernville. Sayles was the leading criminal lawyer of Oneida County in his day, getting off a criminal by the name of Hildreth and his gang who were charged with murder for wrecking an express train just outside Rome in 1896 in which a number of people were killed.

Sayles' advice to his old-time friend was short and to the point. If the league, who then owned the largest private preserve in the East, did in fact own the land, they still had no right to force John off and take his property without some form of due process. "John," he advised, "a man has a right to protect his property, even to the extent of taking a life if necessary. You go back and protect your stuff and I will protect you if you get in trouble doing it." With this advice Uncle John returned. But before he resumed his routine he took new precautions. First, he began construction of a new cabin, temporarily stored his gear in the state barn at Woodhull Dam and asked George Watkins, the gate keeper of the State House, to send one of his boys immediately to notify him if he heard word of when the club was going to make a move against him.

In due time the unwelcome message did arrive, "Uncle John, they've come." John was applying roofing when he received the word. He scrambled down, got into his boat and rowed to the State House landing at the foot of Big Woodhull proper. There he found John Commerford, the preserve manager, in company with the chief gamekeeper and another employee standing by two of John's upturned boats he had removed from the barn. A teamster was also there standing by with a team and wagon complete with a rack used for tan bark. John recalled the wagon was big enough to hold three times the personal possessions he ever owned.

Commerford began, "John, we have come to take your things out. You're situated on league property and we know you've been told to move." Uncle John asked him to "wait a minute" and went into the State House. Securing his rifle and a handful of cartridges he stepped out on to the verandah and in full view of the men calmly loaded the ammunition into the magazine. Then pumping one into the chamber he cocked the hammer and walked out to the men and said, "Commerford, if you touch one of my boats I'll shoot you as sure as there is a God in heaven."

At that assertion Commerford replied, "Now, John, we don't want any trouble. William H. Boardman, the ALC president, sent us after your things and we just want you to be quiet about it and not make any fuss." Van Dyke repeated his threat more forcefully. So much so that Commerford and his men retreated behind to the back of the barn. There a conference was held. Uncle John stood steadfast near his boats. In a few minutes the men reappeared and John Commerford again began to parley by saying, "Now look here John. You must be reasonable in this matter. You don't want to be acting this way. We are going to take your things outside peacefully and you will only be getting yourself into troub—." But he got no farther in his argument for Van Dyke brought his rifle around and aimed it at the dismayed superintendent and shouted, "Commerford, if you touch one of my boats or any of my stuff that is in the barn, I'll kill you and your gamekeeper and the other men, too, if they lend a hand. That's all." His firm, rugged stand with a cocked rifle brought to his shoulder, hazel eyes flashing fire, was too much for Commerford. The result of his positive and comprehensive threat were that the men went back of the barn again for a further conference, this time also being joined by the driver of the team who had hitherto been enthroned on the wagon seat.

The men remained back of the barn a quarter of an hour when the teamster reappeared, wearing in addition to his clothing, a broad grin on his face. He said nothing, however, just climbed onto his wagon, gathered the reins and drove off. Uncle John watched him, suspecting he had won, but as he told me, he kept watch out of the tail of his eye for Commerford and his companions to come out from back of the barn also. Instead, they went directly to the boat landing, got into the boat they came in, and rowed up the lake following the little steamboat route that lead toward the Bisby trail. At that Uncle John, full of fire, shouted, "Commerford, you tell Boardman you didn't get to take my property and for him to come get it himself."

Commerford was a veteran of confrontational affairs and knew when to quit. This had not been the first time he had been threatened. There had been several successful convictions against trespassers that year on league preserve land and all had sworn they would take deadly revenge. The more doughty gamekeeper, rendered surly by this temporary defeat, using semi-profane language eloquent in its expressive brevity, hollered back, "You go to hell, damn you!"

Uncle John Van Dyke, however, did not escape the inevitable reaction from such a nervous strain. It was violent and serious for a little while. He did not realize the strain he had been under and how close he had been to pulling the trigger and killing a man until he saw the men rowing away. Then he began to shake like an aspen leaf. His hands fluttered so that he could not let down the hammer of his rifle. He called to Watkins to come help him. Watkins, as he told me, had kept out of sight fearing a homicide and did not want to be a witness against his good friend. Once he assisted in lowering the hammer he took the firearm from John's shaking hands and led him into the State House. Uncle John was a temperate man but I believed both he and Watkins when they told me John pushed down a quart of liquor within a couple of hours—and with very little ill effect!

Uncle John never heard an echo from his repulse of the attempted rape on his effects. He finished his new camp located on the old Wolf Lake section of Woodhull and continued to receive guests. He also became a temporary gate keeper at the dam for many years. To his credit I will say that he showed no rancor in after years toward the club. He and Mr. Boardman, who eventually ordered the burning of John's original camp, became friendly as the years passed.

Lawyer Sayles was dead when a United States geological survey proved the original survey line wrong. Adelbert I. Sayles' nephew, also a lawyer in Rome, offered to start a suit for damages, but Uncle John declined, saying life was too short for lawsuits if they could be avoided. He died at Westernville in 1928, a friend respected and dearly beloved by all who knew him.

My Elusive Trout

A. L. Byron-Curtiss was a true Nimrod. During a day when most sportsmen would take a one or two-week trout fishing and camping trip in the Adirondacks, B-C enjoyed long periods of time at North Lake. The location of his camp, its easy access to the railroad, his wife's willingness to raise their children and the reverend's ability to juggle his work to fit his out-of-door's schedule all played together to allow him these lengthy stays. There, he fished daily. It was his pleasure to locate the whereabouts of the really big trout that inhabited the remote ponds, lakes, and streams in the Black River headwaters. He clearly delighted in uncovering those pristine gems—the untapped fishing holes.

It was a rare occurrence when his camp table-fare did not include trout on the daily menu even after the season had ended. The savvy, often-times unscrupulous angler's notion of New York State's fishing regulations could be bent to suit his purpose. His sentiments were those expressed by Mrs. Johnson, proprietor of Mother Johnson's famed boarding house located on the Raquette River a few rods below Raquette Falls. When asked, "What kind of fish is that, Mrs. Johnson?" she replied, "Well, they don't have no name after the 15th of September. They are a good deal like trout, but it's against the law to catch trout after the fifteenth, you know."

In "My Elusive Trout" the reverend chortles over his fishing success. He believed in keeping the vast majority of his daily catches for the skillet as compared to today's fishing practices that encourage "catch and release."

"Dick" Camp, an Adirondack guide, was once fishing for bass from a guide boat on Sand Lake with A. Dutton Barber, manager of the Adirondack League Club's Forest Lodge at Honnedaga Lake in 1893. Camp considered bass fishing a silk-stocking sport of the club.

Having hooked a fish, Dick would annoy Barber by the way he would yank the bass aboard. Barber finally could stand it no longer.

130

Squirming around in his seat he faced Camp and scolded, "Now look here, Dick, that is no way to catch bass. You should play them some." Dick's retort was, "Play 'em be damned, Barber. I'm fishing fer fish, I be." In recounting this incident to me, Dick declared he had "half a bushel most in the boat in less'n no time," while Barber lost half of his, "a-playin' 'em."

Camp's method has been mine mostly during my years of trout fishing. If they are fairly hooked I waste no time but get them in the creel as quickly as possible and resume casting for more, only quitting when I have secured a fair mess—usually the legal limit.

One of my favorite streams is the North Branch of the Black River. It is easily reachable from my lodge. The brook is a lovely little ribbon of water that tumbles and babbles down to the lake from the locally famous "Mud Hole" at the headwaters beyond the forks. Many old-timers told me their wonderful stories of the trout to be had there. There are shallows and rifts that as a rule yield nothing and then again, there are tumbling cascades and little pools, some holding scarcely a barrel of water, where one is pretty sure of hooking at least one or two trout. After a night of mild rain, when the trout are running, the sport is thrilling anywhere on this little stream. The trout will run from seven to nine inches, a nice pan variety. I seldom failed in securing the day's limit of twenty-five.

A tote road used in lumbering operations in winter crosses the stream about a mile above the lake. The bridge with its log abutments had caught a lot of logs and other forest debris so that a typical logjam was formed. About thirty rods above the jam at the bridge another log-jam had formed at the bend in the stream. Naturally the trout cannot get over either of these obstructions and I soon learned that the fishing was good above the upper jam and fairly good below the lower jam—at the log bridge. I had just about cleaned out the trout of legal size between the two jams; however, I never failed to fish the thirty rods between, always casting with care and anticipation. What fisherman is there who will not, from sheer force of habit make at least one cast into every likely pool and rift?

One June day I hooked on to a whale of a trout about halfway between the two obstructions. I had hooked him well and following the regulation "Dick Camp Method" I stuck the tip of my rod toward the zenith of heaven, reeled him close and as he swung in to me I grabbed the big wiggling fellow by the gills losing no time in getting him into my fish basket. I then resumed fishing, casting with extra care in the pools as I walked downstream. Just before I reached the last pool above the lower jam against the bridge my foot caught on some hobble brush and I tripped, falling sideways. Instinctively I thrust a straight-arm toward the earth to brace my fall. As I did I detected a "kerplunk" sound but was in no position to pay it any special heed. Righting myself, I continued to the bridge where I decided I would eat my lunch. I clambered to the bridge and sought out a comfortable place to sit whereby I proceeded to first count the trout I had secured and then inspect (and gloat over) the big fellow. But when I pawed in my basket the big fellow was gone!

My face and behavior would had been an interesting study had anyone been there to observe me. I dumped everything out and pawed through the contents. There was the folded-up piece of thin rubber sheeting with a slit in the middle I used as a poncho, my sandwiches, an extra reel, bottles of matches, fly-dope and what-not, and the smaller trout. But sure as night will come, my prize catch was not among the other articles.

I carefully inspected the top of the basket. I felt it had been securely fastened so the fish could not have gotten out by reason of a loose cover. I finally reasoned it had simply wriggled out through the rather large hole in the cover when I had tripped and that the splashing sound I had heard was of him making his getaway. I did retrace my steps to the scene of my spill just to satisfy my curiosity that it had not gotten dumped in the brush. I have since stitched a swath of canvas over the cover with a slit over the hole. I was disgusted by the affair, feeling as if I had lost the farm, and I immediately returned to camp via the tote road that crossed Ice Cave Creek.

A fortnight later I fished that stream again going up two miles and fishing downstream. When I reached the spot where I had hooked the big fellow earlier in the month near the first flood logjam, I became particularly alert and attentive. I cast carefully but never having a strike I moved on to the next pool and the next without a single rise. At the fifth pool I hooked on to what I took to be a water-logged twig vibrating with the motion of the water. I gave a couple of mild twitches and not being able to loosen the hook, I lowered the tip of my rod and began to loop back the line preparatory to reaching down and pulling up the twig I reckoned the hook was impaled on when out of the hole jumped that monster trout with my bait in his mouth and my leader hanging most gracefully from his jaws. His leap was from the pool to the rifts above and I declare now that his mottled back struck out of the water and the stones rattled as he wriggled up the shallows to the next pool. In the excited motion he threw the hook. It all happened before I could get the slack of my line and the rod at a decent angle to properly snub him.

Well, I reeled up my line, telescoped my rod, and quit fishing for the day. If I had felt as if I had lost the farm when I lost that trout the first time, I felt this time as if I had lost the city complete with sky-scrapers! I was anything but in a cheerful mood during the tramp back to camp; it was fortunate that I had no guests there to vent my spleen on.

Well along in August, when the water was low, I decided to go fishing up that way again. Religiously I went to the place on the stream where I was accustomed to begin and fished, this time with fair suc-cess. When I reached the first jam I did as the Scottish preacher once advised the members of his congregation. Figuratively, I took myself by both ears and looking myself squarely in the face said, "Now Byron, attend to your fishing with extra care until you reach the jam below." And I did just that. Forward I moved warily and cast cautiously into all the holes using all my skill. Hole after hole yielded nothing. Not even a nibble.

Finally, in a hole near the lower jam that had never yielded any-thing but undersized trout, my elusive trout struck. He took the lure with a snap and a bang. I promptly returned the greeting with a skillful twitch I had learned in my quarter of a century of stream fishing. As the tip of my rod bowed gracefully to the stream under the strain, the line gave a telegraphic signal and I knew I had sunk the barb of the hook into one of his jaws. He was mine. He looked for all the world like a monster as he turned over in the pool. I did not hesitate a second, but like "Dick" Camp, I yanked him out of the pool, flinging him as far into the bushes on the shore as my line admitted. My tackle is never fancy but it is always strong. I knew it would hold for that sweeping yank I gave. I own that I followed it up by scurrying into the bush ready to set foot on him if he got loose from the hook, but it remained firmly imbedded. Taking no chances, I thrust my thumb into his gills and made my way to the bridge where I goggled over him at my leisure.

Only then did I envision the scene from another perspective. There I was piled in the bushes above the stream. If someone had come along at the right moment all they would have seen was a couple of feet wav-ing frantically above the bushes. After I saw that I hadn't lost my catch, what a good laugh I had—all to myself.

It was a buck trout, a true representative of Adirondack wilderness waters with its bright orange and red markings on its underbelly. It measured fourteen and a half inches and was as broad as my hand. The fish was unusually large for this particular stream. My theory is that having but a small stretch of the creek between the two jams of drift-wood to move in, instead of keeping down his flesh by running along stream all summer, he had fattened up like a stall-fed ox. Anyway, he was my prize brook trout for that year.

Maybe my method of securing him was not up to the ethics of "Dut" Barber and the ALC sportsmen, but when a fellow has lost a whopper like that twice, in my humble judgment, ethics are suspended. As I started to camp with my prize quite secure in my fish basket I forgave him for escaping me twice. I also reflected on the temper I had indulged in each time I had lost him and felt somewhat mortified at my behavior.

Outlying Camps
in the Black River Headwaters

Following my ordination into the sacred ministry and my beginning pastoral duties at Christ Episcopal Church in Forestport in December 1892, it soon became known to my congregation that I had a personal interest in "Nature's sacred temple," the great out-of-doors. The
population of my adopted town had a body of woodsmen, many of
whom were well-qualified as guides. In 1893 I was invited on a June
fishing trip, "If'n you can see your way clear, Reverend." Did I ever! I
had no trouble sandwiching my first trip into the headwaters of the
Black River between funerals, baptisms, marriage ceremonies, and
regular church services.

My new-found companions kept an outlying cabin on Combs
Brook. It was basically the product of Ed Klock, who became a gatekeeper for North and South Lake's reservoirs. The Combs' cabin was
in the best condition of any I eventually came to know. I recall being
wakened just at the gray dawn of morning by the quacking of ducks. I
crawled out of my blanket to investigate and, in the process, my stirring roused my companions. Half asleep, we all went outside to check
on the disturbance. Walking to the stillwater we found a flock of black
ducks swimming in the pool where the creek joins the river a few rods
from camp. Earl Scherer expressed the thought each of us were harbor-
ing, "We've got all the wrong hardware with us; we need a gun." Ed
Klock made a point, though, when he remembered out loud, "Black
ducks are greasy and a bit strong in their wild flavor, anyway." With
that questionable consolation we turned our attention to a standard
breakfast.

Outlying camps (shanties built to offer successive nights of shelter)
were built to withstand the rigors of Adirondack winters and maintained by men who shared a common interest in a particular area where
they fished and hunted. A standard of ethics existed between the locals
and visiting sportsmen in my days of living in the Adirondacks

whereby anyone was free to use any outlying camp. Users were respectful and an unwritten rule placed responsibility on them. Firewood burnt was to be replaced. Balsam tips were cut to replace old bedding. Food scraps were to be cleaned up. Door and window shutters needed to be latched securely. The open-door policy meant help was there for forest wanders in emergency situations. This system generally worked well. Anyone who disregarded the accepted standard procedure was regarded as the "worst kind of lowdown scoundrel."

Before the purchase of my Nat Foster Lodge I had developed an association with headwaters locals, but my move to the area in 1901 began a tight-knit tenure with the North Lake folks. I was a Johnny-come-lately member of a group of men who built and maintained nine tiny outlying camps located at Little Woodhull Lake, Grindstone Creek, Goose Neck Outlet, Twin Lakes, Combs Brook, Hardscrabble, Canachagala, Horn, and Snyder Lakes. The last two were in the "green timber," an unlumbered tract in Township 5, Herkimer County. The buildings were either open-log lean-to's, (three sides with an open front with a bark roof) or four-walled affairs (the side walls of logs and the roof of shakes).

That wilderness construction crew consisted of Ed Klock, Earl Scherer, Byron Cool, George and Lon Wendover, and myself. I will not go in to minute detail of every log we notched nor every spike and nail driven in the building of our outlying camps but I will review the basics for the sake of recording my history. The Wendovers had more need for backwoods camps than the rest of our group members, for in addition to their using them when guiding parties they also relied on the shelters when they gathered spruce gum, which had a commercial value then.

My microscopic investment of money was usually two dollars spent on the purchase of two rolls of roofing paper. We figured it speeded the work. Peeling bark for the roof took a lot of time and we did not always bring a spud with us, just like we never split shakes for shingles right away. A bark roof and shingles were refinements we added as time went on.

Our crew of camp builders started from the head of North Lake loaded like pack horses. In addition to normal camping equipment we also carried everything we would be likely to need in our building operations, including a collapsible sheet iron stove, a drag saw, an old broad axe, and an assortment of penny nails and spikes.

The Wendovers were of slight build, but lean and supple. I shall never forget how, on the day we set off to build an outlying camp at Horn Lake, Lon, after slinging on a huge heavy pack basket, turned his back toward the party and directed us to add and lash well the two rolls of slagged roofing paper to the top of the pack basket. His dad, at fifty-eight years of age, also carried a pack that was amazing both in size and weight. Both woodsmen were capable of toting their big woven packs for miles without a stumble or whimper and without a thought of stopping. Earl and I, on the other hand, were not hardened. We would call a halt every mile or so in order to get our wind and rest momentarily.

The Horn Lake footpath was defined only by axe slashes on trees. The virgin forest with its heavy canopy prevented light from reaching the forest floor. That made walking easy since no underbrush grew. I was happy my feet remained dry for there was only one wet area to maneuver around in a small clearing at the far end of Ice Cave Mountain. We reached our destination, a pleasing mountain lake, within a few hours. I won't say Earl and I were "all done in" but if I compared our eagerness to the rest of the party's willingness to get right into the business at hand, well then, I will have to admit we did have to stay back.

Earl Scherer, though big and husky, spent forty-odd weeks a year cooped up in the cubical of an engine working the controls of a train in New York City. I was almost as soft and in not much better shape. Ed Klock, the oldest of us, was probably in the best shape. Earl and I masked our temporary weakness with a bit of innocent illusion by insisting we take time for a bite and to survey the western shore for the best building site situated away from the pre-existing rough lean-to shelter.

Ed and the Wendovers set to work felling small balsam and spruce trees that would be used for the vertical walls and roof of the camp. Byron worked with Earl and me lopping the boughs from the fallen trees. With them we made a rude camp for our temporary shelter. Byron Cool was a master at building brush camps. Crotched posts were set in the ground, between them a pole was fixed; limbs and brush were angled against the pole eventually forming a water-resistant roof. The sides were filled in with more brush and a fire pit with back logs for a reflector was made. In short order we were done. With our night's abode finished, Byron switched crews with the tyros and set a fire in preparation for the bed of coals needed later.

Supper was nothing fancy, cold victuals, all of a gallon of hot coffee and about a peck of semi-charcoaled potatoes. Once the blackened shell was broken open, salt was added to the steaming white interior.

They were relished by all. We slept well on our blankets cushioned on a bed of fragrant balsam boughs, though someone had to get up a few times to drive off (or kill if possible) a prowling hedgehog.

It will suffice to say that the eight-by-twelve-foot building was up, roofed, and finished in three days. I was surprised how we got such a fairly smooth roof. The Wendovers attended to every detail displaying ingenuity and cleverness. They had selected balsam logs about eight inches in diameter. This wood splits readily and the riving leaves little in the way of shredded slivers. Then they hewed the flat riven sides smooth with the wide blade of the hatchet, fitted them to the top of the log walls with the hewed flat sides up, and spiked the logs in place at the front and rear. We also split and hewed enough two-inch planks to fashion a five-foot door and a table.

Lon had told me to bring along two pair of strap hinges. I knew one pair would be used for hanging the door but I wondered what the second set was for until he secured the back of the three-by-four-foot plank table to the back of the wall. The hinges permitted the surface to be raised to "eating height." When up, the flat top was held level and in place by a single leg.

The little cabin had three rooms in our imagination: the bedroom, kitchen, and living room. The sleeping area was a simple affair. A log the length of the interior width of the building was laid on the ground, five feet back from the front wall and staked in place. A deep bed of balsam boughs filled the entire cavity. The camp stove was unfolded and set up in a corner opposite the table. Ed Klock had donated a sixteen-by-sixteen-inch window sash. It was a luxury he hand-carried through the forest. The light that streamed through the panes of glass established the "living room." It was one of the few outlying huts with a glazed window I ever saw.

With the passage of time new state regulations prohibited the building of permanent shelters in the Forest Preserve; changing values replaced the cooperative spirit needed to keep up remote camps on private land. The advent of automobiles also contributed to the change. Modern motorcar transportation is the explanation of why outside sportsmen come today and don't even stay until tomorrow, whereas when it took a day to get from the railroad station to the heart of the wilderness—over a road only a patient team hauling a buckboard could negotiate—parties planned on staying up to a month.

Little Woodhull Lake

My last active work in the ministry was as the resident chaplain of Willard State Hospital and pastor of a little village church on the east shore of Seneca Lake. It was at Willard that I became acquainted and formed a lasting friendship with the Rev. Ralph S. Nanz of the Department of Plant Physiology at Cornell. We visited frequently; he always stood in and preached for me a few times during Lent. He later went on the faculty of Carroll College, Waukesha, Wisconsin.

Nanz invited me to join him in his rejoicing when he received his Doctorate of Philosophy from Cornell. To help prolong Nanz's celebration of his new degree I suggested that we take a trip to my camp at North Lake the following week. Nanz not only accepted in a heartbeat but was so anxious to get underway he arrived at Willard the next Sunday—almost a full day before our scheduled departure. "Could we start for the mountains this very night if I could break away?" he asked. I demurred. Before daylight Monday we were driving eastbound on the turnpike in his Ford roadster—at one time hitting a breakneck speed of seventy-five miles per hour! He was determined to reach my shanty for supper and long before dark. The long June days gave us the time to meet that schedule.

The fresh, new-to-the-woods doctor of letters Nanz turned out to be a failure as a fisherman. We rowed to the Middle Branch Inlet, one of many good trout streams in the North Lake region. The trout were "running." A gentle rain during the night put trout on the alert for bugs and worms that are knocked onto the surface and washed into the streams. As good as the fishing was Nanz would frequently drop his rod haphazardly on some rock in the stream and head off to a plant he noticed growing along the bank. He'd paw away to expose the one he was after, give it a careful examination and then ask me, "Byron where's my rod?" on his return to the water, having forgotten just where he had discarded it.

Nanz was a typical plant hound. I'll always remember when an eight-inch trout jumped for his lure at a cascade. Instead of deftly

139

hooking it, my fishing buddy dropped his rod at the instant the trout jumped and instead stepped on shore and began carefully examining a mossy spot on a tree with his pocket microscope. Turning toward me with great excitement he shouted, "Oh, Father Byron! I've found a new specimen," indifferent to the fact that the trout that had jumped at his bait had become hooked and was now struggling to get off as it pulled the rod into the water. I slogged over and grabbed his wobbling lance-wood rod from the rifts (by that time the hooked trout was jumping and submerging itself within the limits of the free line), and secured the trout. With incidents similar to this all day we had few trout for supper that night and the majority of what we did have were from my creel.

The next day I promised Nanz we would go to Little Woodhull Lake. I made a hike to Little Woodhull Lake a standard objective for many of my friends who visited. I would always stress they had to be hardy for the route was scarcely more than a slashed trail most of the way with two swamps, each about thirty rods wide, to cross. I also cautioned all that they had to have was physical stamina as well as a poetical enthusiasm for hiking in the forest wilderness.

Those who were up to the challenge found Little Woodhull Lake rewarded them by revealing from a couple to a dozen or even a score of deer as well as raccoons, sometimes a heron or a crane, and numerous birds and interesting plants of the forest and water. Often the wildlife viewed were the first they had ever seen. My daughters never tired of tramping, chattering as they made many a delightful trip to this lake guided by their loving dad. At this lake I first saw a cedar waxwing, a rather rare bird in my part of the mountains. I especially wanted to show Nanz some interesting plant specimens I had found.

Anxious to explore the wealth of botanical specimens there, he had me up before daylight—breakfast was waiting. We were thus able to hit the trail before broad daylight. North Lake was five miles from Little Woodhull—not a terrible distance for a woodsman but for my guest, who rarely got out into the rough, it presented plenty of challenge. We arrived at our destination by 9 a.m. It wouldn't be until 9 p.m. that we would arrive back to our base of the morning. The lateness was due to the diversity of plant life. Nanz quite lost his head in his enthusiasm. He prowled and peeped through his little microscope at every specimen that interested him. My botanist friend even had me gathering whole armfuls of plants and grasses, heaping them up at the lean-to that had been built at the site of the original cabin built next to a spring across from where we arrived on the trail.

The original Little Woodhull cabin had been a haven and shelter for fishermen and hunters since the 1880s. The cabin had an old Northern Farmers brand cook stove with an upright oven. It also had a water reservoir on the back like the old-time Steward stoves. The Northern Farmers types were passing out of usage but the discarded stoves made serviceable equipment for outlying camps both for heating and cooking. The only unfavorable feature was the amount of wood needed to stoke them. The firebox was huge and had a voracious demand for more wood, but with thousands of cords of wood around it was impossible for the supply of fuel to ever run short.

Unfortunately, the snug shelter met a sad vindictive fate at the hand of "Joe" Jenkins, the state game warden. I divert here to tell the tale for it was one I shared with Nanz. The whole thing was a hilarious joke on Jenkins who was one of the breed of wardens who suspected everybody he met on a trail, along a stream, or in the forest hunting as outlaws—game law violators. I've known him to growl, snarl, and demand offensively at me, "What you doing here?" or "Where you going?" when I would simply be walking up the tote road to my camp with neither fish creel, rod, or gun on my person. When Jenkins got himself in a hole by his zeal for actually arresting a party at Little Woodhull Lake there was a lot of merry laughter among the mountain folks and sportsmen along the southern slope of the Adirondacks, for they all were elated that Jenkins had finally got his due.

This was the case in its simplicity. Warden Jenkins and an understudy were hunting the shores of Little Woodhull one night looking for a party known to be there; they were of course outlaws in Jenkins' opinion, and habitual convicts. Lying low, they spotted a light in a boat and heard several shots out on the lake. The doughty game warden and his companion stuck it out until daylight shivering with the cold as the mist began to rise from the lake, the temperature being low that night.

As it began to get light they made their way to the large diameter log-walled camp and found four men fast asleep in the two bunks. Jenkins and his companion woke them up and told them they were under arrest. Why he did not deign to say, and the members of the party were wise enough not to ask him but to submit meekly to their arrest and accompany the officers to North Lake. I happened to be at the foot of the lake while they were there awaiting to be taken out to the justice for arraignment. As I recall they were all from the village of Prospect some fifteen miles north of Utica. I had a talk with them and offered to go out to pettifog for them at the hearing before "Judge" Farr at North

Wilmurt. They thanked me but said they had called for a lawyer to meet them at Farr's and take the legal end of their case in good professional style. Their lawyer did just that.

The case dragged on for nearly a year with adjournments and hearings. Finally it was dismissed for the reason that Jenkins was unable to prove anything at all against the defendants. It was true he and his understudy swore they heard shots on the lake that night; that they had arrested the defendants in the utility camp the following morning, but for connecting up the four men with the shots they heard or producing a carcass or any part of one there was no evidence at all. Any wonder that everyone about who learned the particulars found enjoyment over Jenkins' predicament.

With the failure of the case the four defendants had good grounds for suing Jenkins for false arrest. I was told by those who know that the most hated man in the Black River region did worry a lot about it. We all noticed he did not act quite so cocky after that when he showed up at his old patrol haunts.

But he did one thing that indicated his venom of spite. He returned to Little Woodhull Lake after the case was dismissed by the court and put a torch to the venerable building. His excuse was that it was a resort for outlaws. But at the suggestion of Dell Bellinger, Hobart Roberts and I put our heads together and soon executed a plan that replaced the destroyed camp. We applied to and secured from the Conservation Commission in Albany permission under the law to build at the lake a regulation lean-to camp. As soon as we received it we got busy and had a cooperatively built camp on the site of the old one.

Jenkins came while the work was going on and ordered us to cease, but Dell, who loved Jenkins about as much as the devil loves a monk, produced a signed and stamped permit. I shall always remember how Dell, shorter by four inches than Jenkins, glared up at the defeated warden as he shook the paper in his face and said with a lot of perfumed language, "Now Jenkins, you git and git fast or we'll throw you in the lake and you can swim back to the landing if you can make it through the lily pads." Jenkins did "git." It may appear as unnecessary, yet it must be borne in mind that Jenkins represented a low type of tough character. Dell could be tough, too, and as I regret to record he could use tough language under provocation that rather bent the fourth commandment.

Back to Professor Nanz. He was quite justified in his enthusiasm; he declared repeatedly that the area around the lake had the largest assortment of specimens of botanical life that he had ever seen in any one place. In that statement he was echoing a remark Byron Cool had made to him in the 1880s quoting a professor of the Polytechnic Institute of Rensselaer, N.Y.

As little as I know about botany I was convinced early on during my trips to this site it was extraordinary in many respects as to the flora and fauna. Yellow water lilies, with a few white ones, grow abundantly on the lake as well as on nearby Lily Lake, which a shotgun charge will just about reach. On the spots where the shore is low and mucky with water, plants grow thickly, which I have often seen floral pieces made of in greenhouses and seen in a sprays of those home aquariums fitted out by dealers. I've torn up whole beds of the stuff with my paddle in getting about both lakes. I particularly liked the great blanket of the wild mountain rose that grew close to the bank where the camp was located. It was a glorious sight in early summer when it was besprinkled with the single pink roses about as big as silver half dollars.

The day Nanz and I were there I counted twenty-two deer in sight around the shores of the lake or in the water. I pointed out that it was not the lily pads they were after but their roots. When I spotted a couple of deer with their heads and shoulders under the water evidently on their knees, I told Nanz, "It's not their prayers they're saying but rather they are munching on the tender stems and roots."

From the previous day's experience of playing chase-after-my-companion's-fishing-pole I wasn't surprised to see Nanz's almost indifferent response when I would excitedly say, pointing, "Look, look. There's a big buck in the water of that bay." He would acknowledge by giving a hasty glance and then resume his plant investigation. He had accumulated a fair-sized pile of specimens at the camp. Acting as guide, I fished while my party of one continued to gather, add to the pile, sort and categorize, and study his plant specimens.

Past midday I prepared a fish fry with thick slices of bread with coffee. Following that meal I suggested we leave but he pleaded for more time. I didn't want to return late. Most importantly I did not want to be caught in the woods at dark. I assured Nanz that situation would be most trying. Finally by late afternoon when the shadows had begun to grow long we jammed all the beloved specimens into two pack baskets. Nanz by then agreed it was getting late as he noted it "was really darkening up" as he glanced about.

We hit the trail-of-sorts at a stiff gait for we had two swamp stretches to cross. 'Twas there that he met defeat and disaster. I was leading in the dim twilight. It was none too easy to see the mess of roots one needed to step over to avoid being bogged. I made it across the first stretch but poor Nanz's foot slipped on a wet root and he went up to his middle in the squash black muck. It required quite some maneuvering with my walking staff to extract him and return him to a solid footing. That accident also made him extremely cautious in the next swampy crossing. Needless to say we proceeded slower than I would have liked.

Twilight in June meshes into complete darkness not much after eight o'clock. It was in that darkness that we made the last mile to camp. Our pace, one mile per hour, for even an experienced hiker in a forest slows his pace. Nanz was helpless as to going it alone. I had to lead him three-quarters of that last mile.

Once we arrived at camp, I lit the lamps, started a fire in the kitchen cook stove as well as setting a blaze in fireplace; the world looked more cheerful. I hustled a supper while Nanz stripped down, washed body and clothing, and redressed. The good hot supper I had ready restored his pep and cheerfulness sufficiently to beat me at a game of chess after which we said prayers and retired for the evening.

Nanz was a splendid fellow and exceedingly good company—when he wasn't concentrating on plants. Of his trip to the mountains with me and his experiences he enthused over for many years. Maybe the perspective of time had softened his memory and mellowed his judgment.

*   *   *

The reader may have noted in my telling of this story that they recognized Hobart Roberts' name and realized in my referring to the results of fishing in Little Woodhull or Lily Lakes that I used the word "fish" instead of "trout."

Roberts is noted as a pioneer in flashlight trap nighttime photography. His guide, Del Bellinger, packed hundreds of the sensitized glass plates into the campsite at Little Woodhull. He probably took near to a thousand exposures of the wild things around the lake. Heaps of the old-fashioned glass plates with one side black with the chemical film were abundantly strewn around. He also pitched a canvas-walled tent and did some developing and printing in the field.

As for my use of the word fish. 'Twas very seldom any trout were secured in Little Woodhull, but there was an abundance of the lowly bullheads. We used to keep an old boat up there. It was waterlogged because it was always kept sunk near the landing so it would not fry out or be chewed by hedgehogs.

A few outsiders on hearing of the big bullheads to be had came in for the express purpose of getting a mess of them. Eventually my son and I were responsible for extending the area of the fishing grounds for the toothsome bullhead clear to North Lake.

One time when we had secured a huge mess of the fish we sorted out the small ones, carried them back to camp and planted the good-sized fry off the dock. Seven years later good messes of bullheads began to be secured at North Lake, which before had only chubs and lake trout. When a fisherman came into camp and didn't get a mess of trout they could still boast, "But I still got a grand mess of 'Lily Lake trout.'"

The fact is that in the cold waters of the Adirondacks while it is not sportsmanlike to say so, I much prefer a supper of good-sized bullheads than a supper of trout. They are juicy and the meat has a splendid flavor while trout are something like venison in that both are an exceeding dry meat. I never roasted a saddle of venison but what I slit deep incisions in the meat and put in strips of fat salt pork or bacon to make it a wee bit more juicy than it would otherwise have been.

Horn Lake Region

Approximately eleven miles northeast from the head of North Lake in Township 5 lies Horn Lake. It was a mecca for hardy fishermen willing to make the journey. A strong back was a prerequisite, unless one hired a guide, for the eager and determined invariably needed to "lug out a whacking big mess of trout," I was told. Hearing a claim like that, I naturally was spurred to try my hand someday—and sooner rather than later.

My first opportunity to venture to Horn came about because of an accident to Ralph Merrit, a camp guest, during the later days of Spring 1893. Ralph was a well-to-do Roman, a member of my congregation and an individual who rode a hobby for all it was worth. He was also generous. The first season he came to camp he insisted on buying all the supplies and he hired a team to drive us from the train station to the head of the lake. Once in camp he noted the absence of human comforts and promised on his return more furnishings would be forthcoming so as "to make the little place more comfortable."

The one feature of camp life he did not care for was the deer mice and there were plenty. That month we discovered the rodents never molested the sole hair pillow in camp. With that in mind, the following spring he donated four iron bedsteads with hair mattresses. Included, too, was a power skiff, the first motorboat ever on the lake.

Poor Merrit. He did have some shortcomings. One was the image he had developed at his Rome Club. He had a reputation as a mighty fisherman. When he announced he was off to North Lake on a fishing adventure he also boasted that he would return with enough fish to throw a trout supper for the club. The bluster was sincere and it might have been met had it not been for his tender city feet.

Upon Meritt's arrival he laced on his newly purchased mountain boots, a nice piece of leather had they been broken in. Following a few short hiking and fishing trips wearing these boots, his heels became badly blistered. There was indeed physical pain but the greatest distress came from his psychological disappointment and despair. He whined

146

and whined, "What am I to do, Reverend? I have a reputation to up-hold."

Over breakfast one morning he once again renewed his whining and bemoaned his bad luck. I knew he would be departing shortly. Wanting to help, I was struck with a brilliant idea. "Tell you what, Ralph," I began. If you will hire a guide to accompany me, I'll go to Horn Lake and bring you out a pack basket of trout."

Sore feet or not, old Merrit jumped off his chair and danced a short jig in his bare feet as he exclaimed, "That's the stuff. Let's get down to the foot of the lake right now and hire a guide right away." I will own up that my readiness to make the long trip to Horn was more for the adventure farther into the wilderness and the fun I would get out of it than it was by any sympathy for him and his smarting heels.

Later that day we rowed to the foot and began to make inquiries. Of the twenty-five or thirty individuals there were eight males of the younger variety. We found one available man, named Smith, sort of a handyman at George Crandall's cottage. He was a rather taciturn person and showed little enthusiasm. No, he had never been to Horn Lake, yet he wasn't completely uninterested in the proposal. He named his charge per day and emphasized he knew all about camping, but he would not undertake to cook the meals.

I had suggested a guide because I did not feel it prudent to plunge alone into a region unknown to me. Meritt agreed to pay, so we passed over the man's inexperience and limitations. In the aftermath of more parleying over the fee, Smith agreed to be at my camp by seven o'clock the next morning.

Before the mist of early morning had ceased to hang over the placid waters Smith and I were off. Few first trips ever excited me more than the promise this one held for me. We carried the usual duffel in our pack baskets: blankets, bread, coffee, frying pan, tin cups, and plates. An axe and so forth. I made a mistake by including cans of tinned food such as tomatoes, beans, green peas, and corn. I never made that mistake again. I learned that the weight of a load grows heavy on a long overland journey. In all my remaining years spent on the trail I was content to put up with dehydrated food, the only exception being a small can of evaporated milk. I was going to go light or in the words of Yankee Calvin Coolidge, "Go without."

I didn't realize just how slight Smith was until he slung his pack basket onto his back. The pack seemed as big as he was. We identified the route of the trail and headed out. I gave Smith the lead. He struck an odd picture. All I could see of the man was his legs; I could hear some of the metal hardware in his pack rattle. The wooden axe handle stuck up from within the basket. I couldn't help but laugh silently at the sight for he looked like a walking telegraph pole. But I was too preoccupied about my own footing to think about my trail companion for very long. I began to bend under the weight of my pack before the first hour had elapsed. I did, however, note the absence of undergrowth and tangle of brush typically found in a forest that has been logged. Here one could hike with pleasure in the mature forest. I could see unobstructedly a long distance through the noble trees. The forest floor was a dense carpet of shed leaves and needles. There were areas where the pitch contained in the conifer needles was so abundant that the soles on my boots felt polished and slippery and I felt compelled to watch my step to avoid slipping, as one often did on a wet or icy slate sidewalk in the city.

We traveled less than two miles an hour, the trail being blind, marked by axe blazes about every forty rods. Seven hours following breakfast and our row to the taking off point, we arrived at our destination at about four p.m.

We found a lean-to shelter in fair condition with the usual fire ring in front. Following a rest, I sent Smith down to the lake to explore, telling him to return a little before dark. I added I would hold supper and have the skillet hot and ready. That was his clue to know I expected him to return with a few trout to add to our supper.

As the dear little man slunk away I first busied myself preparing for a couple of nights' stay. With my belt axe I lopped small branches off and carried armfuls of balsam boughs to replenish the withered bed in the lean-to, made my bed, and was just heating water for coffee in a six-quart tin pail when Smith surprised me by quietly strolling in and silently standing before me with four fine fourteen-inch trout in his hands. I noted that he had the good judgment to dress and wipe them dry with leaves—my clue was the bit of green sticking to the gills.

I popped them into the spider as soon as it was heated. Soon the odor of hot bacon grease and frying trout filled the air. Smith with no orders from me busied himself "setting the table" by simply placing our tin plates, cups, and eating utensils along the log settee and crowding all with a loaf of bread sliced up with his belt knife. One habit I especially admired about him was that he was scrupulously careful to wash his hands before doing any work around our log bench-table.

Our sleep both nights of our stay was disturbed now and then by the omnipresent prowling hedgehogs. We took turns getting up and clubbing the prowlers to death. Once I needed to rouse Smith with a little nudge to inform him it was his turn to go forth to the slaughter. And once I crawled out, not being wide awake, seized the pole we used to poke the fire with as it lay in the gleam of live coals and began to belabor the varmint on its backside. My whacks only loosened the quills as it continued on its blundering way. Furious for having to be up, and mad that the wallops had so little effect other than to shorten my pole, I continued after the porcupine clad only in my undergarments and woolen socks.

Realizing I ran the risk of picking up quills in my feet, I called to Smith for help. He appeared reasonably soon, armed with a club. I noted in the dim light Smith had a pipe in his mouth. As we crawled back into the folds of our blankets I asked, "Smith, do you sleep with your pipe in your mouth?" He murmured, "No," as he tapped the spent tobacco out and stuck the pipe stem into a crack in the chinking between the logs. On awaking I learned the rest of the story. My noise had awakened him. Seeing my near-naked form in "hot pursuit" was so comedic he had decided to enjoy the occasion with a bowl of tobacco.

Our third day brought a harvest I shall never forget, for it was the best trout fishing I had ever experienced. Smith had drawn the flat-bottomed rowboat out of the lake following our using it the day before so that it might dry out a little. A long seam between the planks on one side let in water. Not wanting to bail again we planned to caulk it the best we could. Using our handkerchiefs we shredded the cloth and poked it into the crack with our belt knives. Our inventiveness worked but I needed to contribute the flaps from my new flannel shirt in order to make it seaworthy.

The angling was fantastic. Horn had lived up to its reputation. A fisherman without a similar experience would scarcely credit what I write next. Smith and I sat on opposite ends of the boat and faced each other. We were catching fish of the size of about three to the pound. Strikes came so often we quickly evolved a system. When I hooked a trout I simply thrust the tip of my rod over to Smith who next drew in the line hand-over-hand, unhooked the trout, readjusted the lure and tossed it back into the water. When he hooked one, I did the same with his catch.

We had been out on the lake about three hours when I noted that the deer that had been browsing along the shore had wandered in the direction of our camp. Following breakfast we had stowed our provisions in the pack baskets but did not hang them on a limb of a tree. As deer and bear nosed around I was concerned the deer might find the bread and bacon that they are fond of. As I walked to the lean-to, I left Smith to begin to clean the trout. On my return with a pack basket I will never forget the extraordinary sight. The bottom of the boat was literally covered with trout! I'll deny we were game hogs. We did not discernibly reduce the supply of trout in that wild place. I'll wager that not more than one or two other parties even got in that season.

We returned the third day with what I had promised Merrit, a pack basket of trout. Not of solid trout, of course. It was a layer of ferns, a layer of trout, a layer of ferns, another layer of trout, and so forth. At that period the only limit in law was as to the size of each trout. There was no limit on the mess.

Merrit was so pleased he forgot his blistered heels entirely. He allowed me a fair supply of the smaller ones and the remaining he had packed in ice from the ice house located at the foot of the lake. Twenty-four hours later, Merrit hobbled in his city shoes from the bench on the State House porch to board the outgoing wagon. He was going home with his prize and reputation intact. I was left with Horn Lake trout for dinner and a new pair of mountain boots.

Bushwhack to Goose Neck Lake

Nestled deep in a tract of isolated virgin timber exists a remote lake bearing the less than inspiring name of Goose Neck. Wanting to see that out-of-the-way sheet of water I asked mountain man Lon Wendover for directions. Lon had almost no formal education but when it came to getting around in the wilds, he had an extraordinarily keen mind. If I was to be successful, Lon was the man to make it happen.

"Follow the main tributary that enters the North branch," he advised. "An hour's tramp beyond the site of our Goose Neck outlet camp there will be two streams a quarter of a mile apart that feed into the main drainage. They enter from the northeast, your right-hand side. The first one is the outlet of Goose Neck Lake. It will fall into the main tributary from a height of about twenty feet."

In the company of my young son, I made my way up the rocky valley. There, just as it was described to me, we encountered the first stream, but it was a mere trickle. I thought that could not possibly be the outlet of a lake so we pushed on to the second stream. There we found a noisy waterfall with an abundance of water tumbling over the ledge. This seemed more logical to be a lake outlet, but for the next few hours the only thing we saw was a region new to us, eight venison hawks and an impressive view of a grand, high ledge of rock all of a quarter mile long. We returned empty handed, so to speak, to the outlying camp.

The following day we retraced our route to the scanty amount of water that flowed over the ledge of rock at the first falls that we had bypassed the day before. This route proved to be true. Climbing, we soon reached a big stretch of stillwater on the outlet held back by a substantial beaver dam. We lined the shore upstream and noted the bend that most likely gave the lake its name. The little body of water, about thirty acres I estimated, was charming. The forest was undefiled. No lumberman's axe had. felled a single tree. Magnificent giant spruce trees shaded the shore.

We ringed the lake finding the walking easy because of an absence of underbrush. On that circuit we discovered a fifteen-foot rowboat. It had once been painted yellow but had now lost most of its color although it seemed to be in a good state of preservation. But when my son gave it a vigorous kick the toe of his boot went through the planking revealing the disintegration caused by time. Who it had belonged to would remain a mystery. Perhaps the rotting boat had belonged to Atwell Martin, North Lake's hermit. But, no, he had only owned a dugout. It was unlikely this was his. My best guess was that it had been toted there by a guide from the old Bisby Club. Whatever, our tramp through an exceedingly beautiful wild and dense forest had been an exciting adventure.

On returning to our Nat Foster Lodge we stopped to fish a stream or two, then went on our merry way. Not long after that we were met by a member of the Adirondack League Club on his way over the Bisby to Honnedaga Lake trail. He was accompanied by a pack-carrying guide. In a severe but dignified tone he asked me where we were going. I sensed his spirit of hostility and so said, "Oh, we're just taking a walk." His reply was terse. "It looks to me as if you were going fishing."

"Yes," I answered, "We might wet a line." Whereupon he became very indignant and told me, "Then you would be poaching. This is the property of the Adirondack League Club." I denied that I had intended to poach, explaining that I carried a guest ticket. At once he demanded who the gentleman was that had extended me the privilege. I told him Mr. Thomas R. Proctor of Utica. Proctor's name was not one to conjure with. He was one of the founders of the old Bisby Club absorbed by the league. Mr. Proctor was a trustee.

I am positive the man did not believe me for he immediately ordered me to show him the guest ticket. I, in turn, was as firm as he. I stated I had no intention of displaying my pass unless he could first prove to me he was a member of the league. My petition was too much for him or he realized the futility in arguing. He gave me an indignant glare, stepped around me and continued on his way. I didn't expect any backfire from this incident. What resulted, I fancy, was that when he arrived at Honnedaga Lodge and inquired about me, they told him I was an active parson with a will of my own.

Against that incident I can put an occasion when a clerical companion and myself were fishing for salmon at Canachagala Lake when a league member came up to us, offered a friendly greeting, said he hoped we were having success and passed on with his guide with nary a word querying what right we had to be there. The earlier-mentioned member was an example of the handful of cultured prudes the club harbored. We North Lakers didn't see many of them in our neck of the woods until the 1940s. The league's lack of presence, however, did not prevent their game protectors from being ever vigilant to locals who disregarded their posted signs.

Several years following my Goose Neck Lake trip the league discovered our outlying camp in Goose Neck Creek Valley and burned it.

Adirondack Capers

The elimination from the Adirondack Mountains of unsportsman-like and illegal capers, and the scamps who condoned them, was a drawn-out process. More laws were not the answer; public awareness and education proved to be bigger, more effective weapons.

Native sons of the wilderness living in tiny, tucked-away, hole-in-the-wall communities such as Wheelertown knew every out-of-the-way corner of their neck of the woods. When in need of meat, they endorsed any variety of methods to obtain it. Deer were considered plentiful; venison was a staple in the natives' diet.

Tipping the balance toward making trapping, fishing, and hunting practices more recreational rather than occupational or a necessity of life was not the only issue Adirondack folks were challenged to face. When the Volstead Act was passed by Congress in 1919 to help enforce Amendment 18 of the U.S. Constitution, whiskey became hard to obtain in the mountains. North Country natives liked their spirits. It was only natural that a few enterprising woodsmen—such as Jack Conklin—would conceive of the idea that it would be cheaper to make moonshine than to buy more expensive bootleg liquor. Government wisdom carried little influence. Should a neighbor's still be overlooked?

While the entire country wrestled for decades with the pros and cons of Prohibition the newly formed Adirondack League Club spearheaded a movement on their preserve to institute a policy that eventually carried over into accepted practice on state lands, too. The club, having control of a large territory stretching between the Bisbys and Honnedaga Lake districts, added their own rules to the state game laws that regulated the taking of game and fish. Those rules, as reported in an editorial that appeared in the May 28, 1891, issue of *Forest and Stream* under the headline "Jack-Hunting Deer," said the Adirondack League Club forbade "the taking by any member of more than fifteen pounds of speckled trout or ten in number of lake trout in one day." Another rule read: "Jacking or floating for deer is absolutely prohibited." This regulation was adopted because the members were con-

154

vinced that jack-hunting resulted in the wounding and maiming of more deer than were killed, and in the lingering deaths of more deer than were "reduced to possession."

The editorial ended: "[those rule adoptions were] significant and worthy of note, because the attitude of the state toward its game at large should be in no respect different from that of such private organizations toward the game in its preserve."

As a private club, the ALC was acutely aware that its borders were not secure, that neighboring locals carried out many illegal acts on league land and that other capers, such as floating for deer at night with a jack-light, while legal, carried connotations of insensitivity toward the killing of animals. Members and guides employed by the club reached new maturity; people still hunted, fished, and trapped, but they became more skillful at their craft and usually got their limit, if not in such number as formerly.

Following the turn of the century, maps, brochures, and information on how to hunt, fish, and hike became widely available. The monopoly guides once had on knowing how to get around and care for themselves in the wilds diminished. Where once the general public pursued their outdoor activities with little regard—hounding, jacking, luring with salt and meat baits, snubbing trespass laws, cutting wood on state land, and even operating illegal stills—better education and public opinion put values into the sport, improved personal income for Adirondackers, raised their standard of living and led, with tighter law enforcement, to a successful result. The Adirondack Mountains were going to be regulated, but that regulation would ensure the region's preservation.

*   *   *

A long time ago the missionary spirit struck the then-thriving village of Forestport. Villagers learned of the sad plight of people in far-off lands—people who had never seen the "light." Forestporters decided to do something. They organized a canvas of the town to raise funds. Heading their list of prospective donors was the tannery owner known to all as "Brother Hill." Hill was not a Scrooge but he was a tight-fisted, hard-headed Yankee. When the committee approached him about a contribution, he inquired rather pointedly why they were worrying about some "heathen foreigners" thousands of miles away when they had the "Wheelertown Gang" right in their own backyard.

I searched the scanty church records but could not find any hard data to confirm that the local missionary society actually took any apostolic action toward the gang. I was enlightened, however, that it did focus enough attention on the little backwoods settlement to make it the butt of many of the wild capers and ribald humor of the whole region from that time on. According to old-timers' opinions, Wheelertown's isolation attracted a wild, lawless element. The history of Wheelertown is rather nebulous, but what I've gathered indicates most of the inhabitants were members of two families, the Wendovers and the Quackenbushes.

Again, according to local legends, gossip has pointed its finger to some natives of that Adirondack outpost and bestowed on them a reputation that qualified them for a seat in hell. Rumor also had it that Wheelertown natives all grew to a ripe, cheery old age and retained a tireless exuberance that was the envy of their more orthodox neighbors.

Wheelertown traditions were clannish and indications pointed to underground activities. The most apparent evidence was the establishment and maintenance of outlying camps in remote sections of the forest—areas where experienced woodsmen normally would not build shelters—for the sporting public they guided.

The one common characteristic that distinguished those camps from others was a touch of backwoods resourcefulness that was always concealed but easily accessible to the camp: the salt lick, or Wendover salt lick as it was called. The Wendover salt lick was a model of simplicity and camouflage. A tyro (greenhorn) might stand right on one and yet be completely unaware of its existence. Those licks furnished the fodder for many stories told by the boys in the back room or around the campfire but seldom repeated in drawing room conversation.

A salt lick is made by felling a beech tree and salting the stump. There were several methods of applying the salt depending on how long the lick was intended to be used. If a short time was all that was needed, the salt was just spread on the surface of the stump and worked into the bark on the sides and the exposed roots. If a longer use was desired, a dike of clay was built around the top of the stump's circumference and the salt was poured inside the walls and allowed to work down into the wood of the stump.

The inventors of the Wendover model lick deviated from this standard by drilling holes into the stump with a large-bore auger and tamping wet salt into those holes for several weeks, then plugging the holes. A Wendover salt lick would last for years—even the roots would be dug up and chewed clean of their salty content.

Salt licks were lures and as such were located close to a blind where hunters could keep a vigil. The location of the illegal lures was kept secret. If a deer was shot over a salt lick (if the operation was near a road or dwellings), the killer could place himself in a vulnerable position because the report of a rifle out of season would carry a long distance and have the same level of gravity to a game warden that a fire alarm has to a firefighter.

A poacher concerned about detection would not go near a slain deer. Instead he would first conceal his rifle, hasten to the nearest highway, trail, or house and openly show a desire to discover who had violated the sanctity of Saint Hubert, the patron of hunters. Only when the coast was clear would he go back in, dress out the deer, cut it up, and cart it away. If it was a night operation he would usually get help, because darkness brought all sorts of complications in the forest. Venison was always hidden immediately or taken to the "jerk" camp.

The jerk camp was an improvisation, like a moonshine still. It was always positioned deep in the woods. Its name was derived from the operation carried out. Venison was smoked and cured into jerked venison. The process was simple. A fire was started in the pits that were long channels the length of the iron grid above it. The meat was then cut into thin strips, rubbed well with salt and hooked from loops of wire that were wound around poles. The meat hung from the wire hooks and cured slowly over several days in the heat and smoke of the slow fires below. Jerk camps were carefully guarded by lookouts during the processing.

*   *   *

One time when hiking over to South Branch Outlet I got off the trail without knowing it and ran smack into an abandoned jerk camp. From the telltale meat racks and the method the log-wall lean-to was made I recognized the work to be that of Burt Lindsay or the Wendover gang. Later on I mentioned my discovery to Burt and jokingly suggested that the maintainer of the place should share the spoils with their friends. Burt grinned and said, "Reverend, I know you're no prosecuting attorney." I replied, "And I can keep what I know under my hat." The subject was then dropped, but Burt did not forget the matter.

The following summer I was awakened an hour before sunrise by a gentle tapping on my camp door. I came downstairs and there stood

Burt with a pack basket between his feet, his hands resting on the barrel of his rifle. He first eyed me and then asked if I would "look after" his pack basket and "use the contents." I understood at once. "Bring it in, Burt, bring it in," I motioned.

As it developed over a pot of coffee, some state men had been staying at Charley Brown's State House. They had expressed an interest in jacking deer. Burt had guided them to Little Woodhull Lake. Following the nighttime activity Burt put the party on the trail out and then remained behind to bury the evidence.

I reflected seriously on the situation and its moral implications. I hated to see good meat go to waste; it would surely spoil in a few hours. The weather was very hot for the mountains. Finally the science of the conscience, "casuistry" we theologians call it, came as the solution. We hold it to be a sin to waste good food, either fodder for cattle or flesh for man. The law of God is above the law of man, I decided. So I rapped on the stovepipe to awaken the girls, stoked up the kitchen stove, and proceeded to get breakfast. Instead of bacon I prepared venison chops. The girls squealed with delight when they found what was on and took charge of the rest of the meat in the basket. Besides the spare ribs there was a saddle and a lot of meat for stew. They started the stew simmering after breakfast and prepared the saddle for roasting. The windfall provided us with fresh meat for nearly a week, stored in the ice cold spring box out back.

*   *   *

This matter of casuistry came into play another time, too. I had gone on a long hike to fish a stillwater on one of the streams that feeds into North Lake. It was a favorable day and the trout that naturally lie near the confluence of the two streams near where I fished were feeding. After two hours of fishing I ate my lunch and then began to clean my catch. I didn't keep track of my mess. I honestly thought I had about eighteen. The legal limit in those days was twenty-five. I was amazed to find I had thirty-seven "all of legal size," a saying we used to use in speaking of a stream that had a plenitude of trout but which ran small. All mine ran from seven to nine inches—good pan trout.

It was here that the science of the conscience, casuistry, came to me once again. The fish were cleaned; I certainly didn't want them to go to waste, yet twelve trout did not legally belong to me. With my line reeled up, I unjoined my rod, packed the fish—twenty-two in one group and fifteen in another—and headed back to camp. Once there I placed the fish I did not own plus three I added to the mess on a plate, covered them with a dish towel and walked over to my friend and neighbor, a physician from Utica. He was sitting on his verandah relaxing with a corncob pipe in his mouth, his feet up on the railing, looking out at the lake. He greeted me cordially as his eyes stared at the mound under the towel. I explained that I had had fair success fishing and thought he and his wife might enjoy the trout I caught. The dear old man let out a whoop and shouted to his wife, "Come out and see the trout the reverend has brought us."

"Seriously, Doctor, I must tell you," I began to add as he reached out to take the plate, "All of the trout but three are illegal." He gave me a solemn, serious look such as he might use in announcing a diagnosis of a serious malady. Then he assured me that if I had any more of the same kind, he would gladly relieve me of them.

Caucus at Wilmurt

Once upon a time there was a town up in the Paul Bunyan country of New York State called Wilmurt; but the boys up there began to take their legends seriously and grew too tall for their breeches so the legislators down in the capitol at Albany did a little hocus pocus and now Wilmurt isn't with us any more. Of course several other ingredients entered into these arrangements, but why spoil a good story? Wilmurt never did.

Local Adirondack legend has it that in the early 1890s Paul Bunyan's blue ox got a liking for the railroad spikes that Dr. Seward Webb was using to build his "Golden Chariot Route" (the Mohawk and Malone Railroad) and was pulling them out and eating them because the doctor was not feeding the local kitty as expected. So to mollify the wealthy land-holder doctor and cool off the Wilmurt boys, New York State legislators took a part of the town of Wilmurt and incorporated it into the town of Webb, but the Wilmurt boys just asked for more. They proceeded to pile up more trouble and expenses for Herkimer County than any other town in the county so the politicians decided to go another step and just wiped the name Wilmurt off the map giving the remaining land to the town of Ohio.

It was a wild and untamed country, inhabited by trappers and lumberjacks. Life was one brawl after another. In between paydays there was a man's work to do challenging the wilderness, and they did it with gusto. Politics, which treated them so shabbily, was just an incident in the life of Wilmurt, just another brawl, but different in that it was usually organized and a gang affair. You were with the "Boss" and fought for him on election days or you were with the gang that was trying to throw him out and get control of the government.

I had only one direct contact with this Paul Bunyan brand of political activity. I attended a caucus at Wilmurt during a vacation one fall in the early nineteen hundreds when I was roughing it up at North Lake. I suppose that I voted. Later on I was told that I did but affairs were a little confused at the time and I plead innocent of any knowledge. That is the way it was in Wilmurt where they still adhered to the frontier traditions of filling and voting a caucus.

It happened this way. Big Eaf, a tall rangy Welshman with enormous feet, was boss of Wilmurt at that time and word had spread around that the Wheelertown boys were going to bring a gang of lumberjacks down from up north to pack the caucus and throw Big Eaf out on his ear. So Big Eaf put out a frantic call for all his boys to rally around and defend their rights and liberties. He sent word over to Burt Lindsay at North Lake that he wanted him to be sure to bring a load of the boys. There was room for one more in the old buckboard, so Burt asked me if I wanted to come along for the fun.

Henry Paull agreed to drive us over to Wilmurt. It was a twenty-five mile drive so we started out before daybreak driving over rough mountain roads and trails in Paul's sturdy mountain buckboard pulled by a heavy logging team of horses. There were five of us in all. Henry Paull was stocky and easy going except in a pinch when he had to use his head. Seth Lyons was tall and angular, with an eye like a fish and was just about as conversational. George Watkins would pass for any other guy until his oily baritone voice boomed out unexpectedly; then you noticed his polka dot bow tie and walrus mustache. Burt Lindsay was about the best guide in the woods. He had a keen eye and an agreeable nature; but when he got a couple of hookers of bourbon under his belt he felt inspired to assume the role of a man of consequence. No introduction is necessary for the writer.

Henry Paull knew the way and just in case it was necessary for someone else to take over the reins he instructed us all that, "If ye lost the road or trail keep bearing in the general direction until ye hit it again." His directions were comforting! We had tough going on the shortcut from Reed's Mills over the mountain to Pony Bob's, but it saved seventeen miles. That route was worth it for all the shortcomings, for we arrived in Wilmurt about noon.

We put the team in the barn and had taken our dinner at DuGall's Hotel. The caucus was to be called to order in the dance hall of the hotel about one o'clock but there was already general activity with political implications—many negotiations of a secret and confidential nature such as are often involved in dispensing Yuletide cheer under local option.

There were about forty in attendance. George Watkins, a native North Laker, was chairman; Burt Lindsay was the clerk. They were among the few native sons so their appointment was uncontested.

When George Watkins had pounded out a reasonable semblance of order with a pound weight from some old counter scales that stood in the corner gathering dust, someone made a motion that Big Eaf be given the authority to name his own delegates to the county convention. One of the Wheelertown boys immediately offered an amendment that the vote be taken by dividing the house. From there on parliamentary rules were forgotten. Activities started mildly enough with charges of fraud and deceit that clearly indicated the price of a vote at a Wilmurt caucus was a pint of bourbon liquor in a bottle; but there was equal evidence that the bourbon was gone and the promise forgotten as the men sought to align themselves on opposite sides of the room. The shylocks demanded a vote or a pound of flesh and showed little preference as they sought to shove and drag their victims to their side of the room. Soon there was a free-for-all brawl going on with lumberjacks rampant and no holds barred.

My vote was not challenged but it was subjected to involuntary fluctuation several times before I managed to escape the ballroom. Just as the electioneering reached its peak of fury and mayhem someone started hollering, "Dog fight! Dog fight!" The assembled electorate of Wilmurt ceased political activity and came piling out into the road to encourage and abet the hostilities of two mongrel dogs.

I learned later that the dog fight had been staged with the compliments of Mr. DuGall. It seems that DuGall was an astute man and also well acquainted with the volatile political traditions of Wilmurt. He was also aware of the fatal weakness of a lumberjack for a dog fight. So, having read the omens correctly, he took steps to meet the situation and preserve his property intact. He borrowed a couple of dogs and when the zero hour approached, he took them out in the road and sicked them on each other. When nature had answered his plea he called at the top of his voice, "Dog fight! Dog fight!" and another election in the town of Wilmurt passed into history.

When the dogs were done with their fighting the electorate drifted toward the bar room. It was obvious from the brisk business that Mr. DuGall would make enough from the bottle trade to cover the minor breakage. I went back to the ballroom and waited around for a while but the caucus did not reassemble so I started looking for my crowd. I found Henry Paull in the bar room awaiting convivial generosity. Burt Lindsay was in the hotel barn engaged in a weight-lifting contest trying to see who could lift the rusty anvil up. The match was between him and two lumberjacks. They were showing their muscles and bragging.

All three had had their share of spirits; otherwise they would have noticed that the anvil was spiked to the floor. I left Burt in search for the other two in our party. I located George and Seth in the orchard out behind the hotel barn using green pippins for chasers. The entire scene worried me somewhat. I envisioned my riding with that group on the twenty-five mile return trip. I got Henry moving and we hitched up the team, collected the rest of our crowd and started for North Lake.

I noticed that the liquor affected each of the boys differently. Henry Paull was happy and talkative. Burt Lindsay carried his with austere dignity. George Watkins had a crying jag and Seth Lyons was just sleepy. We had not gone far when we hit a stone in the road. Henry complained of a wetness in the region of his hip pocket. We stopped to reconnoiter. The neck of his whiskey bottle had broken off against an iron brace on the seat. About half the whiskey was still in the broken bottle so they finished it off and took inventory of any other supplies. There weren't any.

We had a near fatal accident a little farther on. Seth fell off the seat and slid down between the wheels. We got him back in the buckboard and put him in the middle on the back seat for safety. From there on the journey grew depressing. George had an attack of indigestion from eating those greasy pippins. Burt got out his pipe and filled it with Warnick and Brown tobacco, then he couldn't find his matches so I gave him a box of safety matches that he had evidently never used before. I had just started to explain to him how to light them on the striking surface of the box when Henry gave me the wink and took over. Burt followed Henry's suggestions and tried to light them on everything within reach. Finally Henry had him holding a match on the tire of a revolving wheel so it would light itself. This almost caused another disaster but Burt only skinned his wrist. When he resumed operation he found he had lost his pipe. With that he threw my matches into the brush and lapsed into the silence of offended dignity.

It was dark when we got to Pony Bob's and Henry refused to take the shortcut over the mountains to Reed's Mill. He said it was dangerous in the dark. He wanted to go to the Buffalo Head, water his horses there and then take the new North Lake road. As we argued the matter, Burt turned on his bourbon personality but he was only half-hearted about it because he was beginning to get thirsty himself. So all of a sudden he changed his tune and he was feeling sorry for Henry's team. We decided to go along with Henry; actually we didn't have much choice.

We lost the road a little farther on but never found out about it until we wound up with the horses on one side of a log and the buckboard on the other, so we could neither back up nor go ahead. We got out and unhitched the team, and while we were jacking the buckboard around Henry backtracked until he found the road and then we were on our way again. About this time Henry became disgusted. He wrapped the reins around the whip stock, gave the horses their heads and went to sleep. In due time we were at the Buffalo Head. Billy Mulchi opened up and sold the boys what liquor they wanted while I watered the horses.

My memory of the last lap of our trip from the Buffalo Head is somewhat indistinct. I had been chilled by the cold fall night air. I reasoned I should remove the cold nip from my bones before we continued on the final leg of our trek. For that reason I felt the need to partake of Billy's liquor. The little stimulant worked well but it must have had a little blasting soup blended in with it.

The buckboard run to the timberline was a whirl. I do recall that we could not get Seth Lyon's folks up to open the door so we had to lay him out on the front porch and cover him with a piece of rag carpet; and we laid Burt Lindsay on a pile of hay in the Reed boys' barn. It was just daybreak when we were putting the team up and I remember asking Henry how the vote had come out at the caucus. "Son," he said, "you have got a lot to learn about politics."

It was broad daylight when I rowed across the foot of the lake to my lodge and stole softly in and up to the sleeping loft and to bed. Besides my young son and a couple of church lads to keep him company, there was Rev. Jesse Higgins of St. George's church, Utica. They were all early risers so I got but two or three hours sleep ere I was roused out. Father Higgins was anxious to see what shape I was in. I chuckle now as I recall how he appeared to be disappointed to note that I was fresh and chipper. Then he wished to know if he was not entitled to "half of the swag I got for going to the caucus and voting."

I mollified him and cheered up the boys by getting a good breakfast with pancakes so light one could hang them on a cobweb. One may doubt the last statement. But I've frequently told the story of how one of my pancakes once flew off the griddle and floated over the lake. Upon seeing the brown disk spiraling through the air, Charley Brown was quick to take a pot-shot at it. When he told me about it later, he said he thought it was a duck at first, but I knew Charley was a better hunter than that. I suggested the next time he had a hankering for my pancakes that he just row over.

My Last Visit With John Burroughs

A. L. Byron-Curtiss' observations of the wild things about his camp combined with his experiences ascending heights, skimming lakes and ponds and traversing the forest far into the wilds armed him with information he felt honored to share with one of the foremost naturalists in the United States, John Burroughs.

Rev. Byron-Curtiss came to know Burroughs during his initial stay at Holy Cross, an Episcopal monastery at West Park on the Hudson River. Burroughs' homestead bordered the monastery property.

"He (John Burroughs) had given me a key to his famous Slabsides cabin in the mountains two miles back from the river. I, in the company of other Fathers of the Holy Cross, would hike to Slabsides for an afternoon outing. We obeyed John's instruction to 'Make yourselves at home.' We usually heated a pot of coffee to go with the sandwiches the monastery cook had kindly provided us with.

"I recall the first time I returned the key and thanked him for his kindness, I revealed to him that I was surprised to find Slabsides was truly just a rough cabin. It made me feel chesty. Naturally, he asked why. I shared with him that I had anticipated his building would have had more comforts but that his cabin was more like my rustic Adirondack lodge. He took my comments as well-intentioned and inquired how my own camp was laid out. I explained that I had a separate but attached kitchen with a good cook stove, a sink, a cupboard for dishes, and a hand-driven well with a pitcher pump. The upright or main part of the building was eighteen feet by twenty-two feet and there was a fireplace and a good chunk stove heater. His comment was that, 'It must be very nifty.'"

Shortly before Rev. A. L. Byron-Curtiss' death he authored an article on his visits with John Burroughs. That story appeared in the September-October 1959 issue of Audubon *magazine and excerpts appear here with permission from the publishers.*

My first meeting with John Burroughs was under melancholy circumstances. Mr. Burroughs had come upstate from his home at Riverby on the Hudson below Kingston, New York, in July 1911, to receive an honorary degree at Colgate University. On the upstate end of the trip he was the guest of a trustee of the university, the Hon. Eugene A. Rowland of Rome, New York. On June 19, Mr. Rowland took Mr. Burroughs to see Trenton Falls and its imposing gorge. As they were walking along the path or trail on the bank Mr. Rowland picked up a piece of Hamilton shale, abundant in the region and showed it to Mr. Burroughs as containing a local fossil. As Mr. Rowland turned back on the trail he slipped from the bank into the stream and was drowned. The fatal accident was a shock to me for Mr. Rowland had been a loyal worker with me in the humane work started in Rome. I attended the funeral held from Mr. Rowland's home. There close to the casket was Mr. Burroughs, whom I instantly recognized by his venerable appearance, exactly like his pictures.

At this period I was close to a nervous breakdown, though I did not know it. I only knew I was habitually and fearfully nervous, sleeping but three or four hours at night unless I took opiates prescribed by my physician. I got no better and in desperation I gave up all active work. I realized I could be of no use to others until I was first just to myself, and my first step in this direction was to get well. I had a definite plan in spite of my wretched health. I went to the Anglican Monastery of the Holy Cross at West Park on the Hudson. I soon got a grip on myself, and what I shall ever cherish is that I got to know John Burroughs rather intimately, and to count him as one of my friends.

I found I could be of help to the good fathers by walking to the post office twice daily with the monastery mail pouch. The post office was at the railroad station. As I rounded a corner of the station on my first trip I saw Mr. Burroughs seated on the lowest step of the platform reading a magazine. He wore simple clothes with a dress straw hat of an obsolete style. After delivering the pouch to the postmaster I went up and spoke to him, explaining I had met him at the funeral of Mr. Rowland in Rome two years before. I noted that the great naturalist's conversational voice was exceedingly quiet and his bearing almost shy. As our acquaintance progressed I had to almost lead the conversation, as it were. With my innate verbosity, I fear I must have bored him many times during my visits, but he was ever kind, and in our conversations on nature lore he would let me rattle on and then quietly interpose his corrections or add to the observations I had made.

Mr. Burroughs had suggested I stop in to see him at his "office" as he called it—a frame building a few hundred yards back of his fine stone residence, Riverby proper.

He asked me how I came to know nature as well as I did. I explained that I had a modest camp in the Adirondacks. This interested him at once. He asked me particularly about birds there and I told him all I knew, which was little enough. I did explain how I had left uncut a thicket twelve or fourteen feet high, between the verandah of my camp and the lake shore but ten feet away. This made a great resort for birds and I had thus been able to observe them, from hummingbirds to scarlet tanagers, while sitting on the verandah.

Once a hummingbird had darted from the thicket to within a few inches of the head of my oldest daughter, hovering there a few moments. Helen and I had concluded that the tiny bird had thought a red bandanna handkerchief she had turbaned around her head was a flower. His comment was characteristic. He called my letting the brush grow into a bird refuge clever, but with a sly twist gave my daughter credit for the flower conclusion by saying, "Your daughter must be a very smart girl."

Early one afternoon I waded through the snow on the back way to Mr. Burroughs' cabin. He was not there, so I went on up to the highway, hoping to find him, and had the good fortune to meet him coming down the hill. He invited me to join him and we continued on to his cabin. There he revived the fire on the hearth and took his armchair by his desk and relaxed for a chat. This time he began the conversation and it was in a minor key, as was our first brief exchange at the funeral of Mr. Rowland eight years before. It was the day after the death of his close friend Theodore Roosevelt, and all he talked about was "Teddy." Despite his sighs at his friend's passing he interposed criticisms. Teddy was too hearty an eater of improper foods (Mr. Burroughs was a food faddist), and the President had not taken the proper exercise.

I took the opportunity when he went to replenish the fire to say, "Mr. Burroughs, I would like to talk with you about some observations I've been making of beaver the last couple of years." Mr. Burroughs turned to me instantly, still standing by the fireplace, and looking at me keenly he said: "Do you mean to say you have seen beaver in the wild state?" I assured him that I had; that there were no beaver in the Adirondacks when I began to go there in 1895; but that in the early 1900s a few pairs had been released at the Fulton Chain and that in seven years they had seeped fifteen miles through the mountains to the headwaters of the Black River region. Now there were a dozen or more of their dams, ponds, and houses within a few miles of my camp, and I had seen and inspected them all. He listened to me while adjusting the fuel in the fire, then went to his desk, got some paper and said: "Now please tell me all you have noted about them and their habits." He explained that beavers were extinct in the Catskills before he was born; that the only ones he had seen were in the Bronx Zoo and other parks; that they were a scrubby lot and could not be called wild beaver. I was glad I had been sufficiently interested in this to have made a bit of study of it, and I gave all I knew about beavers, their ways and habits, which I explained to him was not the scientific observation of a trained naturalist like himself. He ignored my blarney and indicated I should go on.

I explained that the brush in their dams weighted down by stones was invariably laid with the butt ends downstream, thus the lacy tops caught all the debris that floated down resulting in the dam being strengthened and made more solid. All the flotsam, from slivers as big as a match to billets as big as drumsticks, contributed to the solidity of the dam. Their houses were not the symmetrical domes depicted in pictures but rough mounds of earth with small stones appearing here and there. I told him that I could judge if any of the family were home by paddling around the house to where the submerged entrance was indicated by bubbles coming to the surface. If many bubbles came up I judged the whole family was home. The previous autumn my son and I had seen where a group had accumulated their winter supply of food in the shape of a big pile of the branches of poplar trees. It was heaped by the house partly submerged; probably before ice formed they would have it all submerged and weighted down by earth and stone.

As he made notes from the above Mr. Burroughs said, "But what about the little animals themselves?" I explained I had observed them when fishing from a raft on a little glacial lake several times and had seen a pair swim past my camp every evening for weeks at about the same hour—between seven-thirty and eight o'clock. I had seen but one carcass of a beaver taken one autumn when trapping them was permissible. Their tails, not unlike the blade of a small paddle, were about fourteen inches long and covered with a thick, corrugated skin. I did not believe they used their tails as trowels as alleged by fairy tale writers. Their dams and houses were too rough and untidy to admit of any trowel work on them.

I had noted a singular use of their tails in giving the surface of the water a resounding slap but an instant before they began to sink out of sight, and since the tip of the nose was the last thing to disappear, they very evidently were going down backward. I had satisfied myself of this one evening by launching my canoe and chasing the pair that was coming down past my place. I had chased them around a lagoon by my place compelling them to submerge several times and it was the same every time—a vigorous slap on the water with their tails, then their sinking out of sight, with the nose the last thing seen. At this Mr. Burroughs pointed out that by thus agitating the water a little area was filled with air bubbles facilitating their sinking out of sight, adding they might well use their tails as paddles to hasten their going down.

Mr. Burroughs took notes with care until I finished. Then I added an item he appeared to receive with avidity, indicated by his resuming taking notes. It was that the meat of beaver is delicious eating. Mine was of the sole specimen I had seen during the brief open season the autumn before.

I was staying a few days with C. H. Brown, the custodian of the state reservoirs in the region. A trapper whom I knew was skinning a beaver he had taken at a colony at Grindstone Creek a few miles back. As he removed the pelt, I said, "Why, 'Slim,' the meat looks good enough to eat!" Slim answered that it was, that he and his brother often ate beaver meat, adding, "I'll give you this if you want it." As I was staying with the Browns, I did not wish to impose on them, but I went to the house and asked Mrs. Brown if she would cook it for us. She said, "Sure, Reverend, I'll cook it for supper tomorrow night." Experienced in cooking and serving wild meats, she served it hot for supper the next evening perfectly cooked. Its flavor was similar to the dark meat of barnyard fowl and Mr. Brown and I ate heartily.

And here I could not resist the temptation to weave in a hyperbole that so often goes with the telling of fish and game stories. I said: "Mr. Burroughs, a singular thing resulted from overeating so heartily of that beaver meat. That evening it gave him and myself an awful hankering for wood. I chewed up all the lead pencils in my pockets and Mr. Brown rummaged in the wood box for chips and slivers to chew on." The only rebuke the dear man gave me for my temerity was to lay down his pencil quietly but firmly and say: "I'll write a fresh article on beaver sometime and use all the details you have given me, giving you credit for the information; all but your hankering for wood to eat."

He also thanked me most heartily and in this quiet way had chided me for jesting. Mr. Burroughs had a sense of humor but it was a quiet one, like himself. He bade me a kind good night and I hustled over to the monastery. I had missed the five o'clock vespers but arrived in time to line up as a guest and follow the good fathers in the march to the refectory.

That winter he sent me a splendid glossy snapshot of himself and his autograph on a separate slip of paper. I had asked him for them to paste in a copy of his book, *The Story of My Boyhood*, which I had just secured. Mr. Burroughs did not live to write the article. I've often thought of how narrowly I missed a little fame in the reflected glory of the greatest naturalist then living. A trip to California the following winter brought no restoration of his ebbing vital forces and he died on a train on his way home as it was passing through Ohio. Thus he passed on to the realms of nature's Creator.

My recollections of my last visit with Mr. Burroughs are most fragrant. Free of all guile the great naturalist had been willing, even eager to learn from an obscure parson the details of something he himself knew little of, and had taken my jesting without annoyance or undue irritation.

Uncle Jack's Bear Story

We were gathered in the very comfortable sitting room of Charley O'Conner's hotel located in the village of Forestport. Within the village proper, as well as far beyond, the land was poor and the people poorer back in 1932. It was the last day of the hunting season. Tom Nightingale, the town constable, came in as a group of us were sipping hot toddies. A hearty greeting rose from our ranks to welcome him to join us. Then, who should walk in but Jack Yeoman, the very pioneer of pioneers. He was an old-time woodsman who knew every rod, furlong, and mile of land back from Forestport to the timberline. "Uncle Jack," as everyone called him, had been the town assessor.

Uncle Jack was a typical "Uncle Sam" type, tall, straight as an arrow in spite of his eighty-seven years, and complete with chin whiskers.

"Uncle Jack. How are you?" I exclaimed, happy to see him again.

"Ah, young man," he replied, "I'm fust rate, fust rate. How you be?"

Considering that he had known me for forty years, that my hair, too, was well turned gray, his reference to my youth was a decided compliment. I suggested that he and Tom be served hot toddies, too, their favorite drink for this time of the year, a protection against the frost of the autumn night. They agreed, and while they were being prepared, a strange coincidence occurred. An old commercial traveler friend of mine from Syracuse happened at that moment to enter the pool room, next to the sitting room where our provincial renewal of old acquaintances was taking place. I waved to Tom Switzer to come join us. Since he had never met my old Forestport friends, I was anxious that he should. Tom and Uncle Jack were most cordial in their greetings and soon both seemed to be on the most friendly of terms.

The storytelling hour of the night was upon us. It was Tom's turn to spin a yarn but in my eagerness to introduce the latest city yarn I had heard, I was on the point of butting in when Uncle Jack also spoke. Kindly in his manner, he, too, was interrupting the order as he said, "Now the year Lon Denton and me killed the bear. . . ."

Tom looked at ease, not caring if he had the floor or not. Knowing

171

Uncle Jack's proficiency for pertinacity, I sat back saying I had heard the story before.

"Ah, um, yes. Maybe so," he assented. "Who did you say told it to you?" he asked quite innocently.

"Well, I just can't say," I ventured. I could not tell the dear old man that he had told it to me many times. "I think possibly it was Jess Withers."

"Humph!" He snorted in his disgust. "Why he never got it straight. Why he was over to Wendover's camp the fall that happened."

"Well, it might have been George Abbott who told me then," I countered.

At my mention of Abbott's name, Uncle Jack, giving a greater snort of disgust, declared that I had never heard the story right and that if I had but five or ten minutes to spare, he would, "git it straight with no ifs or ands," adding that if we were not satisfied, we could ask any of his friends or relatives in the village. But inasmuch as this would include practically all the inhabitants, we declined the taking of a poll and assured him that we would believe every word that he spoke. At that we settled back and listened as he related his bear story—his eyes glistening all the while. I thought this retelling was pleasurable, and it provided a stage that refired his lively imagination.

"It was in November 1887," Uncle Jack began deliberately, "that me and Lon Denton was scaling lumber near Big Woodhull close to Sand Lake when we come across that bear you've heard tell of but ain't never heard right. Perry had a lot of logs left in the woods from the previous year on account of the open winter last. There was thousands of feet left on skidways, way back in, the slashin's scattered over the whole woods. Me and Lon went in the following October and scaled logs for two months. I remember we didn't even come out for the elections — though that was an off year anyway. We was tryin' to get Perry's stock of logs straightened out. We wanted to get 'em ready for movin' if the new season brought enough snow to get 'em to water so's to drive 'em to the sawmill at Mc Keever. There was so much stock left over Perry even cut his logging plan for that winter right in half.

"Well, one afternoon we was scaling a lot of logs that was just left as they fell. The trees was sawed proper enough but there hadn't been no top trimming to speak of. More'n half the time we had to crawl around in to a tree top or under 'em to measure the end of the log's top.

"Lon was doin' the measurin' and calling off the number for me to record in the book. We come to a big old hemlock about three foot at the butt. It had originally been more'n seventy-five feet high, I remember that 'cause Perry was cutting twenty foot stock in them days. Long, he goes walking along the log to the tip and stooped down some to measure. And all of a sudden, like he got bit by fire ants, he straightened up and he yelled out such a hoot that I never heard before or since. He jumped off'n the log sprier'n a cat and legged it towards me as if the very devil hisself was after him.

"'Why Lon,' I sez, 'what's ailing you? You got a cramp in you or somethin'?'

"'Cramp nothin', he yelled back. 'I can tell you one thing, Uncle Jack, you aint going to get me back on that top for all the tea in China. There's a varmint in there that ain't got no business bein' there and while it's there I ain't goin' back! There's a powerful lot of tops that ain't been lopped off and likely enough there's more of the critters around.'

"I looked at Lon for about a minute then I said, 'Why Lon Denten! Ain't you ashamed of yourself? Here you be scaret of what you ain't even seen yet.'

"'Ain't seen yet!' he snapped at me. 'Well, I have and you ain't.'

"Seeing he made such a fuss about it, I handed him my entry book, gripped good on my axe and went forward to take a view of the situation. And I'll be goldarned if I couldn't blame Lon one mite. Under the top of that mighty hemlock was the biggest, all-fired whopper of a black bear I'd ever seen in all the years I've been in the mountains. Why he looked bigger'n an elephant. As near as I figured he had gone in under the toppings to hibernate for the winter. But Lon had done disturbed the critter, upset his calculations and sleep.

"I set my eyes on him and I'm here to tell you he seemed to have an ugly streak. He was squeezed in among the limbs so all you could see was part of his back and head—the head, mind you, was big as a flour barrel. He raised up, growled and snorted, drawed a long breath and then humped his back. The tree was a risen' up and down regular as he breathed and arched.

"I looked at the situation from my position on the truck, course I was holdin' on good and all. Lon kept sayin', 'Come on, Uncle Jack, let's skip this lot.'

"I jest stood there sizin' up the situation. Then, I made up my mind how I would take him right in the coop since he had got himself into this fix. I recollected as how Lon was a veteran of the war between the states he ought'en to be a hesitatin' and beatin' a retreat. So I said to him, 'Let's open an assault on the enemy and take his hide.'

"But Lon wanted to show the white flag. 'No. No. No,' he allowed. 'It would be better fer me to go over to Abbot's camp and fetch me a gun. You stay and keep a watch on the critter so's it won't get away.'

You can bet I poked fun at him for that.

"'Here you be,' I sez, 'a veteran of the War of the Rebellion. A-fightin' to free the slaves. Facin' the Rebels without a tremor, but now you can't join me in tacklin' an ordinary bear that's gone and cooped his self up afore winter. Really! And besides, Lon, while you was serving in the war I hadn't even been in the draft riots, cause I was busy growing oats to feed the Union mules. There's no cause for you to be showin' a white feather on account of an old bear that wuz woke up.'

"Lon braced up and listened to my plan agreeing to help carry out any generalship that I might devolve during the skirmish. Our council of war resulted in being that I would go straight at the bear with my axe while Lon would execute a rear flank movement and irritate the bear with a pole from behind.

"While Lon was cutting himself a stout pole I busied myself chopping some of the branches right over the bear's head and shoulders so I would have a good clear leeway of a hole about three feet big. As Lon would poke the bear, it was natural to assume he'd lunge up toward the hole. When he do that I'd whack him one 'tween the eyes with the butt of the single-bitted axe and lay him out. Then we could get at him and stick him proper for butchering.

"Taking a last survey to see that everything was all right I gave the word to attack. Lon poked once. That was all he had time for because that bear doubled himself up, performed a somersault quicker'n greased lightning, and roared as he clawed Lon's pole free of his hand. It all happened before either of us knowed what was up.

"'Hold on over the hole, Uncle Jack,' Lon yelled. 'I'm going to cut another pole.'

"About then as I looked down at the frothing mug I thought perhaps I had cut too big of a hole. But being we'd started the fight I was prepared to see it through.

"Lon's second pole must have been twenty feet, I swear. A bit scandalous, too, him being a warden of the new Episcopal church that Elder Jewett had recently started in the village. Lon wasn't particular Episcopal himself but his wife's brother's sister had married a 'Piscopal deacon out in Ohio. Lon allowed that if that particular religion was fine for his sister it might do for his family here, too. So he joined the church and was appointed warden by the bishop when he made his first visit to the village the year before he died. That bishop was an uncommonly fine man and liked to stop at Lon's. Lon said the bishop was so plain and friendly, no more of a gentleman than he was in fact. 'I ain't never joined no church myself but if I was to, it'd be Episcopal 'cause you can join it without getting all excited like you've got to if you join the Methodists or Free Will Baptists. Then, too, the 'Piscopal preachers don't come down on you so hard like if you make a slip up like a bit of cussin' or degenerated swearin'.'"

At this churchly digression of Uncle Jack's, Tom Switzer spoke up and proposed that we all have another round of drinks on him. Uncle Jack said the night was getting cold. Another drink would take away his hoarseness as well as enable him to proceed more readily with the story.

"Lon's dander was up and with it he gave a good strong jab at the bear's ribs with a mild sort of cussing. The bear knew ole Lon weren't just a tickling his underside. As he clawed at the pole the broad side of his back came under the opening in the limbs. That was my opportunity and I seized it without delay, giving him a tremendous whack but it only seemed to loosen up his fat a mite.

"The next few minutes events was mighty interesting all around and come along without any lollygagging. Lon kept on a poking and the bear kept a squirming and revolving as I kept a whacking and hacking as the opportunity presented itself.

"I swear that bear was as fast as a king bolt of lightning the way he'd whirl around. His head would come up and I'd take a whack on his face. My idee at this point was to chop off his jaws so's he couldn't do no chawin' on us. Then his back would be up like I explained it was the first time and I'd fetch down another awful blow with the iron axe head fixing to break his back. But it was as if I was pounding on a feather bed; he had so much fat on him.

"I managed to slice off the tail clean as a whistle in a single stroke and chopped one paw off and clipped the nails on the other paw. After that it heated up 'cause he got his head and shoulder clean out of the hole I was facing. I had his front feet already out of commission, as I said, with two well-placed blows, but the situation was still ticklish as he squirmed out of that hole as ugly and wild a specimen of an animal as I ever care to see or think of ever again.

"It was then that a surge of strength came to my aid. I've thought of it a good many times since, too. From somewhere deep inside me I landed a proper blow with the blade on his forehead and split his head as clean as I'd split a block of maple. His brains splattered all over. He died so quick he didn't have time to shut his mouth or eyes.

"The conflict had last more'n an hour. Then it took Lon and me until dark before we could get his carcass untangled from the mess of boughs and limbs.

"You should have seen him dressed out. He had fatted up like a hog next to the swill barrel. He had a layer of fat so thick that you could stick a jack knife in at the tail, run it right up his back to his head and not strike a bit of lean meat at all. Fust rate. Fust rate.

"'Course the best part was the bear hunt itself. We had no more got the hide off before a rip-snorting snowstorm came up. We packed the hide down to Abbott's camp. Towards the close of the second day it stopped snowing so's to allow us to return on the third day on borrowed snowshoes and with Charlie Cunningham's big sled. We didn't propose to lose the carcass of that bear to the foxes and wolves. It had turned so cold that the bear's carcass had frozen hard as flint, but that didn't make no difference. We just rolled the very stiff dead body on to the sled and pulled it, hitching a pull from a sleigh that come by.

"As we passed into Bellingertown word began to get around. Everyone's excitement was mighty big—as big as the bear. Word even got passed down to Forestport and the school teacher brought the children up to look at the great skinned wonder.

"We rendered the fat using Sam Utley's large sap kettle for a week. W. R. Stamburg said the carcass was as big as an oxen. It was after hearing his comment that Lon and I struck on the idea to have a bear barbecue on Thanksgiving. The idea struck us most proper and we put the word out to all the folks at Abbott's camp, the boys at Perry's #1 lumber camp and a whole lot of folks from the village came. I believe it was the only bear barbecue ever in our part of the country."

At the end of his long narration Uncle Jack, abstemious to a degree, consented to another glass of warm whiskey while an impressive several minutes of silence fell over our group. No one, I presume from experience, dared utter a word of skepticism. Friend Switzer, whom I knew to be a veritable iconoclast, was hitching about in his chair but he wasn't saying anything as yet. It wasn't like him, I thought, but then he was just newly acquainted.

Tom Nightengale, a dozen years younger and Uncle Jack's junior in all other respects, was the first to break the silence in defense of his old friend's absurd tale. Eyeing the salesman Switzer twitch, he vouched that every detail of the story had been true. He well remembered the winter referred to. He had heard of Uncle Jack's and Alonzo Denton's memorable encounter with the bear at the time—had even been at the barbecue.

Tom Switzer couldn't hold back any longer. He began to remark that he believed the axes commonly used in lumbering operations of that time were of the double-bitted variety. I tried to get his eye to dissuade him from questioning the validity but failed. Uncle Jack agreed, acknowledging his knowledge of the tools of the lumber craft. He was obviously sucking Tom in for he got him going on a discussion of axes, peeves, cant-hooks, skippers, and grabs.

'Ere long Uncle Jack led the conversation back to his bear encounter. Switzer, eventually more profane than I first thought, began to apply higher criticism of the telling, pointing out other serious discrepancies. My city friend was putting his neck on Uncle Jack's chopping block by questioning Jack's "sacred Scriptures" as we all called his tales. Switzer had just questioned the week's encampment to secure the oil and had begun to float doubts about the barbecue when Uncle Jack came at him with his fine, effective, imperious, dogmatism that was ever the refuge of guide and Adirondack native of the woods.

Rising with a glass of farewell toddy in his hand, Uncle Jack addressed him severely. "Stranger, let me tell you this. Lon Denton's second wife's daughter's son wuz ordained a 'Piscopal preacher out in Ohio and he's got that bear skin now on the floor of his study for a rug. And what's more, it's a perfect specimen of a bear pelt, tanned in these mountains. If you don't believe me, ask the preacher," as he pointed severely at me.

Having delivered himself of this sally and finishing his glass, Uncle Jack buttoned up his coat and took his departure, followed by the village constable.

It took me many set-me-up's and a good-natured effort to square myself with old Uncle Jack for ever introducing him to a man who questioned his veracity. And that IS the whole truth of it.

In Search of Ice Cave Mountain

Monday morning, August 16, 1926, Scudder Todd and I boarded his power boat and rode to his company's landing near the head of North Lake. From there we tramped the remaining eight miles over the rough tote road to Lumber Camp Number 7 of the Gould Paper Company. John B. Todd, superintendent of Gould's forest operations and Scudder's father, had invited me the previous year to be a guest of the camp while we were on a fishing trip together. This was my first opportunity to avail myself of Todd's hospitality. I planned to use the camp as my base from which I would leave to search for the often talked about but rarely seen Ice Cave and the snow and ice on the mountain of the same name. Camp Seven was positioned at the northern side of its base in a valley between Ice Cave and Canachagala Mountains.

On my arrival, I found the camp so unusual and possessing so many varied departments and enterprises new to me for lumber camps that I tarried there all of one day—postponing my ascent of Ice Cave Mountain until Tuesday morning. I had seen a good many of the older shanty lumber camps in my day and slept a few nights in them as a guest. (John B. Todd two years later hired Byron-Curtiss to work at Camp 10 as a bookkeeper during the winter of 1928.) I would always rise early in the morning, secure a piece of yellow soap from the cook, seek some secluded creek or pool for a vigorous body scrub and carefully search my clothing for cooties.

My usual ritual was not necessary at Camp 7. I found the office, constructed in the usual log style, and the bunkroom to be clean, attractive, and equipped with many modern conveniences ordinarily considered impossible or impracticable for a camp devoted to the enterprise of getting pulp wood for paper mills. The camp was a hamlet in itself. The complex consisted of fourteen buildings from the superintendent's modest log cottage to the standard bunkhouse-cookhouse combination. This latter building was more than one hundred feet long.

A little before five o'clock Tuesday morning, August 17, 1926, I was awakened from a peaceful slumber by a gentle shake on my shoulder. It was my bunkmate, the bookkeeper of Camp 7. I speedily dressed, for I found I shivered more at this elevation, which was several hundred feet higher than my camp on North Lake. My clothing was a tad damp from the forest's penetrating moisture which did not add to my immediate comfort. I glanced out the small single-paned window and noted the morning mist beginning to rise on streamers of heated air where the warm rays of the sun were already shining. The scene gave the appearance of great clouds in the sky rising from the surrounding bushes, grass, and forest. The morning appeared to be the beginning of one of those spectacular Adirondack August days. Deep blue skies. Bright sunshine. Comfortable temperatures. No flying, stinging insects.

I had no more completed my toilette, having combed my thin thatch of hair with the towel, when I heard the clang of the breakfast bell ring out.

I hurried through the dewy wire grass of the camp clearing to the fine complement of food I knew was awaiting me. Sitting where I had been placed the previous evening, I was soon eating my favorite breakfast foods, flapjacks, bacon and eggs, and drinking as good a coffee as one could secure in the best city restaurant. My companions were mostly the peelers and crews whose work of the day was to peel the bark from the cut logs, haul the skinned logs to skidways, and build or improve the woods roads.

I had expected that my younger host, Scudder, would accompany me on my climb of Ice Cave Mountain and help me search for the cave that reportedly held ice and snow year round. Unfortunately his plans had changed. His father had asked him, instead, to go to the foot of North Lake that morning to supervise the transportation of several tons of supplies that were expected to be brought in from the Forestport rail station.

Nothing would daunt my ambition that morning, not even Scudder's hint that perhaps the "cave" did not exist. He was all for my finding its location, if indeed it was there, for its discovery would put to rest the persistent rumors he had always heard. Scudder being a lumberman, of course, did not have the leisure to investigate whims as I did.

I sensed success that morning in spite of doubts some cast my way for I held an ace up my sleeve. Since coming to North Lake I had talked to many an old-timer, notably Wolcott and, who built camps at the head of the lake during the 1870s as stopovers for their fishing sojourns at North Lake. Both men confirmed there was a rock opening, not so much a cave, that held perpetual ice and snow. It was for me to find it.

Undaunted, I arranged with Ed Wheeler for a lunch. While he gathered food that was light and portable I was treated to observe (done for my benefit, I'm sure) Musty La Fountain shaving the bull cook in lumberjack fashion. The razor was a highly sharpened double-bitted axe, every bit as keen as the finest Swedish steel when stropped over a leather belt.

Receiving my vittles, I fashioned a pack bag from a gunny sack Musty had given me from the machine shop. In it I placed my cameras, field glasses, a poncho, the lunch, and a sweater. I twisted the excess material, making a neck, and tied a short cord around the material, leaving enough length so that I could sling the bag over my shoulder and hang on to the rope much like a traveling hobo. A sheathed hatchet on my belt completed my equipment. With a goodbye to Ed, who good-naturedly joked for me to bring him a snowball, I was off at exactly 7 a.m.

Camp 7 was situated in a valley but elevated on a low shoulder of Ice Cave Mountain. I calculated I had no more than a couple of miles to go ere I would be atop the dome from which I could then look down and see the camp. Ascending was not difficult for I had any number of slashed trails and open easy skidways that lead me upward. The top of the mountain is easily many acres long. About one-third is exposed granite, the remaining two-thirds is covered with a sparse growth of low bushes, shrubs, and small trees no more than six inches in diameter, being mostly spruce.

A vast quantity of red raspberry bushes, loaded with berries, were intermingled with other bushes. Their presence would account for the many black bear signs I noted and the one bear I espied just as I rose from my smoke. He was sitting like a cat when I first saw him. I shouted and he made off in a great hurry down toward the eastern end of the summit. As far as I know he probably did not go far for the berries were plentiful. I continued to note much excrement and bushes trampled over the four to five hours I wandered the tabletop-like summit.

I was greatly impressed by the panoramic views to be had. While they do not compare to those which I viewed from the Rockies, they had a beauty all their own. The tops of the forest cover gave the land below a great rich green pile carpet look; I sensed I could almost sink my hand into it up to the backs of my fingers.

Early in the afternoon, the sun being fairly strong, I bethought myself to take pictures. Away to the west stretched a great valley with noble mountains receding to the horizon. One of the mountains, the furthermost I am satisfied, was Woodhull Mountain by Big Woodhull Lake where I had fished for land-locked salmon and bass and where Uncle John Van Dyke, a well-known and fine character had lived for years. Woodhull Mountain had a tower on it for a fire warden's observations. However, the atmosphere was hazy enough that I was unable to observe the tower even with the aid of my field glasses. But a picture I did try, anyway. I was also able to locate to my satisfaction the location of Canachagala Lake and the Bisby Chain although I could not actually see them either because of the closeness on Canachagala Mountain.

Having satisfied my scenic curiosities I returned to my pack I had left on a rock when I descried a black hole in a thicket. Thinking it might be a spring from which I could draw some sweet water I moved toward it. As I drew closer I realized it was no spring but a depression.

Could I actually be approaching the site of perpetual ice and snow? I began to hurry, in the process barking my shins and scratching myself. Within minutes I was standing at the edge looking down into the darkness. How lucky I was, both for finding the site so easily and for preserving my life and limb. The large fissure and several smaller ones were well-hidden in the tangle of underbrush. Had I not been paying good attention to where I was going I could have easily stepped off into space and been injured or instantly killed. The latter I would have preferred if given a choice between the two, for a slow death would have resulted from an injury. I would never have been able to climb back out and there would have been no hope for rescue.

I made my way forty feet toward a thicket of spruce and there discovered a great yawning hole. I was exhilarated. My search was over. As far as I could ascertain only two people had seen the ice and snow. Both men had told me they saw it a half-century ago.

Since I began coming to the North Lake region I had always heard the legend that there was perpetual ice on the mountain, but it was not located by the present generation of inhabitants of the lake. The mountain is in a little known area. The terrain is a tangled, dense, and absolute wilderness and therefore little frequented. It is most plausible that I am the first person to have seen Ice Cave since Frank Wolcott's last trip forty some years ago.

I was soon poking my head into its chasm. The entrance was about as big as the door to a hayloft, only it was well grown over. The granite walls dropped down while at the same time they towered above me. I was careful about extending my body over the edge. I wanted to see farther down than I could, yet I was concerned about loosing my eyeglasses and falling. If only I could get down safely and then have the means to get back up again.

I spied a large rock wedged between the walls below me. I would be able to have a better view if I used that as a perch but it was about eight feet below the surface. I hemmed and hawed. I readily saw I would need to get down to that lowest boulder if I was to see the bottom of the fissure, but concern for my safety was a given. I backed out of the bushy tunnel I had made on my belly and reconsidered. After careful consideration I decided the best I could do this time was to carefully lower myself onto the boulder wedged in the wall. But how to get down onto it?

I chopped a small spruce tree with my hatchet, leaving several inches of the limbs extending out from the main trunk to serve as a sort of ladder. This I lowered to the boulder, got down on it and had an outstanding view of the ice and snow. It was a keen disappointment that I had to content myself with just looking at it. I resolved then and there to return with rope, light, and help so that I could further explore the hidden recesses.

There I was, viewing ice and snow in a great fissure or natural crevice on the top of one of New York State's more remote mountains in the Adirondacks. It was fully seventy feet from the top down to the ice. The fissure looked like a great trench with a dirty white bottom.

I was eager to determine if it was solid ice, snow, or just slush. I climbed back up to the surface and found a cobblestone about as big as a man's head. Returning, I pitched it down into the depths below. It landed with a dull thud and remained two-thirds exposed, showing the frozen surface to be quite solid. As I sat on the rock perch I also noted how my breath would vaporize from the cold air coming from the depth below. I took two time exposures while the sun was shining into the shaft but my pictures were both failures.

I noted two things about the interior of the shaft as I sat upon my chilly perch at the southern end. Besides the moist or sweating condition of the granite walls both above and below me, they were a very positive salmon pink as to color. Water was continually dripping down, so depressing the crown of my felt hat I placed it under the most promising drip on the ledge mentioned and got about a tumbler full of water during the hour I spent there. I suppose that only by boring could the actual depth of the ice be ascertained.

After getting down into the real forest below the granite-domed top, a good hour's tramp took me to Camp 7, which I had left so blithely that morning. Ed Wheeler was the first to greet me. In his quiet way he asked where the snowball was and I explained that while I had seen the snow and ice, it was many feet below and therefore beyond my reach. Ed began to brew me a pot of coffee and assembled a hot supper even though it was not yet five o'clock.

Following the good cook's substantial meal I retrieved my pack basket from the office, packed all my duffel and bade good-bye, starting off on a fourteen-mile hike to my own Nat Foster Lodge. By the time I reached the head of the lake, midpoint in my trek, Luna was just lifting herself into the dome of heaven. There I ran across an old man we affectionately called Grandpa Getman. He was well over eighty years old and had been going to North Lake some forty-five years. When I told him I had been to the top of Ice Cave Mountain and had actually seen the ice and snow he looked up at me and said, "Well, Reverend, you have done more than I have. I have hunted for that place a dozen times but never found it. I only know of two men who ever claimed to see it and they were Sim Fuller and Frank Wolcott. Sim's dead and Frank is almost as old as I be. I'm glad you found it just to keep the truth alive."

Following my original discovery I guided many parties to the cave in the ensuing two decades. I will attempt to describe the place of perpetual ice and snow from the notes I took on my initial visit as well as from my second investigation during which, in the company of a fellow detective, I was lowered down to walk on the ice, follow the crevice, and return with a sample of ice as proof the spot did exist, for there were many nonbelievers.

The mountain I have mentioned was named from Indian legend. It lies mostly in Township 5 of the Adirondacks and is far removed from popular routes. North Lake is where my own lodge is and it, too, is not a popular resort being occupied in season by a few cottagers, the dam keeper, his family, and a few workmen and natives. If one wishes to reach Ice Cave Mountain he will have to get off the beaten track.

The fissure is from ten to twelve feet wide at the top, the walls of granite receding very gradually to the surface of the ice. The top is overgrown with shrubs and bushes. Among them are yellow birch, some as large as one's wrist. Other forest shrubs are intermingled while a few small trees cling to the edges of the top. The fissure is about seventy feet long, extending to the north, and receding. As to depth, I had noted just a fleck of light to the north and upon exploring this part of the fissure found it shallow and filled with much forest debris.

There is a smaller cavern here, about as big as a state room in a steamer. Here I thought I had made another and remarkable discovery. For far back in the little cavern, among the broken pieces of granite on the floor I saw a remarkably white stone about as big as my two hands. But upon crawling down and securing it and bringing it into the full light of day I found it was only a rock covered with "fox fire" or phosphorescence common to any moist or wet region or condition. When I looked up from below I noted about halfway up the crevice the rock that I first sat on. Actually it was two pieces of granite about thirty inches in size (the lower one hidden from view from above) that had been caught in the glacial eddy, so that they formed a sort of natural bridge. From down below the rocks seemed more like a great buttress wedged there to keep the fearful walls from closing in and crushing me.

The *Boonville Herald* and the Utica *Daily Press* ran interesting articles of how the ice cave was conquered again and again. Someone from almost every party was lowered by rope to the ice in the granite crevice so that they could chip out a huge block of the ice that was then hoisted to the surface. Photographs were taken and the cavern explored. The ice was wrapped and then packed out. I also began to sign an affidavit, being a notary, telling of their experiences and of the finding of the cave. This was done to substantiate the truth of my statements previously made telling of the mountain deposit of ice, which few people credited in 1926. When I next took a party in to see and explore the granite bed we brought out thermos bottles containing ice, but we were accused of securing the ice from the Atwell ice house.

Jailbirds

One criminal incident had an intriguing angle. It involved a number of my Forestport friends and acquaintances.

Charley O'Conner was my faithful "Man Friday" during my first missionary work at Forestport. A few years after my coming to that town he became implicated in a scandal over breaks in the canal feeder that ran from Forestport to Boonville. It was one of those situations when one needs to understand the background to appreciate the circumstances. It involved the sabotage of state property so it violated the law but it solved an economic problem that gave it that inevitable Robin Hood touch.

Between 1897 and 1900 there were several breaks in the banks of the feeder. The repair work to each of those breaks brought close to eight thousand dollars into the town of Forestport. There was the labor, gravel, lumber, and other construction essentials. The resulting income was a real lifesaver to the town. By that time, the turn of the century, the bottom had dropped out of the lumber business and the big steam mills were not sawing the logs they used to. State canal inspectors sent to appraise the damage suspected the first break was not exactly an act of God. It was the general opinion that the opening was due to the work of muskrats that undermined and weakened the feeder's bank; the evidence also seemed to indicate that the muskrats had a lot of human help. There was enough doubt to the cause that the state decided to do some investigating.

The Attorney General placed an undercover detective in town; he masqueraded as a promoter and organizer. He got the village all stirred up about incorporating and forming a town water company. The sneak boarded at the Getman house, renting a room over the hotel lobby that was near the bar, where the affairs of the town were often discussed in semiprivacy. In the ceiling of the lobby was a register for radiant heat to travel upward off the ceiling surface and heat the room above. The detective spent much of his time lying on his stomach eavesdropping—gathering evidence against the participants, who during the time he was there executed two additional canal feeder breaks.

It came out during the trial in Rome that there had been much quarreling and disagreement among the conspirators. Clark, one Forestport livery owner, wanted the break to be located five miles down the feeder so there would be a demand for his rigs. O'Conner and Sandy Denslow wanted the break only one half mile from the village proper, close enough to boost their bar trade.

The records indicated that a boy discovered the second break while getting the cows in from the pasture early in the morning. Thinking he was doing a good deed he reported the leak and the tender was instructed to close the locks. Thus that washout did not cause too much damage. The undercover man even heard that someone had suggested censuring the lad to prevent him from reporting another break.

At the time the "Canal Feeder Scandal" broke I was in charge of a mission church in Rome. During the trial I experienced one brief anxious personal moment. It all began one Sunday as I was walking over Stanwix Street past the jailhouse on my way to hold services at the County Home. Someone hailed me from an upper window in the cell block of Rome's Bastille; he asked me to come and see him. I recognized the prisoner. It was my loyal buckboard driver Fardet of Forestport. I called with some tobacco the next day. There I learned his two cronies Root and Jones were in jeopardy with him. Root had been member of my church at Forestport.

I had come to know Fardet well; he drove for Clark's livery. I often rented a team from Clark when I went to North Lake. The embarrassment I spoke about had to do with an experience I was afraid might be brought up during the proceedings in court. The reflection it could have brought on me and, more importantly, clergy in general came from my careless banter on a trip into the lake with Fardet.

It had been very cold when we started out during the wee morning hours prior to daylight. There were four in my party: Besides myself there was Rev. Meisenhelder, a Protestant pastor; Rev. James Burd, father of Holy Cross church in Utica; and my tight-fisted, stingy little brother-in-law Gus Hossfelt. I remember it was very nippy that autumn during the pre-dawn hours. We crossed the Black River at Bellingertown about daybreak. In unison we tried to rouse Del Bellinger with a friendly "hello" hoot but our efforts failed. Our failed attempts showed us how cold and shivery we were. As we climbed the long, sandy hill out of the valley someone had the bright idea that as long as we were as well-prepared as St. Bernard dogs with their keg of spirits (we all carried a pint or so for emergencies in our duffel bags) we would poke a little fun at my brother-in-law's expense. Gus had a flask on his hip. We had seen him take a swig in the cold gray dawn because he was sitting up with the driver, Fardet. We united in badgering Gus for "just a nip" until he handed over his precious flask. By the time the three of us had passed it around twice there was not much more than two good shots left in the bottle. I handed it up to our driver and directed Fardet to finish it up for he had to be as cold as we were.

Gus eyed Fardet as he tipped the bottle, drained it and then flung the empty container smashing his once-full flask into a million pieces against a boulder at the side of the road. Then we commiserated with Gus over his great and tragic loss. I had forgotten about the matter until Fardet began his testimony.

Clark was on trial as one of the co-leaders. Fardet was a stool pigeon turning state's evidence against his employer in return for a reduced sentence. Since Pastor Meisenhelder and I knew all the principals and their accomplices we decided to attend the court sessions.

Fardet had been arrested on a warrant at Old Forge and he admitted that he was gloriously drunk on his arrival at the Rome jail. He claimed the arresting constable had permitted him to buy a pint at the village before leaving for Rome, but he denied that he was accustomed to carrying a bottle with him although he did admit to occasionally taking a nip or two out of a flask when he worked. The defendant's lawyer was trying to discredit his testimony. The lawyer persisted in this line of questioning but Fardet continued to claim he was innocent of any real drinking, illustrating by offering, "When I took parties into the mountains they often asked me to join them in a sniffer. When that happened, I never refused their good intentions."

As he said this Pastor Meisenhelder gave me a sharp poke in the ribs and whispered excitedly, "As there's a God in Heaven, Arthur, what happens to our good names if Fardet identifies us in telling an example?" It was as though the lawyer must have heard Meisenhelder and had mercy because he shifted his questioning. Thus we narrowly escaped having our names associated with the Canal Feeder Scandal.

For their role Clark, Monahan, and Basset served prison terms in Auburn while O'Conner and several others paid stiff fines. Years later Timothy Curtin, the Oneida County district attorney who prosecuted the case, told me that Tom Wheeler, the Republican boss of Oneida County and then superintendent of canals, tried to supersede him as prosecutor of the case, pushing instead for an attorney from the State

Department, but he told the political boss, "Wheeler, the people of Oneida County elected me their prosecutor and I am not going to abdicate for the attorney general and his Albany crew."

In 1902, following this affair, my friend Charley O'Conner stayed with me a few days at my camp at North Lake. We relaxed and whipped the North branch with our fly rods. It was lousy with trout but they were all small and we did not pay much attention to the golden rule. When we came within sight of the lake we saw two men land from a boat at the inlet.

They were strangers to us and O'Conner's imagination started working overtime as he started for the brush. I followed him into the bushes where I gave him my rod and creel with its share of short trout and told him to lie low while I investigated; then I casually strolled down to look the men over. They were two vacationers from Ilion who were stopping at the Mitchell camp nearby. They were so innocent it was ridiculous. They showed me a small mess of chub and five trout between four and five inches long. I gave O'Conner the "all's clear" and he came down with a worried look still on his face. We gave the men enough of our short trout to make a mess and told them to throw the chubs away, cautioning them to not show the trout to anyone, rather cook and eat them at once. The trial had spooked poor Charley more than I had realized.

*   *   *

Several years later my luck held out in a Forest, Fish and Game Commission scandal that involved cutting timber at Twin Lakes—on state land. The case involved "Moody" and "Skinny" Harrig, a pair of harum-scarum Lutheran affiliates who some claimed had a deal with "higher up" officials within the commission to attempt an extensive logging operation on state property.

On one of my trips through Forestport that summer (I had no knowledge of the strictly hush-hush rape of state land that the Harrig brothers had committed) I stopped at the Harrig's Forestport mill. The hedgehogs had chewed up my camp floor pretty badly in places; so I gave the Harrig boys an order for five hundred feet of spruce flooring.

Along about October Moody Harrig stopped by when he was in Rome to tell me the flooring was ready. When I asked him for the bill I noted Moody cleared his throat rather nervously. I conceitedly accepted his body language to mean the flooring was a tribute to the cloth, especially with his following request: "Reverend, me and Skinny are planning a little vacation around North Lake to do a little hunting. If you will let us use your camp we will not only cancel the bill but we'll take the flooring in and lay it for you." I had no knowledge an investigation involving the boys was underway. His proposition was reasonable and very much in my favor. I thought no more about it; I readily gave him the key to the camp and wished him and his brother the best of luck on their hunting trip.

A few weeks later I read a report about the illegal cutting of an alleged twenty thousand cords of pulpwood in the Twin Lakes region. The authorities were looking for the Harrig boys; common hearsay tossed about Forestport placed Moody and Skinny somewhere in Canada looking after some lumber interests. Of course other rumors circulated that they had simply slipped out of town to avoid prosecution. Either way they did not appear for the trial. I attributed no special significance beyond a little convenient shyness on their part.

The following spring when I arrived at North Lake to open camp I found the floor had been laid and ten cords of firewood was laid up handy to the door. Later on Moody told me how snug and comfortable my camp was. They had been holed up there the entire winter. The brothers were not convicted. The outcome of the trial showed the principal culprit in the cutting to be a man known as "The Fox." The Moodys, upon learning they were only fined, "returned from Canada." I think it had been an intelligent ruling.

Old-Time Mountain Law

North Country natives shared a code—a private law that did not look on hunting and fishing as a sport or pastime. Contrary to city sportsmen, Adirondack families relied on those activities to sustain life.

Liquor occupied the most important place in the pharmacopoeia of the wilderness. Woodsmen often needed to be their own doctors, make a diagnosis, and prescribe the medicine. Who could blame them if they were partial to the flavoring?

You might think these subjects have nothing to do with each other, but there is a common thread they share. When a legislative body in some distant capital city declares hunting and fishing a sport and the Anti-Saloon League declares liquor a curse (for the good of the country Prohibition was the answer) every red-blooded Adirondacker reared back on his hind legs, threw out his chest—and kept his mouth shut. Did you expect hell fire?

There was nothing baneful in this form of defiance. Working and living among the locals I saw graphic examples of their indifference to outside influence time and time again. Natives were staunch individualists. They distrusted a faceless system that made decisions that affected them. Their response was simple; they continued to follow *their* ways. However, the continuation of old customs did mean they could not leave any clues.

If the law frowned upon any of their activities, they were forced to go underground. The range of the resistance system often dictated venison be masqueraded as lamb or goat and if it got a little ripe—hash or croquette. The mechanics of this subterranean program often showed an inventive genius. A hollow tree, a collapsible stump, some loose boards in the floor under the bed, a step in the stair screwed on instead of nailed and a wood box with a false bottom; all those and more clandestine devises were employed to accommodate illegal meat and "medicine" (whiskey) from the prying eyes of those who would betray.

The first challenge to the North Lake folks of the Black River country I was privy to came when a group of well-to-do sportsmen took control of a vast tract of forest land and then attempted to keep the public off by posting their property. I am referring to the Adirondack League Club land acquisition in the 1890s. A hatred toward the "city slickers" evolved due to the lack of any mutual understanding. Both parties held each other in open contempt. The boundaries of the private tract were considered indefinite because the first surveys were decades old. Trees on which the surveyors blazed their marks were gone.

More confusion was added to the picture by the patriotic gesture made long ago by John Brown, the merchant of Providence, Rhode Island, who purchased thousands of acres, divided his holdings into townships and attempted to encouraged wide-scale settlement. In each of those townships were lots set aside for church and school purposes. Forever. The old deeds were the only evidence of the existence of those public lots. A new survey would have been necessary to relocate them. In the absence of that being done in many instances those locations did not show on maps. Many a canny woodsman had told a game protector, "Hell, son, this is one of old Brown's church and school lots," and gotten away with it. [Editor's note: B-C's slant show his adherence to the local view—one that generally opposed the ALC. The John Brown Tract he refers to was northwest of the Moose River Tract on which ALC lands were located.]

Deer meat was the most important contraband and because of its size it was the most dangerous to handle without instituting elaborate safeguards by poachers. Wrapping cloths and razor-edged butcher knives were always found in a pack basket. When an unlawful kill was made it was usually shared with the neighbors because of the lack of refrigeration and the amount of meat involved. Transactions were conducted in a way that under oath on the witness stand there would be no evidence of collaboration. A mythical third party always acted as the agent. The witness is merely a Samaritan of the wilderness.

The distribution system was simple and worked in this way. A visitor dropped by a neighbor's cabin and casually asked why a package was lying out on a stump or set on the well curb. Some noncommittal answer was given and no further mention was made of the subject. If there was any barter involved, an old knife was stuck into the meat. That alone was considered in the negotiation. It was considered good etiquette (and also evidence of good faith) to leave the knife lying on the ground when the meat was taken away. Small game and fish were usually handled in a tin pail or other container. The container was the only item involved in the deal. For example, I witnessed, at the Buffalo

Head, nine pounds of brook trout in a tin pail change hands for five dollars—the price of the tin pail.

Almost all legal action for trespass or game law violations were brought against outsiders. The intentional invasion of private tracts was seldom discovered in time to prosecute, so the accumulated anger of the guards and wardens was heaped on the unfortunate they did catch. Numerous stories circulated about those conflicts with the sporting clubs.

Many lawyers spent their vacations in the North Woods and sat around an evening campfire talking shop while their guides listened with due respect. At such times it was not difficult to lead the conversation around to the subject of trespass and the illegal taking of game. Every sporting shamus was loaded with strategic information and little by little the guides added to their libraries until the archives in their heads were well-stocked with pertinent legal lore. Some of them had thought on their material and developed into successful pettifoggers and reliable novice advisers on law. Not only did they know the vagaries of the legal code but more importantly the peculiar behaviors of the local justice of the peace. One of these mountain pundits was Dick Camp, who lived in a cabin on North Lake.

One summer relatives of Camp's wife who had run into hard times came to live with them. The North Lake stationed ALC game warden caught them red-handed fishing in a club lake. When they told Dick about it he knew at once they were going to be up against a cold deck of cards. He rushed the violators over to Gid Ferris, the nearest justice of the peace who lived about nine miles away. Camp took along a quart of bourbon to discuss the matter "off the record but under a mellowing influence."

The first question Gid asked the men was what luck they had had fishing. When they admitted they had not even had a bite the justice's attitude seemed to undergo a subtle change. He was awful sorry that any of Dick's folks were criminals. He committed that their downfall came when they left the woods and threw their lot in with city folks. He instructed them to reform, "Depart from your evil ways."

He lectured, too, on American citizenship and their duties in upholding the laws and the Constitution of the country. Gid was always convincing on such occasions. Before the bourbon was finished Dick's relatives had stark visions of prison bars and a fare of bread and water. When the bottle was empty Gid used it as a gavel and opened his court. Dick Camp offered a plea of guilty on behalf of his erring kinfolk, who remained silent, and promised their future would be guided by the excellent fatherly advice of His Honor. The judge fined them one dollar each and dismissed the case. He also remitted the fines.

A day or so later a constable arrived with warrants to arrest the men. Camp had advised his relatives this would happened. They were once again taken before Gid Ferris. Following the formalities of opening court the club attorney charged the men with trespassing on private property. Gid adjusted his specs on his nose, picked up the warrant and thumbed the used copybook pages. He compared the names of the accused, the date and charge on the warrant with his own records, then slowly removed his specs, cleared his throat, leaned back, and glared at the attorney. "Counselor," he said sternly, "this case is closed. My records show the men in question pleaded guilty to these charges days ago. The prisoners are discharged." The futile legal action cost the club money for transportation and legal services and gave Dick Camp something to brag about for the rest of his life.

I think the most famous case in mountain jurisprudence was the one that involved "Uncle" Jack Yeomans. Uncle Jack was tender on the number one feeder lock on the Black River Canal at Forestport. He was a shrewd, pious little man with Uncle Sam chin whiskers. He had a reputation for enjoying a friendly game of poker, had a fine memory, and was fond of telling stories that he seemed to always improve in the retelling.

Isaac Cohen was a Jew and unorthodox in many ways. He spent his vacations in the woods, minded his own business, and was considered, "all right" by the locals—which meant more in the North Woods than it did on the outside. The ALC game warden had caught Cohen dead to rights. Cohen would probably have been convicted also if the club lawyer had not started pushing him around, but that is exactly what made the Isaac Cohen trial famous.

Isaac had been caught fishing in a club lake. Twenty trout (two of which were a fraction of an inch under size) were in his fishing basket. He was tried before a jury in the court of Justice of the Peace Seth Lyons in the fall of 1901. The date is significant because it associates with the day of Queen Victoria's funeral.

The lawyer for the ALC, smarting under several humiliating defeats at the hands of local pettifoggers, was determined (for personal revenge) on hard justice. He nailed Cohen to the wall with a mass of evidence. It seemed as if no one could get him off, or so it appeared, until the lawyer in a taunting manner heaped an insult on his victim.

Everyone knew Isaac's fondness for pork sausages with his morning flapjacks and this fact became known to the lawyer, too. As the club lawyer wrapped up his case he sneered in his final arguments to the jury, "Give this miserable pork-eating law breaker a good dose of the punishment he deserves."

The entire courtroom fell silent; it was not the silence that gives assent. Judge Lyons reached for the piece of stove wood he was using as a gavel, weighed it carefully for balance in his hands, then thinking better of it, he laid it down on the table. It was then that Uncle Jack got to his feet slowly. He made some sounds—the way he usually did as he collected his thoughts. Then he spoke. He first commented on the weather, complained querulously about his rheumatism, then as inspiration seemed to get the best of him he started talking about Queen Victoria, for that very day she had been put to rest. Yeomans mentioned some of the highlights he had read about her long reign and they were told in the quaint way he was known to tell his stories.

No one ever left the room or was inattentive when Uncle Jack told a story. Two of the jury started sniffling. Uncle Jack felt the sympathetic reaction and began to pour it on as thick as any tale he had ever told. "The Queen had been generous," he pointed out, "generous toward Benjamin Disraeli, her prime minister. The empire owed their glorious position to him. He was Britain's brightest star."

After a brief pause, Uncle Jack continued. His voice was quiet. "Benjamin Disraeli was a Jew. So is our friend Isaac Cohen. Queen Victoria thought Disraeli was all right. We think Cohen is all right." Then in a booming voice he declared, "God save the Queen!"

The verdict of the jury that night was "Not guilty."

If you ever hear a North Laker muttering "God save the Queen" when the law is breathing down the back of his neck, he is not being profane or facetious. He is just sending a brief supplication to the spirit of Uncle Jack Yeomans.

Horn Lake's North Star Lean-to

Fine trout waters were once found throughout the Adirondack Mountains. Just where the best localities were for fishing was debatable. Any guide worth his salt, proud of his turf and armed with personal knowledge, could assure the sportsmen in his party he would direct them to any number of remarkable transparent gems, none of which, he would claim, had been disturbed since the previous fishing season. And, proving his word to be true, he would still have kept in seclusion the choicest nooks of his North Woods domain to himself. Horn Lake was counted among the best trouting waters in Herkimer County. For locality and surrounding scenery none excelled.

The building of North Star, a tiny outlying camp at Horn Lake, added comfortable shelter but did not add to the region's usage. The fine trout lake was tucked miles back in the woods, reachable only by foot. All equipment was packed in on the backs of humans, who, once doused in tar oil or other "fly medicine," were required to make a long march through a magnificent unlumbered forest and celebrated black fly country. Guides and woodsmen-in-the-know knew that if the schools of brook trout were stirring about and happened to approach a lure amazing results could occur if the angler was both alert and quick. I have seen first hand brook trout hauled in one after another faster than a man could say, "Atwell Martin."

Horn Lake, indeed, had a reputation as a consistent producer of trout twelve to fourteen inches long—there were larger ones but they tended to be large-headed and in poor condition. It wasn't the excitement of the click of a reel changing to a chirr-r-r that always provided my most outstanding fishing excursion memories. Rather the most impressive incidents were experiences my party encountered while in the wilds. The following incident occurred while we were trouting in the Black River headwaters.

North Star camp was new; I recognized it would offer excellent protection from weather, annoying insects, and roaming nocturnal mammals. The way to Horn Lake was not a well-chopped trail that one would often find between lakes, but having gone the distance several times I felt confident of the route. Thus crowned with successful fishing on the tributaries of North Lake over the last days I promised my party I would take them to a good place where very few anglers fish, but where many fine trout subsist.

My group was comprised of Drs. Hyzer W. Jones and James W. Flemming; Roy S. Brockett, a friend of Jones'; my son, Joseph; and Albert Coram, a printer from Utica and somewhat eccentric character; and me. Coram was not an initial member of our party. To those who know of him he had a reputation as one who loved to wander, enjoying outdoor ventures all over the world. His most recent trip to Egypt had been reported in the Utica newspaper. This good man of high adventure had been banging around the forest of Township 5 when he stepped into the clearing of the Horn Lake camp. We suggested he join us for supper and stay the night.

The camp was not designed for a party of six, but we managed by covering the floor with a huge pile of balsam boughs. Lulled by the aromatic camphor of balsam and feeling the fatigue from our long tramp we would all have probably slept soundly until daylight had it not been for Dr. Flemming.

Flemming was one of those men who was ever concerned about his health. Earlier that day he had promulgated he had not had a proper evacuation of his bowels. At that time he had taken several cathartic pills from his tin box of medicines and washed them down with a cup of bubbling spring water. The trivial incident had been forgotten until the disturbance during the night.

"Byron, where's Joseph's little .22 caliber rifle?" whispered Dr. Jones as he gently shook my shoulder wakening me from a sound sleep. I pointed to a peg over our quarters. Then, realizing the boy had broke the gun to assure there was no charge in it, I roused him to learn of where he had placed the ammunition. Half asleep Joseph took his jacket from under his head and fumbled for the cartridges in the pocket.

"What's up?" I asked the doctor. All he answered was, "Rabbits," as he stumbled over Brockett and Coram and disappeared into the dark night.

By that time everyone in the crowded "dog kennel" was wide awake. We crawled out into the night to see what was going on. The embers in the campfire were warm. In order to place some light on the nighttime activity I snatched an armful of balsam boughs and tossed them on the live bed of coals. The flashing light that resulted revealed a comical scene and brought on loud laughter and guffaws from us.

There, a rod or two from the camp, was Dr. Flemming positioned over a moss covered log, his hanging shirt tails covering his buttocks. With his pants down around his ankles, his pale legs and white shirt glowed in the ruddy blaze of the replenished fire. On one side of the log was a lantern. On the opposite side of the doctor who was manfully holding himself aloft also sat a good-sized rabbit. Add to that picture Dr. Jones aiming Joe's little rifle about to take a potshot at the rabbit and you have one zany scene. As the doctor's rifle cracked, the rabbit jumped from the log and made off in the direction of the river.

The excitement being over, all six of us gathered around the smoking fire. Naturally the four wakened sleepers wanted to hear the particulars. During that next half hour I also returned to the cabin to fetch armfuls of balsam tips that I nonchalantly kept adding to the fire. It seemed that the medicine Dr. Flemming had prescribed to himself earlier that day had manifested its efficiency in his gut in good and proper form after we had all gotten well into our slumbers. Severe grips and pain followed that caused him to groan and awaken his buddy. Naturally Dr. Jones was sympathetic to his fellow and accompanied him to the outer air. With ample space available to expel the results of the strong cathartic taken, Dr. Flemming assumed the proper position for effecting relief when a rabbit jumped from the bush and landed between Flemming's legs. Jones, startled for an instant for the imperfect light from the lantern gave no real clue to what had just happened exclaimed, "My God, Doc! What on earth did you just pass?" It was then they both espied the rabbit that had by then hopped up on the log as friendly as could be. Seeing the animal, Jones had bounced into the "kennel" for Joseph's gun.

All this was told as we stood around the fire. The retelling brought on good humored guffaws about Jones' ambition to slaughter little bunnies and to his being the worst shot in the North Woods. Flemming was not exempt from our chiding, either. Sleepy again, we retired to our beds only to find I had inadvertently burned most of the bedding. All the snickers and giggles moments ago changed to grunts and groans. My camping companions, however, were soon overtaken by sleep.

Fishing the next morning was indifferent and anticlimactic compared to the happening the night before. Four of us decided to follow the slashed trail to the Indian River and fish down to the waterfall above the first stillwater not far from Balsam Lake. We caught a couple of good sized trout each but the most intriguing part of the day came when we ran on to the iron stake that marked the line between Hamilton and Herkimer Counties. The trees in the vicinity of the boundary stake had been felled into a long lane about forty feet in width. The decaying timbers were being overgrown by brush and saplings. I walked into the forest a few rods so that I could say I had been in Hamilton County.

Returning to base camp we compared catches. Among us we did not show more than four pounds of trout, which brought a good-humored chide from my son. "You should have killed that rabbit last night, Doctor Jones." With our larder down our "Committee of the Whole" voted to return to North Lake the next morning "after the Reverend says the prayers."

In all my tramps and camps I have had with my secular friends, my companions have always cooperated with me in observing our duty as Christian men on Sunday. A prayer book was always with me. At Horn Lake, following breakfast, we assembled as a group to join in repeating each prayer. Dr. Jones, a veteran of my outdoor Sunday services, forewarned dear old Coram, "Don't worry, Byron will give you something to do." Which I did.

Our return was uneventful until we reached the skiff we had left moored in a safe place in the mouth of North Branch. It had been well-loaded with five coming up the lake; now there were six to return. The wind was blowing briskly and the water was rather rough. When we were loaded and ready to start I delivered a warning that although the gunwales of the boat were less than three inches above the water, we would be perfectly safe—if we sat perfectly still. We arrived safely at camp although not a one let out a peep all the way down the lake. To this day I don't know if their silence was because of my admonition or if the threatening weather conditions depressed the group.

Wilderness Gadgets

I have seen a bewildering assortment of useless gadgets toted into the Adirondack wilderness. Purchasers must really believe the items will contribute to their comfort and well-being, accelerate their getting about, save their lives under particular circumstances, maybe even help them to acquire game more easily.

I recall one occasion when I invited a party camping in tents below my camp to fish the Middle Branch. It turned out they didn't have fishing permits, but they came along just to watch me fish in a mountain brook. When we arrived at the first falls, I took great pains to cast into the seething pools and frothy eddies; my companions sprawled as comfortably as possible on convenient boulders. After picking up several eight- and nine-inch trout I decided it was time for a drink. I removed my old felt hat, crumpled up the rim and dipped it into the well-aerated water, placed the rim of the hat to my lips, and was about to pour the water down my throat when the oldest member scrambled to his feet with a warning shout. "Here, here! Don't do that. Use this," and produced from the pocket of his very clean regulation hunting-fishing coat a rubber tube with a bulge in the middle about the size of a butternut. I finished my drink, then gave heed to what the well-intentioned man was trying to impress on me with the patented back-aching water pump gadget he was waving. "The bulge contains powered charcoal," he exclaimed. "It will strain all the impurities sucked through the tube. Drinking water the way you're doing it—why you might get typhoid fever."

What a strange bird, I thought. I pointed as impressively, as I could toward the direction of the High Peaks in Essex County and lectured, "You can go in that direction seventy or eighty miles and never see another human being. Where in the world would the sewage come from?" He sheepishly grinned. I suppose he reflected on how green he appeared.

In 1920 my total investment in fishing tackle represented two dollars and a quarter. (A dollar steel rod, a fifty-cent line and any reel that has a drag and ring hook with a long shank.) I had friends with high priced rods, Shakespeare reels, five-dollar line, and snells and snell hooks—tackle often totaling as much as twenty-seven dollars! Often, when eager camp guests call, many bring useless gadgets into the woods. The fishermen are always anxious to show me the fine assortment of fishing tackle: rods, line, lures, and gaudy flies as well as unnecessary clothing. In their innocence they would ask me, "Is this any good?" I was always tempted to tell them that its chief value was with the dealer who sold the mess to them but I always refrained.

Frugality and common sense are principles I adhere to. It carried over toward my entire way of living and that included guns. I had an old seven-shot Winchester rifle all of sixty years old. The bore of the barrel was somewhat worn and pitted but I still used it successfully shooting large game.

Along about 1930, desirous of judging how it and my own marksmanship held up, I gave it a test that I have always considered superior to any shooting at a standard bull's-eye target. On this occasion, with a slight breeze rippling the water, I aimed at a block of wood floating forty rods out in the lake. After a couple of tries to get a line shot I was able to hit and knock the block out of the water repeatedly. It proved it was not so much the gun but the way it is held, handled, and fired.

Marksmanship depends on the man behind the gun, just like fishing has more to do with skill than equipment. Frugality, frugality, frugality. How can anyone argue man needs more things? Mild deceptions, the genius of capitalism, can be called the halftones of life—I suppose.

Tiddlywinks, the Not-So-Speedy Fox

Dr. William Sessler, his wife Grace, and daughter Milda, parishioners from my former Willard parish, first began visiting North Lake in 1920 when Milda was ten years old. Thereafter, for well over ten years, the family continued to spend a part of every May or June with me at Nat Foster Lodge.

Following Milda's graduation from high school she began her career at Willard State Hospital and she continued to vacation with her parents, eventually arriving accompanied by Francis, her special gentleman friend, who was a plumbing contractor in Waterloo. On June 9, 1930, I had the special privilege of marrying the couple at my North Lake Saint Catherine's Outdoor Chapel.

Francis was a fine type of young man. He also had great physical strength and endurance. Without a doubt Francis could butcher more firewood than the average person. When brushing the undergrowth around camp, I might be turning to get an axe to cut off a small tree or bush when he would grab hold of it and rip it roots and all from the ground. In addition to being a powerhouse around camp he was a splendid companion hiking trails and on fishing trips. Following a trial period, he eventually became my equal in taking trout.

One Sunday following our proper prayers inside the camp (it was too cold to have them in the open chapel) the Sesslers and I were sitting about the fireplace, when Francis bounded in panting like a spent hound and looking as if he had fought in the trenches in World War I. His clothes were covered with black muck, his trousers were torn, his arms were scratched, and he had small trickles of blood running down his cheek, but that was not what we noticed first. Clutched tightly to his chest he held a beautiful young red fox about two months old. Of course our party was at once full of excitement. "Where did you get him? What happened?" we curiously demanded.

When his wind returned he told of moseying along the foot trail that lead to the tote road that skirted the lake. There he espied the fox in the brush and took after him. "When I started in, I realized I might be able to catch it. It was just a question of which of us could run the fastest and the longest." From his description it sounded as if the fox might win the contest. The fox, seeing Francis, leaped into the brush, dashed across the tote road and started nimbly up a "hogs-back" with Francis in hot pursuit. Francis fell down several times, became snagged on fallen limbs, tripped on rocks and slipped when crossing a moss-covered log. Once he stumbled headlong into one of those shallow black muck-filled pits that prevail in the Adirondacks. He scratched his face on brush getting out of that. He lost a little each time he stumbled and tumbled but Francis continued to get back up and keep after the fox. They raced along the top of an open ridge but he was never able to gain on his prey. The fox eventually turned, dropped off the ridge, and headed back down toward the tote road.

One might wonder why he put so much effort into a seemingly fruitless endeavor, but Francis could be a very focused person; he wasn't one to give up, but rather enjoyed putting a dogged determination into things that require a physical challenge. He was also determined to catch the fox because he had decided upon first espying it that when the prime season came, its pelt would make a fine neck piece for his fiancée.

Once the fox had plunged off the ridge and closed in on the road Francis lost sight of it in the brush along the side of the tote road. In fact he was almost certain he might have lost it for good as well as losing the match between man and animal. Standing on the open course of the roadway, breathing hard, he surveyed the terrain. Just as he was about to give up the chase he spotted a spot of red color where none should be a dozen feet away. Both were probably close to done in (Francis more so than the scared pup). Francis made for the red color in a spurt and in a moment's time had drawn up to the fox, seized it by the nape of the neck and clutched it tightly. It didn't put up a fight once he had a hold of it. Panting, he stumbled into camp as I have described.

The kit was at once name Tiddlywinks. We built a large crate for him to live in. The young animal became quite an attraction, it being the only "pet" fox ever gracing my lodge. Throughout the rest of the vacation period Francis turned to shooting black birds for the little fellow's meals and also feeding it bacon rind, eggs, mice, bread, and the like.

Tiddlywinks left the woods when the Sesslers returned home. By early winter his fur had approached a prime grade. Tiddlywink's life was going to be sacrificed on the altar of fashion, but in the nick of time his less than prosaic demise was averted. Along about February, the mating season for foxes, Tiddlywinks, the not-so-speedy North Lake fox, showed his species' cunning and intelligence and disappeared.

I can't say what ever happened to the fox but being the romantic I am I would like to think it found a partner and made a den in a sand hill or rocky district. There a litter of four to nine would be born. By day they would all lie in some clump of brush or weeds, or on top of a stump or log and at night they would visit a valley area in search of food.

Romance on the Waters of North Lake

The Harrisfields were a contrasting pair who came to my camp for a month's outing in the mountains. Spencer, the father, was tall, angular and gaunt, bald-headed and hatchet-faced. His son, Floyd, in his mid-twenties, was short and stocky, of flaxen hair, with a ruddy complexion and chubby face. The father would scarcely tip the scales at one hundred fifty pounds, while Floyd was fully another one hundred pounds. Withal, Floyd was a handsome man and as universally good-natured as the majority of fat men are.

The tall, thin frame of Mr. Harrisfield was an asset in negotiating the trails and tramping long distances through the forest. His long legs permitted him to straddle logs and step over streams and obstacles with ease while his long arms enabled him to grasp an overhanging limb of a tree to keep himself from falling when by any chance he tripped on a root.

Floyd's heavy frame on the other hand was a positive drawback; an office executive who did not exercise, he was soft and flabby. No amount of earnest effort after he arrived at camp seemed to harden him. His hands blistered at butchering wood and he would invariably return from hiking with blisters on his feet, legs bruised and cut, and generally be completely bushed. Not even a good catch of trout would lighten Floyd's footsteps or loosen up his muscles. While he was eager to do his share of camp chores, his grunts and groans would accompany his filling the wood box for the night. Overbalancing and outweighing his lack of physical endurance, however, was the fact that Floyd had an everlasting good nature. He would take all our banter and chaff without any resentment. He was a most likable chap.

Once, after instructing him on how to aim and fire a rifle, I sent Floyd, in the company of my son, Joseph, to hunt at a known deer area. Unknown to either myself or my son, a colony of beaver had built a dam near the outlet of the small lake. The impounded water had raised the stream depth and widened the stream's width that prevented the boys from crossing. A detour required a complete encircling of the lake in order that they could strike the homeward trail, adding approximately three miles to their tramp. Poor Floyd was done in on his arrival. After offering him a refreshing swallow from one of my pre-Volstead camp flasks, I asked him the cause of his distress.

"Why?" he said. "Joe and I have walked twenty miles through the worst tangled underbrush and witch-hoppel that grows in the Adirondacks. If I've fallen once I've fallen a hundred times. My legs are stripped and as raw as a piece of beef." He pulled up his trousers and uncovered limbs that did show a liberal number of marks made by coming in violent contact with logs, stumps, and rank underbrush. Joseph filled in the details regarding the beaver dam diversion. I was most interested in another matter and shoved off Floyd's minor injuries for the bigger question. "Did you see any deer?"

"See any deer!" Floyd piped up. "Why, we started up a bunch as big as a herd of dairy cows; but I didn't hit a one." That disappointed me. We had been eating salt-pickled and smoked meats. Fresh venison would have been a most welcome change. "Joseph!" I exclaimed, looking for an explanation. To my sound of exasperation he replied in his customary quiet way. They had started up two bucks, three does, and three fawns after they had gotten around the water obstacle created by the beavers. Wishing to give Floyd the honor of securing meat on the hoof, he had told him to pick off the smallest buck. Floyd had emptied the rifle at it but the whole herd had disappeared in a flash. "I guess Floyd's hand trembled so that he could not get in a good line shot," replied my son.

"My hand didn't tremble; it doesn't tremble," exclaimed Floyd extending a very thickset right hand. "The trouble was it was too dark in the woods; the shadows there under the trees made it seem like twilight so that I couldn't see the sights on the gun." He repeated my instructions given to him (as all amateur hunters who visited me) about never squeezing the trigger until a patch of fur showed on the end of the gun. "I never saw the dern fur, Reverend. Honestly," he retorted. The incident of the missing fresh venison passed with the serving of a supper consisting of broiled bacon, johnny-cake, smoked herrings, and coffee.

Although Floyd had his limitations we discovered that month that his avoirdupois was a lifesaver for him in the water. Floyd Harrisfield was incapable of sinking. If he foundered beneath the surface of the water, he would quickly bob up and float like a cork. I saw that with my very eyes when we were crossing a small lake in a grossly overloaded boat.

We were paddling a small flat-bottomed scow—one we kept safe by sinking it on the edge of the lake in the late fall and keeping an inch or so of water in it all summer. It was serviceable for several years. On this particular morning it was decidedly overloaded and navigation was a ticklish matter. However, all went well until we had nearly reached a landing on the opposite shore. There we struck a submerged rock. The boat at once capsized. We were all thrashing in the water—all except Floyd that is. He had first disappeared instantly beneath the placid flood but as quickly reappeared and began bobbing, rolling, and splashing about like a side wheeler.

Once we righted the boat, splashed out water with cupped hands and retrieved lost gear that hadn't sunk we made our way toward shore. Floyd first paddled after the oars that had floated toward the middle then made his way back to meet us at the shore. Once on land we roared until our shouts drowned the calls of the hawks in the forest and the loons on the lake.

A fire was kindled and in an hour's time we had dried our clothing. Spencer and I pushed the boat back into the placid waters of the lake and proceeded to fish for bass. The boys were to deploy along the shore and cast from the best places they could find. As Harrisfield and I were casting near a projecting rock I paused a moment to look for the boys. I saw Floyd making his way along the trunk of an old tree that overhung the water near us. I mentioned to my fishing partner that his son would have a good place to cast from once he reached the far end of the large branch and resumed my casting when we were startled by the sound of rending wood, a splash, and a gurgling yelp. Turning, we saw Floyd's hat on the water amidst bits of wood bark and moss. Floyd's weight was too much for the tree trunk.

Mr. Harrisfield very calmly shifted his pipe in his mouth and said: "Just watch and wait, Reverend; he'll come up head first, then his great hulk will surface." And so it did. By the time we reached him he had made the shore and had wafted up among the pitcher plants growing along it to reach dry ground. We had compassion enough to forgo fishing and assist him in starting yet a second drying fire of the day.

Naturally, Floyd's exploits of the day were the subject of animated conversation by our own party and of our neighbors, the Wilkinses, whose turn it was to visit us that night.

The Wilkins ladies were vacationing in the camp across a small bay from my own Nat Foster camp. There was the widow, Mrs. Wilkins, and her three daughters: Helen, a self-possessed young lady of twenty-three; Amy, a young maid of sixteen; and Ruth, the youngest at nine years of age. They had taken the camp for the summer being strangers to me until their advent in June. They were refined, cultivated people and their company was a pleasure. Mrs. Wilkins had confided to me that she had decided to rent having learned from the landlord of my professional reputation. "For," as she offered, "with you as a clerical-naturalist and philosopher living next door I feel we would be protected from any possible danger and my daughters safe from designing men."

I later learned her main idea seemed to be that her daughters were to never marry, but to grow up to be what she had been: a professor in a woman's college. She seemed to forget that if they were to emulate her entirely, they must each marry a rich professor and have him die leaving them sufficient money to retire in middle life.

With the advent of the Wilkins women and the Harrisfields and my son's arrival from college, that particular neck of the woods around the tiny bay developed socially during the month of June and some of July. The distance between our cottages was a moderate hailing distance and there was always the tote road around that side of the lake facilitating informal calls and walks back and forth. Added to this was the boating on the part of the young people, by day and by moonlight—particularly by moonlight. It was a delight to hear their young voices come floating across the water as it reflected the silvery light of Luna. Helen had a rich contralto voice, Floyd was a splendid baritone, while Joseph's rumbling bass and the soprano of the other two girls gave a harmony that was magnificent. Add to that the fun the young men and women had around a campfire and their animated talks on the porch under the soft glow of Japanese lanterns, the atmosphere was most bewitching.

To my observing eye, it was easily seen that Helen and Floyd were drawn to each other. Eventually everyone saw what I had first noted. To me it was an opportunity for study of human nature, but it was a distress to Mrs. Wilkins. Spencer watched his son with the keenness of an old fox, while Joseph generously threw every opportunity possible to the young couple to carry on their courtship.

I do not know if Floyd would ever have plucked up the courage to propose to Helen had it not been for my Old Town canoe.

The red painted canvas canoe was among the water vehicles at camp. Like all canoes it was a delicate craft, tipsy to handle but safe enough to one who knew how. Mine was also capable of safely carrying several hundred pounds. Floyd's two hundred fifty pounds, added to the weight of a slip of a girl, was not the kind of cargo for the canoe, however. Following Floyd's two baths on our fishing trip I warned him to be careful going for a paddle. The lake was very still and the afternoon charming. I didn't have the heart to discourage them although I knew the weight ratio was iffy at best. I steadied the canoe as they took their places, remarking as they did so, that it was too bad that in paddling they could not face each other. Giving the canoe a hearty shove from the dock I watched them paddle out into the quiet bosom of the lake. Helen made little dabs at the water with her paddle at the bow while Floyd gave the long sweeping stroke from the stern. Widow Wilkins joined Spencer and me on the porch; we lazily watched them as they leisurely paddled across the lake to the opposite shore. The widow had let off a little vocal protest when they started but she finally calmed and seated herself.

As they entered the bay on their return, widow Wilkins began a mild commendation on their exploit. She thought they went much too far from the adults. They were adults themselves but that made no difference to her. For our part, Spencer and I shouted our approval. Just as they were within two canoe lengths of the dock Floyd attempted to shift his great bulk. This would not have been disastrous had he not also rolled his eyes around! The movement yielded to the law of gravity. The once-graceful Old Town made a roll pitching Floyd and his fair companion into the water.

The upset caused wild confusion and alarm. Helen's mother let out a weird scream while Spencer and I rushed to the dock. As we ran Spencer kept his head and expressed a conviction that proved true. "Leave 'em be, leave 'em be," he commanded. "Helen can swim and Floyd will float like a piece of dry bass wood; they'll save themselves." His sagacity was proven true in just about two minutes. For together they came to the surface, together they threw their arms around each other and together they arrived at the dock. Each had an arm fondly around the shoulder of the other, both paddling with their free hand with Helen vigorously kicking.

"Well now," drawled Spencer with an affected voice, "aren't you two young people ashamed of yourselves, hugging each other right in front of your ma and pa?"

"Yes," I chimed in, "you'll have to get married now. I've a notion to marry you right here on the dock."

Both of them blushed handsomely and, showing a bit of bashfulness over our jibes, exchanged a look of relief to once again be on shore. Then, as they stood dripping wet, Floyd grinned at me and in the next instant bent and gave Helen a resounding smack on her own wet cheek. It was a magnificent show of courage for such a shy man.

"Well, now, I guess its all over except the shouting," said Spencer with a broad grin on his face. Mrs. Wilkins had been a silent and speechless witness of it all. Hustling Helen into a wooden boat she told Floyd he best get into dry clothes, too. Returning to camp I meditated upon the wonders of Providence in human affairs.

That fall Helen and Floyd were married. The service was not held on my dock but in the bride's parish church with her mother as a re-signed witness, Spencer as the enthusiastic father of the groom, and me, the clerical naturalist-philosopher, as the officiant.

Two Lumberjacks Ride Niagara

During a visit to Forest Lodge on Honnedaga Lake, Byron-Curtiss tried this yarn out on some Adirondack League Club members who had assembled in the lounge of the main club house. One in attendance was an ornithologist. Upon hearing the preacher's story he commented that Anthony reminded him of a Rocky Mountain ouzel, a tiny bird that lives near and gets its sport around waterfalls.

"The League Club member helped my improvements on the preposterous yarn," *he penned at the end of his draft.* "Anyway, it was a popular story and eventually my tale got around. In time, and because of the fabrication, folks who knew the real Anthony recognized his most outstanding characteristics and began calling him the 'Adirondack ouzel,' a label that stuck to the end of his life."

I observed a keen rivalry between the Americans and French Canadians in Gould's Adirondack operation where I worked for a brief period in logging Camp 10 as a bookkeeper and filled in when needed as another bull cook. The friendly rivalry was widespread in the forest, felling trees, peeling bark, skidding logs during spring on the river drive. At night, in the bunkhouse, I noted braggadocio was whetted by the mountain air and by the stimulus of work in the field so that if one were listening in, as I was, to the conversation of the men gathered around the stove in cold weather or congregated back of the bunkhouse in summer, one would be reminded of this ancient verse:

> "Regally they spat and swore
> And fearsomely they lied."

At Camp 10 the honors for feats of strength, daring, and telling huge stories lay between Anthony Coleman, a native of New York State, and Alex Compo, whose place of nativity was the Province of Quebec. Anthony was of a large build with shoulders nearly a yard wide and hands as strong as bear paws. He could fell trees with a double-bitted axe unaided, and was so fast he kept two gangs of bark-peelers hustling just to stay even with him.

Alex was short and stocky. He could hew timbers for sluices faster than any man in the camps. Withal, both men were of the very best during the spring drive on the Black River. Anthony claimed to have once ridden a log over the dam at the Lyon's Falls Paper Mill. Both he and the log had shot beneath the apron of water instantly, but in spite of his heavy build and thick clothing he was wearing at the time, Anthony surfaced at the same instant the log did. The momentum had shot man and log skyward. For a moment both were suspended in the air, so claimed Anthony's supporters who were there. After his feet cleared the water by some yards Anthony gave a mighty leap and jumped onto the peeled log next to him, jammed his caulked boots into the slippery, smooth, fibrous surface and gently guided the thirteen-foot-four-inch timber to a gentle splash landing on the surface of the mill pond.

To offset Anthony's piece of bluster, Alex claimed he rode a log through the log sluice at North Lake's reservoir. At a point several rods from where the log discharged out of the impoundment it struck a hidden rock just as it began to dash into the current of the river. Striking the large boulder squarely, the log turned end over end twice. Alex claimed he had remained calm throughout the adventure. He simply turned a somersault in the air each time the log flipped and landed solidly, and in a serene-like posture, on the peeled log as it moved along in the fast moving river. Of course that was nothing, Alex's buddies claimed, when you compared it to the time he was laying a charge of dynamite in a logjam. When the explosive blew in a loud BOOM Alex was rocketed into space. When he began his free fall, the pull of gravity was great. He fell with such force that he plunged smack dab onto the kingpin in another nearby logjam. His downward force was so great he sprang the pin, which broke that jam, freeing the river all the way to the mill.

The banter continued all winter, Anthony and Alex bragging, as well as their supporters telling of acts of bravado they swore they had witnessed, until the principals each claimed he could run the Niagara River and shoot the falls. At this heightened moment, everyone listening took a renewed interest and egged the men on until a date was arranged when this feat would actually take place. Bets were to be placed with the bookkeeper before the spring drive. When the logs were safely within the booms at the sawmill and the final checks had been cut, An-

thony, Alex, and the rest of the crew went to their respective homes—
Anthony to his native village on the edge of the Adirondacks, Alex to a
little family farm in Quebec. Half the men in Camps 10 and 7 managed
to save enough money from their pay to cover the railroad fare to the
falls. Those who had no money by reason of their loss at card games or
having posted a bet from what disposable money they had left with the
bookkeeper beat their way thitherward to the meeting place in any
manner of ways.

The preparations of the contestants, though hundreds of miles
apart, were simple and similar. Anthony hand-picked a log from the
Lyon's Falls mill and had it shipped by freight to the city of Niagara
Falls. He checked his heavy rider's "Croghans," replacing the caulks in
the high-heeled boots with their correspondingly pronounced instep.
He also selected a new pike pole that was nicely balanced and put it to
soak, then sat tight and waited for the moment he would be careening
down a major waterway. Alex followed practically the same course
save that he picked a log from the forests of his native Canadian province.

Each with their backers met at the predetermined city that is normally a mecca for well-heeled tourists. In comparison, the crowd they
formed was a motley one comprised of bronzed and bearded huskies,
most of whom wore cheap store-bought clothes.

For fear of interference from the authorities the affair was kept
quiet; the two logs being hauled from the express office to the main-
land side of Goat Island bridge during the night. Before dawn Anthony
and Alex, friends, and onlookers gathered at the bridge. At daylight the
logs were rolled into the seething river. Both Adirondack lumberjacks
sprang on to their respective logs with the agility of cats and the great
affair was on. A committee of would-be officials was stationed at the
brink of the cataract, another had assisted at the launching; the specta-
tors were along the bank between the bridge and the brink of the falls.

The residents of the city whose homes were in the proximity of the
river had become accustomed to the noise from the volume of moving
water in the river but on this morning they were awakened by a new
and strange uproar. Many left their comfortable beds to investigate.
There they witnessed a dangerous but exciting duel that exhibited the
rivalry and combativeness the lumberjacks often showed. The test was
a tribute to each man's athletic ability. Their hardened biceps were
building just below rolled-up sleeves made from buffalo-checkered wool
fabric. To be sure they were a picturesque pair, quite typical for lum-

berjacks who liked to pit their skills against each other. It was reminiscent of the many spur-of-the-moment contests between rivals in the woods or of any barroom that often served as a ring for bare-fisted matches.

A short time was consumed in the mad race down the boiling, churning channel. Both logs were tossed and turned in the torrid waters but each man rolled and danced to keep his balance while directing his singular craft in a most frightful manner downriver. Folks said Anthony and Alex "rode 'em pretty," with pike pole in hand as they clung to the careening billets of wood with their caulked boots. Both men, it was observed, seemed controlled, their rugged, weathered faces appeared calm with a set determination frozen in their jaws.

The men were riding like fast-moving pulp wood does in a channel sluiceway above a river. When the men-on-logs reached the terminal end they were neck and neck. Together they pitched over the precipice like cascading pulp wood dropping over a trough into a river below where the water would then carry them to their ultimate destination.

As Anthony's log shot over the brink of Niagara Falls, he was seen to take his pike staff in his teeth, raise his arms overhead, and make a mighty leap in the air. Flipping end over tea kettle, he grabbed himself by the seat of his stout Malone pants and held firm, rigid, motionless for a full minute. He then released his death grip hold on the seat of his britches and dropped through the mist to his log below that was, by then, bobbing in the froth.

Alex was seen to throw away his pike pole after trying to take hold of it in his teeth but, alas, his mouth was too small to hold the wooden handle. He somersaulted three times. The mist enveloped him before he struck the plunge pool. Alex was never seen again. His body was never recovered. It's believed it was jammed with such force so that it became tightly wedged between the rocks below the water's surface.

Two days afterward Anthony, nearly famished but still manfully treading his log, grasping his pike staff and gracefully maintaining his balance without frantically waving his arms or bucking at the waist, was picked up by a passing boat miles downriver. While Anthony won and poor Alex lost his life neither river runner would have had it any other way. Both knew from professional experience a log driver doesn't save his life unless he "rides her out" (holds fast to a bucking log when a jam gives way). They were members of an elite few whose nimbleness, precise judgment, and top-grade poise meant life or death. A river driver's job involved no window-dressing or ballyhooing.

Postscript: *Rev. Byron-Curtiss said this of his tale. "I told this hyperbolic yarn after I had thought it out to some of the mountain people around the headwaters of the Black River. It immediately spread all through the region. The two heroes were well-known in all the lumber camps. Alex Compo was one of those men who confound the best philosophy of wise men as to formal education, for while he could neither read nor write he eventually became a jobber who oversaw three hundred men in his scattered camps. His many antics when young and his later success set me to speculating if a formal education would have spoiled him."*

Anthony Coleman spent most of his life as a lumberjack but once or twice branched off into other occupations, still woodsy in nature. In his later years he served as the game protector for the Adirondack League Club stationed at the head of North Lake. His job was to shoo any of us freelance fishermen or hunters off the club preserve. In Herkimer County, there is a Coleman Dam built across Bear Creek located northeast of Granny Marsh or southwest of Bear Pond. It was named after him.

Forest Trails, Tales, and Destinations

Trails in my neck of the woods often originated as herd paths, trails beaten by animals. Some were deer runs that led to springs, salt licks, and feeding places. But there was another type of deer run that was more deceptive. I could never find a reasonable explanation but learned early on in my forest tramping that some runs just seemed to start in the darnedest place and lead nowhere. Knowing that was often the case I avoided the habit of blindly following those runs.

A defined forest trail was one marked by axe slashes, called blazes, on tree trunks, usually placed from two to three rods apart. Any further human refinement would be the result of the amount of use the trail received. With regular use a trodden pathway will appear on the forest floor. Moss on the ground and on the trunks of fallen trees will be scuffed and torn loose. Twigs and branches will be broken and tossed aside. If the trail is used for portage by buckboards, fallen trees will be removed, dangerous pitch holes are filled in, and side brush will be cut back. A corduroy matting made of small tree trunks laid side by side is placed to span long swampy sections; branches and brush are placed in wet areas. Trees will be felled across streams and foot bridges built where convenient. The "blind" or blazed path has now been changed to the commonly known "open" trail.

Knowledge of woodcraft is required to follow a "blind" trail. Properly blazed, it will indicate the direction going in and coming out. This is accomplished by slashing opposite sides of a tree so the mark is visible from either direction. The outgoing blaze is made with a forehand slash while the ingoing blaze is made with a backhand slash. It is usually smaller and different in shape. Blazes need to be clear, and if properly made they will not be invasive to the woodland yet will direct the traveler without causing any confusion that might lead to losing the trail and walking useless miles or wasting time backtracking.

Blind trails are safer than open trails because few woodsmen will attempt to use a blind trail without always remaining alert. On the other hand an open trail breeds carelessness because a traveler often plods along conscious only that there is an open avenue through the forest ahead of him. However, Nature has a habit of forming avenues, and woe to the unfortunate who wander off on one of them.

A human hazard in the woods is the "jackknife" guide. He is an example of the old maxim that a little knowledge is a dangerous thing. A jackknife guide is one who knows enough about the woods to blunder his way around and eventually get back to camp. He can take care of himself after a fashion but doesn't operate on any set of rules or procedure. His greatest danger is that he may deceive others. I say this because sometime in his novice career he will attempt to guide others or become public-spirited and attempt to improve trails. He'll "freshen" a blaze on a blind trail. Straighten the path. Remove certain natural obstacles. His unthinking actions obscure the original landmarks, confuse the picture and invite the public into his confidence.

There is seldom any concerted effort to drive jackknife pests out of the woods no matter how flagrant their offenses. The forest has a law unto itself that dictates only the fittest survive. If they stay in the woods they usually do a little trapping and poaching or work as porters or as handymen for camp owners. I recall a few of them.

One, the name has been lost in the passage of time, landed a job acting as porter for a party of campers who were going on a summer fishing trip to Horn Lake. The greenhorn placed all the provisions in a large pack basket, lashing a kerosene lantern to the top. When they made camp the first night miles from the point of entry into the woods they discovered the oil had spilled from the lantern and saturated their entire stock of provisions.

Another jackknife episode occurred at North Lake. This tyro borrowed Kettle Jones' raft to fish. The pole raft, crudely built to begin with, was staked in the bay across from my camp. Without first observing that the binders had begun to rot, he placed the party's gear on the surface, equally distributed everyone's weight and poled out into the lake. Before they reached the wide waters the raft came apart and everyone spilled into the water. Luckily all that was lost was the fishing tackle and the day's supply of food.

Another episode involved Billy Dunbar. Billy had been a tailor in far-off Brooklyn when he felt the call of the wild. He started for the Adirondacks, stopping where his money would take him. The rails ended and the trails began for him at the Forestport Station. Billy was an affable, easygoing, towheaded fellow with a lot to learn. He had the good fortune of securing a job with a party of United States government surveyors who were about to make geological survey maps of the southwestern Adirondack region. They hired him to be their axe man and general chore boy.

He was the brunt of their good-natured pranks. They had him sawing basswood, cutting ironwood, and splitting sugar maple knots. He learned much about wood. One evening he spotted a porcupine and only once did he approach a "pretty little kitten with a big white stripe down its back" that he thought had become lost in the woods. He learned a lot about animals. The survey party, camped at North Lake, sent him out to the Forestport general store for a package of blasting pills and some pucker fuse. He learned a lot about medicine.

When the government job was finished Billy stayed around, taking possession of an abandoned camp in the area. As long as I knew him I never observed him learning to think in the language of the forest. He was never sure of himself. One time he started out on a trip that should have only covered seven miles but he took three days!

*   *   *

Charley Brown spent his life in the woods around North Lake. He earned the reputation of being one of the best guides in the business in spite of his short comings. Charley got lost only once. It taught him to avoid roosters except in the presence of biscuits and gravy. His story happened like this:

Charley was the gatekeeper at North Lake. His duties included acting as guide for the New York State officials when they made inspection trips. Those trips were conveniently timed to coordinate with the fishing and hunting seasons. One time Superintendent Wooley of the old Black River Canal and several of his friends decided to "inspect" the trout in a particular headwaters lake. They expected to be gone for just a day so traveled light.

The trip in was uneventful. The fishing was so good the officials ignored Charley's oft repeated warning that they had best be starting back. About a half hour before dark he finally convinced them to get started. He tried to hurry them along but darkness came as he knew it would. The trail walking turned rough. Irregularities became hidden traps sending the inexperienced men occasionally reeling like drunken sailors. Branches slapped them and briers clawed until their tempers grew ragged. They began telling Charley what they were going to do with him when they finally got out of the woods.

Charley was having enough trouble trying to safely guide these nimrods out. His disposition did not improve when they informed him that he "might just lose his job."

In the dark he had lost the blind trail, not exactly sure where he had slipped up. He pressed on hoping to sight a landmark that would give him some bearing. He did not announce he was lost but the party knew it. They also admitted no responsibility for it having happened. With shins barked, knees trembling and ankles aching, and being scared as well, they voiced to Charley they could not go on. A smudge fire was lit to keep the biting insects at bay. Unwilling to participate in building a temporary brush shanty, they shivered and dozed throughout the night. In the wee hours of morning before daylight reached the deep woods Charley was awakened by the distant crowing of a rooster. Anxious to redeem himself he roused the weary men announcing, "I know where we are. Let's get moving. I can get us out of here, have DuGall drive us to North Lake and be there in time for breakfast."

The officials gave him a sour look. They would not move until broad daylight came to their rescue. Charley slumped back for the sun to shine down upon his humiliation.

As it grew lighter the roosters crowed more often; so, too, did a cow moo. Daylight revealed a barn and a house but Charley made no move nor spoke another word. When blue smoke began climbing out of the house's chimney, Charley's party was again roused by the smell of wood smoke. When they saw the distant farmhouse they told everyone to hasten to break camp. "What's the hurry?" Charley quizzed in disgust, "Anna has just started the fire. We have plenty of time to get there for Anna's famous eggs, bacon, and chicken gravy with biscuit breakfast."

Charley did not lose his job but ever afterward this episode was a delicate subject to him. Whenever it came up he tried to talk about something else. Most often he deflected the heat by reminding me of the time I lost my way. I had crossed Bull Moose stream, gone beyond the edge of an old burning, a clearing that had grown to brambles, and crossed it. Later, on my return from fishing a nearby stream, I found I could not locate the blind trail so came out the long way by following the stream to where it joined the Black River. "Hee, hee, hee," Charley would chide. "That's a good one, reverend. Got lost. Couldn't find the trail. Even lost his sweater." Whereby I straightened up and replied, "Charley, my old friend. At least I returned in time for supper." Old Charley probably squirmed inside but he gave no sign. He just clammed up and stared blankly into space.

*   *   *

Losing my direction is an experience I have had a number of squeaks with, but I can pride myself that I have always landed on my feet and reached my shelter. I will admit I have reached North Lake and my boat a number of times after darkness had settled in, necessitating a row to my landing guided only by the contour of mountains against the night sky. But I feel gratified that after spending a half century in the headwaters of North Lake Country I have never spent a night out unless I planned to.

One day I took my youngest daughter, who was then twelve years of age, berrying at a burnt tract. We approached it from the dirt roadway about a mile beyond the foot of our lake. The burning was caused by a forest fire that had raged around the headwaters in 1903. We had followed the line of least resistance to reach the red raspberry patch. As the day wore on the sky clouded and peals of thunder warned me we should leave immediately. We had wallowed around in the brambles so much I lost my direction. I picked Catherine up, setting her on my shoulders. She, holding on to my head, maintained her balance while I carried the two pails of berries. I acted confidently but if the truth had been revealed I was not confident I had set out correctly. I confess I heaved a sigh of relief when from her perch she exclaimed, "Papa, I can see the telephone wire."

*   *   *

Another trip—when I was accompanied by my neighbor Dr. Hyzer W. Jones—took us to Mud Lake. It was both an enjoyable and rewarding day for Dr. Jones for he hooked a prize two-pound trout. We began our return over an infrequently used blind trail that led over Sugarloaf Mountain's summit and angled down toward Panther Bay Spring. I led and, unwittingly, as we proceeded, I steered us wrong, for I talked more than I paid attention. The doctor was the first to notice the way seemed wrong and told me, "Byron, you're off the trail." I assented. I indeed was and turned in the direction we felt would correct the error. That evening I was rewarded when his wife served us the big trout browned to a turn. Later that year we returned to the high lake and I landed the last two trout ever to be caught from Mud Lake.

Rev. Burd, Rev. Allen, and I had fished Mud regularly since I had purchased my camp in 1901. Previous decades of fishing there had always yielded worthwhile creels full of trout. Allen was a fine scholar, a Dublin University man, but he was the most laughable man in the wilds—exhibiting less sense than a jackknife guide. When he hooked a fish, he would become greatly excited. We would yell instructions and warn him not to let "that whale get away." He would loop the line in until the splashing, fighting trout was alongside the raft and then offer his rod to one of us asking, "Now tell me again. What'll I do next, Byron?" Following further instructions he'd lay prostrate on the deck and run his thumb up into the gills and draw the trout in. Next he'd rise to his knees and hug the whale close to his chest so it would not slip away.

Those days of fishing at Mud Lake are gone now. The wild lake has slowly filled up with sediment; there is almost less than half the volume of water there once was. The gravel bed the trout need to spawn has been covered with forest silt, too. This, I believe, explains the disappearance of the trout.

*   *   *

Another great change I have witnessed has been in the mouth of the South Branch inlet. In 1896 the inlet on North Lake was at the base of a high bank that was overgrown with scrub spruce, wire grass and other wild plants. Now the bank has been eroded away by spring freshets. The bank has crumbled, rocks have slid down into the stream and the course has forked and currently drains in two directions with high water. This second outlet has resulted in the wearing away of the point of land I once landed at to take the trail to Hardscrabble Lake.

Hardscrabble Lake was famous for trout, but known only to a few. I always understood it was named by Colonel Fred Dent Grant, son of General Ulysses S. Grant, our 18th president. Julia Dent Grant, Grant's widow, and her family vacationed at Honnedaga Lake after it became part of the Adirondack League Club. Grant would have been guided to the little glacial lake. The fishing trip would have followed a long approach—a tough, scrambling adventure through wild forest land. The homesite of his parents near St. Louis where his father struggled so bravely against the bottle and poverty after marrying Julia was named Hardscrabble. As the story goes he saw a relationship between the homesite and his journey to the steeply rimmed mountain lake.

Bibliography

BOOKS AND ARTICLES BY A. L. BYRON-CURTISS

Byron-Curtiss, A. L. "The Mystery of the Ice Cave Mountain." The Adirondack News Co., August 22, 1900.

———. "Life and Adventures of Nat Foster: Trapper and Hunter of the Adirondacks." Utica, N.Y.: Thomas J. Griffiths, 1897. New edition with second preface by author, Boonville, N.Y.: The Willard Press, 1912. Reprinted Harrison, N.Y.: Harbor Hill Books, 1976.

———. "The Story of a Pass in the Adirondacks." Boston, Ma.: The Gorham Press, 1917.

———. "Voices Tribute to Forestport's Past." Utica *Daily Press*, September 2, 1924.

———. "Couple Married in Rustic Setting." *Boonville Herald*, June 12, 1930.

———. "Water at North Lake Lowest It has Been in Many Years." *Boonville Herald*, October 23, 1930.

———. "Mr. and Mrs. Brown Honored at Atwell." Utica *Press*, September 7, 1931.

———. "Silver Wedding at North Lake." *Boonville Herald*, September 10, 1931.

———. "Bear With Cub on Back Swims Across North Lake." Utica *Press*, May 21, 1933.

———. (?) "Bear Swims Lake With Cub on Back." *Boonville Herald*, May 25, 1933.

———. "North Laker Finds Ice and Snow at Ice Cave Mountain." *Boonville Herald*, June 1, 1933.

———. "Adirondack Cavern Yields Perpetual Ice." *Boonville Herald*, August 29, 1935.

———. "Women Visit Ice Cave Mountain Geological Phenomena Caused by Convulsion of Nature." *Boonville Herald*, September 5, 1935.

———. "Syracuse Women Explore Deposit of Perpetual Ice." Syracuse *Herald*, September 5, 1935.

———. ed. *Poems of North Lake Adirondacks*. Privately printed, 1938.

———. "Forestport—Fifty Years Ago." *Lumber Camp News*, November, 1942.

———. "Tall Stories/Tall Tales." *Lumber Camp News*, October, November and December, 1941; February and March, 1942.

———. "The Roaring Harmony of Nature." *North Country Life*, Vol. 8, No.1, Winter, 1954.

———. "Forestport Days." *North Country Life*, Spring, 1955.

———. "My Last Visit with John Burroughs." *Aubudon*, Vol. 61, No. 5, September-October, 1959.

———. "Tragedies in the Wild Life About My Camp." Town Topics, date unknown.

———. "The Service of Socialism and Its Present Place." Privately printed pamphlet, date unknown.

OTHER BOOKS AND ARTICLES

Ackert, Patricia Avery. History of Forestport, New York. The Town of Forestport Centennial Celebration 1870-1970. Albany, N.Y.: Hooper Productions.

Allen, Mart. "Ernest Blue Loved the Woods and Made a Life of Forestry." *Adirondack Express*, November 11, 1997, Old Forge, N.Y.

Avery, Hilda. "Forestport—Fifty Years Ago." *Lumber Camp News*, December, 1942.

———. The History of Oneida County 1917. "Forestport." Utica, N.Y.

Bird, Barbara Kephart. *Calked Shoes: Life in Adirondack Lumber Camps*. Prospect, N.Y.: Prospect Books, 1952.

Blankman, Lloyd. "North Woods Profile: George Wendover." *York State Tradition*, Vol. 20, No. 2, Spring 1966.

Brenning, Lee M., William P. Ehling, and Barbara McMartin. *Discover the Southwestern Adirondacks*. Woodstock, Vt.: Backcountry Publications, 1987.

Brumley, Charles. *Guides of the Adirondacks*. Utica, N.Y.: North Country Books, 1994.

Comstock, Edward, Jr. and Mark C. Webster, eds. The Adirondack League Club 1890-1990. Old Forge, N.Y., 1990.

Donaldson, Alfred L. *The History of the Adirondacks*. Harrison, N.Y.: Harbor Hill Books, 1977.

Dunham, Harvey L. *Adirondack French Louie: Early Life in the North Woods*. Boonville, N.Y., The Willard Press, 1953. Reprinted by North Country Books, Saranac Lake, N.Y, 1970.

"The Forest Preserve of New York State." Compiled for the Conservation Committee of the Adirondack Mountain Club, 1985.

Grady, Joseph F. *The Story of a Wilderness—The Adirondacks: Fulton Chain-Big Moose Region*. Boonville, N.Y.: The Willard Press, 1933. Reprinted by North Country Books, Old Forge, N.Y., 1972.

Hungerford, Edward. "Black River, Its Praises Are Least Sung." *North Country Life*, Vol. 1, No. 4, Summer 1947.

Keller, Jane Eblen. *Adirondack Wilderness: A Story of Man and Nature*. Syracuse, N.Y.: Syracuse University Press, 1980.

Lane, David F. "'North Lake Bishop' Writes Woods Lore." The Watertown *Daily Times*, Saturday, July 11, 1942.

McDermott, Marion H. *Abundant Harvest*. A Syracuse Catholic Press Association Book, 1991.

New Century Atlas of Herkimer County New York with Farm Records. Philadelphia, Pa., Century Map Company, 1906.

O'Donnell, Thomas C. *Snubbing Post: An Informal History of the Black River Canal*. Boonville, N.Y.: The Willard Press, 1949. Reprinted by North Country Books, Old Forge, N.Y., 1972

O'Donnell, Thomas C. *Birth of a River: An Informal History of the Black River Headwaters*. Boonville, N.Y.: Black River Books, 1952.

Peter, John. "John Peter Goes Away," *Boonville Herald*, July 24, 1894.

Pomeroy, Mark M. "The Great Adirondack Forest." *Pomeroy's Advance Thought*, Vol. IV, No. 1, August, 1890.

"Private Grounds and Parks." *The Fish and Game Laws of New York*, Article IX. Albany, N.Y., 1893.

Raymond, Edward R. *Adventures of Uncle Hatchet*. Edward R. Raymond, Forestport, N.Y.: Boonville Graphics, 1989.

Reed, Frank A. *Lumberjack Sky Pilot*. Boonville, N.Y.: The Willard Press, _____ Reprinted by North Country Books, Old Forge, N.Y., 1965.

Slusarczyk, Stanley. "To South Lake With Lloyd Mortice." Remsen City-Steuben News, Fall 1994.

——. "Through Rain, and Snow, and Dark of Night." *American Snowmobiler*, October 1994.

Spears, E. A. "Hermit of North Creek." Utica *Observer Dispatch*, date unknown.

Spears, Raymond S. "Byron E. Cool's 'Good Work.'" *Lumber Camp News*, March, 1944.

Sperry, Charles. "Passing of Old Golden." *Angler and Hunter*, Vol. 2, April, 1910.

Sperry, Claire, and Charles Sperry. *North Lake: Jewel of the Adirondacks*. Whitesboro, N.Y.: privately printed, 1981.

Sprague, Ken. "History & Heritage." *Adirondack Express*, Vol. 15, No. 11. June 26, 2001, Old Forge, N.Y.

Sylvester, Nathaniel. "Not Guilty: An Account of a Murder in Herkimer County a Century Ago." *North Country Life*, Vol. 1, No. 3, Spring 1947. Reprinted from *Historical Sketches of Northern New York and the Adirondack Wilderness* by Nathaniel S. Sylvester. Published by William H. Young, Troy, N.Y.

Thomas, Howard. *Black River in the North Country*. Prospect Books: Prospect, N.Y., 1974.

——. *Tales from the Adirondack Foothills*. Prospect Books: Prospect, N.Y., 1971.

Stoddard, Emily. "The Woodland Hermit: Old Atwell and His Camp." *Gameland*, January, 1895.

Thompson, Harold, W. *Body, Boots and Britches*, J.B. Lippincott Co., 1939.

Unsigned. "One of Smallest U .S. Post Offices Is in Northern Herkimer County." Newspaper clipping from unknown source.

Unsigned. "Veteran Boatman Recalls Busy Days on Black River Canal." *Watertown Times*, date unknown.

Unsigned. "A Beautiful Wedding Solemnized at North Lake." *Utica Press*, date unknown.

Unsigned. "Old Atwell." *The Adirondack News*, 1894.

Unsigned. "Game Protection." *Boonville Herald*, November 9, 1899.

Unsigned. "Adirondack Deer Hounding." *Boonville Herald*, November 9,1899.

Unsigned. "North Lake." *Boonville Herald*, August 29, 1935.

Unsigned. "The Pack-Basket Trail." *Buffalo Courier-Express*, September 20, 1936.

Unsigned. "Clergyman's Article in Magazine: Rev. Byron-Curtiss Tells of Visit with John Burroughs." *Rome Sentinel*, October 27, 1959.

Unsigned. "Deaths in the Woodlands Parish." *Northeast Logger*, Vol. 8, No. 7, January, 1960.

Wallace, Edwin R. *Wallace's Guide to the Adirondacks*. Syracuse, N.Y., 1894.

Wells, Robert A. "Big Tracts in Three Counties." *The Watertown Daily Times*, February 13, 1928.

OTHER SOURCES

Byron-Curtiss, A. L. Unpublished manuscript and personal papers warehoused in the Rome Historical Society's archives, Rome, N.Y.

Byron-Curtiss, A. L. Personal papers, letters, and camp logs. Owned by Doris and
    Thomas Kilbourn, Rome, N.Y.
Gray, David V. Unit Management Plans for Black River Wild Forest, Pratt-Northam
    Memorial Park, J. P Lewis Tract Easement and the John Brown Tract Easement.
    New York State Department of Environmental Conservation, June 1996.
King, A. H. Map from 1917 showing the Blake Lot of Adgates Eastern Tract.
O'Donnell, Thomas C. Personal papers housed in the George Arents Research Library
    at Syracuse University, Syracuse, N.Y.
Personal interviews with:
    The Reverend Dr. Stanley Gasek, Clinton, N.Y., 1989.
    Robert Buell, Camden, N.Y., 1989.
    Harold McNitt, Atwell, N.Y., 1996
State of New York: The Forest, Fish and Game Commission. Adirondack Maps, 1900
    and 1908.
Wood, D. C. Map Number 8, Blake Lot State Land, 1917; Map R487-B, Blake Lot
    Tract.